D1429352

The Moth and the Candle

your faithful and affectionate humble servant James Boswell

James Boswell, pencil drawing by Sir Thomas Lawrence, c. 1790–5

Iain Finlayson

THE MOTH
AND
THE CANDLE

A Life of James Boswell

Constable · London

First published in Great Britain 1984
by Constable and Company Limited
10 Orange Street London WC2H 7EG
Copyright © 1984 by Iain Finlayson
ISBN 0 09 465540 5
Set in Linotron Ehrhardt 11 pt by
Rowland Phototypesetting Ltd
Bury St Edmunds, Suffolk
Printed in Great Britain by
St Edmundsbury Press
Bury St Edmunds, Suffolk

This book is for my father,
JACK FINLAYSON

Contents

	Acknowledgements	xi
1	The Newmarket Courser	1
2	The Moth and the Candle	27
3	Boswell and the Philosophers	55
4	Passion, Pandaemonium and Piety	89
5	Mr Corsica Boswell	105
6	Boswell in Love	129
7	Boswell and the Bear	156
8	The Hypochondriack	191
9	The Laird of Ulubrae	215
10	Boswell and *The Life*	238
11	*Envoi*	259
	Bibliography	265
	Index	267

Illustrations

James Boswell, pencil drawing by Sir Thomas Lawrence c.
1790–5
(*National Portrait Gallery, London*)   *frontispiece*

Euphemia Erskine, Boswell's mother, by William Mosman,
1742   2

Lord Auchinleck, Boswell's father, by Allan Ramsay
(*Yale Center for British Art*)   3

Extract from Boswell's journal for 16 May 1763, in which he
records his first meeting with Dr Johnson
(*Yale University Library*)   50

John Wilkes, a satirical portrait (*British Museum*)   57

'La Belle Zuylen': Isabella Agneta Elizabeth van Tuyll van
Serooskerken, portrait by Jens Juel
(*Stichting Inconographisch Bureau, The Hague*)   63

Jean-Jacques Rousseau, portrait by Allan Ramsay
(*National Galleries of Scotland*)   78

James Boswell in his finery, portrait by George Willison
(*National Galleries of Scotland*)   80

Voltaire (*Mansell Collection*)   84

The Savage Man, a caricature of Rousseau, apostle of nature,
with Hume and Voltaire. A contemporary engraving, based on
an original sketch by James Boswell   86

Lord Mountstuart, son of Lord Bute, portrait by William
Hoare (*Thomas Agnew & Sons Ltd*)   94

General Pasquale Paoli, portrait by Richard Cosway
(*Mansell Collection*)   108

James Boswell dressed as a Corsican Chief, engraving by   119
J. Miller after S. Wale
(*National Portrait Gallery*)

Dr Samuel Johnson, painting by James Barry, c. 1777   158
(*National Portrait Gallery*)

A literary party at Sir Joshua Reynolds': those present are   174
Boswell, Johnson, Reynolds, Burke, Garrick, Paoli, Warton
and Goldsmith. Engraving by W. Walker after James E. Doyle
(*Dr Johnson's House*)

Walking up the High Street, Edinburgh from The Picturesque   177
Beauties of Boswell, a suite of etchings by Thomas
Rowlandson (*Victoria and Albert Museum*)

Wit and Wisdom making preparations for dinner from The   178
Picturesque Beauties of Boswell

Dr Johnson in a Highland hut   180
(*John Rylands University of Manchester Library*)

Highland Dance on the top of Dun-Can from The Picturesque   186
Beauties of Boswell

The Recovery after a severe drunken frolic at Corrichatachin   187
from the Picturesque Beauties of Boswell

Scottifying the Palate at Leith from The Picturesque Beauties   188
of Boswell

Boswell, his wife Peggie and their children, a family portrait by   201
Henry Singleton (*National Galleries of Scotland*)

Hester Lynch Piozzi (Mrs Thrale), portrait by an unknown   239
Italian, 1785 (*National Portrait Gallery, London*)

James Boswell, portrait by Joshua Reynolds, 1785   241
(*National Portrait Gallery, London*)

Edmond Malone, portrait by Joshua Reynolds, 1778   245
(*National Portrait Gallery*)

James Boswell, engraving by William Daniell after a drawing by   255
George Dance, 1793 (*British Museum*)

Sculpture of James Boswell at Auchinleck   262
(*Scottish Tourist Board*)

Mr Samuel Johnson and Mr James Boswell passed the night of 5 August 1763 together at Colchester. A moth fluttered round the candle and burnt itself. 'That creature,' said Mr Johnson, 'was its own tormentor, and I believe its name was BOSWELL.'

(*Life of Johnson* by James Boswell)

Acknowledgements

No biographer of Boswell can fail to be influenced by, or hope to rival, three previous attempts on the life of James Boswell. First, Boswell's own record, in the form of journals, memoirs, memoranda, letters, books, poetry, and essays, should be a more than adequate resource. Second, *The Hooded Hawk* by Mr D. B. Wyndham Lewis is such a prodigy of erudition (lightly worn) and style (one is tempted to praise the book in the words he uses to recommend Boswell's *Account of Corsica*) and adds so significantly to our understanding of Boswell, that it is difficult not to pick at its wealth of detail. Thirdly, a debt has to be owned to *James Boswell, The Earlier Years*, by Professor Frederick A. Pottle. Here is Ulubrae, his the *animus aequus*. No sooner does one conceive an idea about Boswell, than one discovers it to be but an echo of an insight already fully considered by Professor Pottle.

That there are errors in this present attempt to chronicle the life of Mr Boswell, I don't doubt. But we all four – Boswell, Lewis, Pottle and I – have at least one thing in common: we find it difficult to be disobliging towards James Boswell.

I should like to thank Yale University, Messrs Heinemann and McGraw-Hill for their kind permission to quote from 'The Yale Editions of the Private Papers of James Boswell' (listed in full in the Bibliography) and in particular from his 'London Journal', his 'Journal', his 'Inviolable Plan', his 'Agreement between James Boswell and Margaret Montgomerie', his 'Review of My Life during the Summer Session 1775' and his letters to John Johnston, David Dalrymple, Lord Auchinleck, Mme Skarnavis, Rousseau, Oliver Goldsmith, Rev. Thomas Percy, Mrs Thrale,

Francis Barber, Edmond Malone, Sir William Scott, and to and from Zelide and her father.

I have other debts to discharge: first and foremost, Elfreda Powell must take full credit for suggesting Boswell as a suitable subject for biography and giving him to me: with patience and resilience she supported my progress to publication. Over a period of months, a number of people gave generous support, though their patience was sorely tried: I have to thank Susi and Jasper Jacob for a good deal more than the loan of their Somerset cottage, and my mother and sister for considerably more than providing a place to write. George Robinson and Dr Anne Smith will each know, I hope, how much I relied upon their strengths and how inadequate my thanks can be. Then, too, the 'brickettes', Emma Parsons and Liz Bland, were tireless in their confidence. I must particularly thank Gladys Bickerstaff.

Mrs Vera Rigg supplied the quotation from Auchinleck House, and a translation.

The London Library supplied most of the books I required: it is the most charming and indulgent Library in London, and its work deserves generous support.

This book was born at the same time as Georgia Jacob: I'd like to think that they will both give pleasure to their friends.

IAIN FINLAYSON
Somerset and Ayrshire, 1983

[1]

The Newmarket Courser

Fond as James Boswell was of claiming to descend, as Laird of
Auchinleck, from an ancient and distinguished line of Scotsmen,
it was a conceit on the part of a man who generally despised his
countrymen and would have preferred to go as little as possible
among them. Yet there is no snob like a Scots snob, particularly
when abroad, and Boswell could and did claim descent from,
among others, Robert the Bruce. At Flodden a Boswell fell, with
so many others of his countrymen, in company with his king. But
the male line failed in the early sixteenth century, and the estate of
Auchinleck was granted to a cadet branch of the family. Thereafter, for seven generations, the Boswells were untitled landed
gentlemen until judicial office bestowed on Alexander Boswell,
who was appointed a Lord of the Court of Session in 1754, the
style of Lord Auchinleck. It was a courtesy title which did not
necessarily confer upon his wife, Euphemia, the right to be styled
Lady Auchinleck, and it was not heritable by his eldest son,
James, who had been born in Edinburgh on 29 October 1740.
Euphemia Boswell had previously borne a daughter, also chris-
tened Euphemia, who died when her brother James was three
months old. Both Euphemia and James had been seriously ill,
though the illness has not been identified. In the late summer of
1743, John Boswell was born, and, in 1748, a third son, Thomas
David, completed the family. In 1754, the Boswells had lost a son
at birth, and it is possible that other children may not have
survived. Infantile mortality was not uncommon and, often, taken
for granted. Though some provision might be made for younger
sons, and dowries given to daughters, the eldest son could expect

Euphemia Erskine, Boswell's mother, by William Mosman, 1742.

to inherit the father's title (if it were hereditary), the estate and income. More, he would assume the dignity of a laird and, with it, the responsibility for the welfare of his tenants. The dignity was often more eagerly sought than its accompanying obligations, particularly as the century advanced and gave way to the nineteenth.

The Boswell family was well-connected enough through Alex-

Lord Auchinleck, Boswell's father, by Allan Ramsay

ander's marriage in 1737 to Euphemia Erskine whose father, the Deputy Governor of Stirling Castle, was a grandson of the Earl of Mar and Lady Marie Stuart, daughter of the Duke of Lennox. Both Alexander and Euphemia descended, too, from the second Earl of Kincardine whose wife was of the distinguished Dutch van Sommelsdyck family. The Boswells were solid burghers, landed gentry, who had not featured significantly in the history of

Scotland or been honoured in its service. Their name was said, by a Bosville cousin, to derive from the French 'Boisville', and could be variously spelt as Boswell, Boswall, or, as James Boswell's father would have it, Boswel. James restored the second 'l'.

To James, the blood of the Boswells, tinged with blue and enriched by royalty, flowed through the veins and capillaries of his character like a bright thread of pride. On his travels he was Mr Boswell of Auchinleck, but suffered himself easily to be described as Baron Boswell or Monsieur Boswell d'Auchinleck. At the time of Lord Auchinleck's death in 1782, the Auchinleck estates brought in an income of £1000 per annum, and this had been supplemented by Auchinleck's judicial income of £900. In total, this was a good deal, though not lavish. The estate itself was large enough, though not extensive: its proprietor could ride in a straight line for ten miles before coming to the boundary. The tenantry amounted to some six hundred souls. The Boswells, for generations solid and worthy, have been distinguished by their improbable sprig. Until recently, however, they have preferred, in the dour Scots way, to cluck their tongues rather than to take any great pride in him. Nobody took pride in Boswell but Boswell himself.

It is occasionally said that, had it not been for Boswell, we should have heard, and thought, less of Samuel Johnson. It is true that, had it not been for his biographer, our view and knowledge of Johnson would have been different and less detailed. But he exists as a forceful character in the memoirs of other contemporaries and as a man of learning and letters through his own works. It is perhaps more accurate to say that without Johnson we should have heard less of James Boswell except as a source for social historians of the eighteenth century, and as a minor character in the obscure history of Corsica and the little-known career of General Pasquale Paoli.

Yet Boswell does exist very much in his own right as a superb journalist and diarist, as a tuft-hunter (if he had not pinned himself to Johnson, he might well have been the intimate of some other great man), as a lawyer, as a lover, as a rake, and as an eccentric of more than usual tenacity. Without the benign and moral influence of Johnson, Boswell might have been more intimate with John Wilkes, and even more dissipated. He was permanently fascinated by Wilkes, and Wilkes found in Boswell a source of endless amusement, 'The agreeable scatterbrain, the gay drinking-companion, the quaint Scots chatterbox, the admirable and untiring listener.' And too, under the influence of Johnson, the repentant sinner with recurrent urgings towards Christianity and a better life.

Boswell, ever prone to self-advertisement but wholly incapable of revealing less than the terrible truth, wrote a description of himself in 1773 and included it in the published *Journal of a Tour to the Hebrides*:

I have given a sketch of Dr Johnson: my readers may wish to know a little of his fellow traveller. Think then, of a gentleman of ancient blood, the pride of which was his predominant passion. He was then in his thirty-third year, and had been about four years happily married. His inclination was to be a soldier; but his father, a respectable Judge, had pressed him into the profession of the law. He had travelled a good deal, and seen many varieties of human life. He had thought more than any body supposed, and had a pretty good stock of learning and knowledge. He had all Dr Johnson's principles with some degree of relaxation. He had rather too little, than too much prudence; and, his imagination being lively, he often said things of which the effect was very different from the intention. He resembled sometimes 'The best good man, with the worst natur'd muse.'

He cannot deny himself the vanity of finishing with the encomium of Dr Johnson whose friendly partiality to the companion of his Tour represents himself as one, 'whose acuteness would help my inquiry, and whose gaiety of conversation, and civility of manners, are sufficient to counteract the inconveniences of travel, in countries less hospitable than we have passed.'

This 'best good man,' beset constantly by the demands of a turbulent and self-revelatory character, was educated from 1746 to 1748 at Mundell's School in Edinburgh, more progressive in its breadth of instruction than the High School where the sole staple was Latin. James would have been taught (in addition to Latin) English, Writing, and Arithmetic. He thoroughly disliked the school, and from the age of eight, until 1752, he was tutored privately at home by John Dun, a young man of twenty-five who introduced his pupil to reading the *Spectator* and Roman poets, and offered a more optimistic view of Boswell's chances in the afterlife which, according to more orthodox opinion, were dicey. Dun was relieved of his duties as tutor when Alexander Boswell appointed him, in 1752, as minister to the parish of Auchinleck. His place was taken by Joseph Fergusson, a man in his early thirties, whom Boswell clearly disliked and feared.

His governors depressed him: they 'were both men without manners, men of the meanest sort of education . . . I saw them treated with contempt. Yet they had authority over me, the power to inspire me with cowardly sentiments. I thought that everyone who was a little better dressed than I was and could speak without fear was my superior. I trembled before a lord, and would have thought myself honoured to be a duke's coachman.' Boswell's father was an even more substantial figure, whom no man treated with contempt: in 1748 he had been appointed Sheriff of Wigtownshire, and the official authority of the judge seems likely to have become confused in his son's mind with natural paternal authority. Alexander Boswell succeeded to the estate of Auchinleck on the death of James's grandfather and namesake in 1749, and built a fine neo-classic house to lodge his family and his impressive library. Over the front of this edifice, on the pediment, he inscribed a motto from an epistle by Horace to whose writings, and those of Anacreon, he was devoted:

> *Quod petis hic est,*
> *Est Ulubris, animus si te non deficit aequus*

This, translated, runs, 'What you seek is here, at Ulubrae, if you have but equanimity.'

Alexander Boswell's mind was perfectly calm, and his equanimity as Laird of Auchinleck and as ornament to the legal profession was sustained by the orthodoxy of his political views and the convictions of his religious attitudes. He was a Whig and a Presbyterian, both attitudes conformable to the pre-Union tradition that King William had preserved Protestant Scotland and the established virtues and order. His portrait by Allan Ramsay depicts a long, heavily-built face with a satisfied look, a *nemo me impune lacessit* challenge in the forthright stare of the eyes. It is not a gay face, though there is no indication of melancholia. There is little trace of any emotion, save the suspicion of dry humour around the lips. He is said to have been ironic, in the Scots manner, uttering devastating but deadpan sallies.

In his youth, Alexander Boswell is alleged to have affected modish red heels and stockings, but the sober man would have soon put away such childish delights, along with frivolities such as modern literature, and he certainly disregarded the fashionable tendency towards Anglicising the vernacular Scots tongue. A lack of gentility in this respect was to pain his son James throughout his life. Alexander continued to address the courts in the fashion that was good enough for the coarse and brutal Lord Kames and the disgraceful Lord Braxfield, just as he would speak in his private life with equal force and dispassion, if with a little less patience.

He was not, perhaps, a cold man, but he was undemonstrative: he was circumspect and respectable, a man of distinction and deliberation, a man of law and learning, conscientious as to his duties as a landlord, lawyer, and exemplar to his sons. It may be possible to love such a man, though it is a good deal more difficult to like him. But he had his enthusiasms: his library of finely-bound classics, his collation of Anacreon editions and the Greek Lyricists, his classical tenets of gardening, and his pedigree. Even in his pleasures, Alexander Boswell was not light.

His wife, Euphemia Erskine, was portrayed by William Mosman in 1742, five years after her marriage when she would have been in her mid-twenties, and two years after the birth of her son James. The face is almost perfectly round, fair and delicate. It is difficult to read character into such demureness. Her notions, says her son, 'were pious, visionary, and scrupulous. When she was once made to go to the theatre, she cried, and would never go again.' She does not emerge with any vivacity from behind her piety, which may mean that it was not merely conventional but deeply held and felt.

She was kind to young James, indulgent even, and he was ready to take advantage of her docility. 'I was brought up very tenderly . . . If I did not feel well, I was treated with excessive attention. I was not made to go to school, which I detested. She gave me sweetmeats and all sorts of pretty things to amuse me.' Her concern for the physical health of her 'delicate child' was softer than her care for the boy's soul. As a duty, she inspired James with religious devotion; but 'unfortunately she taught me Calvinism. My catechism contained the gloomiest doctrines of that system. The eternity of punishment was the first great idea I ever formed. How it made me shudder! Since fire was a material substance, I had an idea of it. I thought but rarely about the bliss of heaven because I had no idea of it. I had heard that one passed one's time there in endless praise of God, and I imagined that that meant singing psalms as in church; and singing psalms did not appeal to me. I should not have wished to go to heaven if there had been any other way of not going to hell. I imagined that the saints passed the whole of eternity in the state of mind of people recently saved from a conflagration, who congratulate themselves on being in safety while they listen to the mournful shrieks of the damned.'

This is amusing: it was meant to be. It was designed to appeal to Rousseau for whom Boswell, as an adult, wrote a sketch of his life. But the prospect of damnation for eternity was a real enough horror to a young child raised to be delicate and with imagination or cunning enough to seize the opportunities that the delicacy pressed upon him presented. Euphemia Erskine believed in salvation through faith and an act of conversion. James was to prepare himself to receive and be a fit vessel for the operation of Divine Grace. Meanwhile, the terrors of hell were supplemented by the servants' gossip of witches and ghosts, murderers and robbers. Mundell's Academy was in the West Bow, a street said to be haunted by the ghost of the warlock Major Weir and his sinister sister who were reputed to ride about on a headless, flaming horse. Though the boy never saw Major Weir, who had been officially strangled and burned in 1670, the West Bow was also the route of some regular melancholy traffic when condemned men were led from the Tolbooth to the Grassmarket gallows: the noise of their passage, if not the sight, would have been heard at Mundell's.

'I was born with a melancholy temperament,' wrote Boswell to Rousseau, 'it is the temperament of our family.' He believed that a strain of madness or melancholia had been imported into the Boswells through his ancestry. 'I preferred being weak and ill to being strong and healthy.' Fortunately, Dun stepped in to allay some of his pupil's timidities. 'He told me that if I behaved well during my life, I should be happy in the other world . . . and some hope entered into my religion.' From eight to twelve years of age, he asserts, 'I enjoyed reasonably good health.' Dun delightfully developed Boswell's literary tastes and young James became romantic. Enthusiasm for classic literature swelled in his young mind, which was at least a route to his father's heart, had he time to pay much attention to his son's education. But Dun disappeared, and his successor Fergusson flew into a temper when James thought to find pleasure in poetry rather than mere instruction.

At the age of twelve, James became ill: he caught a bad cold and cunningly resisted every attempt to relieve it so as not to have to go back to his tutor. He was sent to Moffat, a spa, to drink at the sulphur springs and recuperate. That he did recover is evident: he never again refers to delicacy of constitution, though depression and doubt will dog him the rest of his life. Feeble-mindedness, not to say actual insanity, is a recurrent theme in Boswell's ancestry and, indeed, his immediate family. It contributed to his anxieties about his own mental stability which he considered precarious. The third Earl of Kincardine was feeble-minded, and both Alexander and Euphemia, Boswell's parents, descended from that family. Alexander's younger brothers, twins, were certainly eccentric: one of them, Thomas David, known as David, took to idling in his bed for long periods and was finally confined in a strait-jacket; while the other, John, joined an extreme religious sect that preached salvation by faith, and was excommunicated by his fellow-Glassites for immorality. James's younger brother, Johnny, became mentally deranged when he was nineteen and was thereafter subject to periodic fits of insanity, and often confined.

In 1753, James Boswell entered Edinburgh University. It was usual for students to begin a course of study there from the age of fourteen, and James was coming up to his thirteenth birthday: he was bright, but not precociously so. He already had a good grasp of Latin, which he never lost: he could, for the rest of his life, write a letter in good, grammatical Latin without reference to a dictionary. Greek was another matter: though he now began classes in that language, he never achieved the standard of his fluency in Latin, but his competence enabled him to identify a passage in the original Greek when seeking to compare it with a translation, and to be able to summon up an occasional quotation. He studied Logic under John Stevenson, a course of instruction that included, in addition to logic, the unnerving study of metaphysics, the history of philosophy, and readings from poets ancient and modern to illustrate the theory of criticism. The philosophy of Locke was introduced, and that of Aristotle adduced. Among the other subjects leading to an Arts degree were Mathematics (in which Boswell had no facility), Physics (Natural History) and Moral Philosophy, and he opted to study Botany, Astronomy and Roman Antiquities which dwelt upon Roman institutions (a useful class for a lawyer, since the law of Scotland was based on the principles of Civil Law, a subject still taught to law students at Scottish Universities).

In all, Boswell studied for six years at Edinburgh University and acquired some learning in the humanities and the law, though he considered his education narrow and inadequate, lacking the leaven of gentility which, at Eton or Westminster, he might have acquired by association with teachers and students who were acknowledged to be gentlemen: as it was, Robert Hunter, his

Professor of Greek, could be relied upon to refer to 'jelly' as 'jeel'. If his command of English was thus suspect, what trust could the sensitive Boswell put in his ability to instruct a class in the pronunciation of Greek? That James was high-flown in his expectations and ideals is clear from the fact that, now as later, he regarded himself as apart from, and very likely above, the common ruck. 'I found myself always a little different from my companions, and as I advanced in years, the difference increased. I found in none of them those indescribable ideas of grandeur of soul and delicacy of taste which I believed within the reach of humanity, and which I hoped I might myself one day possess.' Lacking the longed-for stimulation, he was shy.

He did, however, discover two friends with whom he was to remain on close terms for the rest of his life. The first was John Johnston, some ten years older, a fellow student who first attracted Boswell's attention by the straw-coloured lining to his coat, from which James took him to be 'quite the genteel gentleman'. He had evidently got over his inferiority in the presence of anyone better-dressed than himself, or perhaps his own clothes by this time were more appropriate to a young gentleman of ancient lineage. Johnston was older, already a laird in possession of three farms in Dumfriesshire, and could claim remote descent from an aristocratic line. Johnston was attractively hearty and masculine, a romantic Jacobite, a Tory, enthusiastic about the history and topography of Scotland, and a depressive.

They walked the streets of Edinburgh together, drank tea together in the afternoons, and talked long hours together. Johnston visited his friend in the fourth-floor Boswell flat in Parliament Close and, very likely, dined with the family. It was a vivacious age and a drinking society. Breakfast was early, at about seven, and consisted of porridge, herrings, and ale. Tea, by the middle of the century, was served as a matter of course, though it might be fortified by a little brandy. Until about 1745, it was usual to dine at about one o'clock, though by 1760 the dinner hour had advanced by degrees until three o'clock, or four in fashionable circles, was the time by which well-to-do households were at table.

Supper might be served at about eight in the evening, a substantial meal of the kind we now think of as a good dinner, but often enough a gentleman would spend the evening with congenial friends, eating little but drinking a good deal. It was a convivial age and the masculine social life of Edinburgh was largely conducted with the utmost sociability over ale or claret in coffee houses, clubs, inns, and cellars. The magistrates, by an old Municipal Act, were enabled to penalise anyone found still carousing in a tavern after ten o'clock, but later in the century ten o'clock passed and the topers tippled on, among them the magistrates themselves, disobligingly disregarding the Act that had indicted 'abounding drunkenness, uncleanness, night revellings, and other immoralities both in the houses and in the streets,' which was 'a great hindrance to sober persons in the worship of God in secret, and in their families . . .'

'Clubs there were of all kinds,' remarks Mr H. G. Graham in his *Social Life of Scotland in the Eighteenth Century* '. . . for wits and cits, for solid traders and spendthrift youths, for judges and clerks, for men of law, men of letters, and men of leisure . . . In such cellars they were happy; lords, lawyers, lairds met and had their high jinks, and the mirth was loud and the stories and jests were broad. In one room might be assembled judges relaxing their intellects after deciding subtle points on feudal law, while in the other their clerks caroused, retailing their lordships' Parliament House jokes of yesterday. Lords of Session might indulge with impunity in bacchanalian nights, and waken with brain clear to unravel an intricate case of multiple poinding next morning; but such ongoings played havoc with feebler constitutions.' Burns, on his deathbed, is said to have lamented, 'O these Edinburgh gentles – if it hadna been for them I had a constitution would have stood onything!' Johnston may have introduced Boswell not only to the dangerous immorality of the theatre in the Canongate, but also to the social drinking and vivacious, gossipy huddles in the dirty, dark dives and dens where worthies went cheerfully to the devil and drink and then, unsteadily, home.

Johnston was affectionate, staunch, and conventional. He was imaginative, otherwise Boswell would not long have been detained by his company, but he was content to let his fancies remain fantasy. Boswell was a more ardent spirit. Ideas and urgings no sooner entered his head and animated his senses than he began to seek out ways in which they could be affected or satisfied. His enthusiasm was such that, no sooner had he begun, than he was anticipating the pleasures of achieving his fantasies. Boswell was the dominant partner throughout his intimacy with Johnston, who was not himself corrupt and certainly had no thought or intention of corrupting his friend. Indeed, he did not do so: he may only have introduced Boswell to some possibilities, but for Boswell the possible immediately became the probable.

The foil to hearty and masculine Johnston was Boswell's second friend, the 'amiable and worthy' William Johnson Temple, an English youth from Berwick-upon-Tweed where his father had been mayor. He was of an age with Boswell, loved literature, was a pious Anglican. As his 'grave, sedate, philosophic friend,' Boswell walked and talked with Temple until the summer of 1758, after which they rarely saw one another but continued their warm friendship in an exchange of correspondence. Temple, too, like Boswell, had intimations of greatness, but he was disappointed and his sole service to posterity was to father a son who in turn fathered an Archbishop of Canterbury who gratifyingly fathered another. Temple introduced Boswell to Episcopalian services in the Church of England chapel in Carrubber's Close, an enterprise as fraught with danger as Johnston's peepshows of tavern and theatre. The Presbyterian Church of Scotland tottered and never again quite recovered firm ground in Boswell's emotional theology.

Terrifyingly, too, at about this time Boswell became aware of sex or, at least, of the physical appetite of his body for pleasure. He had found the experience of climbing trees inexplicably exciting, and falling from them ecstatic. He had first fallen in love at the age of eight, a distinction he shares with Byron. At the age of twelve, he had been in love with a Miss Mackay, but Fergusson, his governor, had jeered at his infatuation. He discovered masturbation ('I learned from a playmate the fatal practice') and, although this was a minor sin compared with horrible fornication, he thought himself nevertheless damned. He considered the example of Origen, whose doubts about the efficacy of self-discipline in the matter of animal passions led him to castrate himself, but 'that madness passed' though there was another to follow. 'A terrible hypochondria seized me at the age of sixteen' and he returned to the sulphur springs of Moffat.

Sexual anxieties or fantasies do not adequately account for his sudden debilitating depression: metaphysics too confounded his mind which dwelt laboriously on the vexed question of determinism, of divine foreknowledge and man's free will: it was never decided to Boswell's satisfaction. Necessity, he always suspected, governed his actions. Intuition, not logic, was always Boswell's stronger card. The moral verities and virtues of his parents were being assaulted, their limited vision enlarged by Boswell's adventures: he could no longer trust to their piety and respectability as a defence against the snares and entrapments of his own thoughts, feelings, and moral predicaments. But he made an attempt to do so: he turned to the comfort of the hope offered in childhood by his mother – the prospect of salvation by faith, by an abandonment of the self to the operations of divine grace. As a refuge from the disturbing rationalism of metaphysics and logic, he turned to religious fervour and evangelical sureties, 'Methodists next shook my passions.' He cannot have been wholly won over, because this further addition to the conflicting pressures upon him resulted in melancholia and, thus, the trip to Moffat in the summer of 1757.

Gentlemen and ladies, out of health or spirits, would resort to Moffat Wells and there they might meet the eccentric geologist John Williamson who preached vegetarianism, polygamy (though he remained a bachelor), the inadvisability of moving dust from the house, and the doctrine of the transmigration of souls: many were the imprudent riders or coachmen who were, very likely, even now whipping the souls of their grandmothers along the roads. He had read deeply in alchemical lore, mysticism and mineralogy. He inclined to the belief that the love of God could more appropriately be invoked and celebrated out of doors, preferably on a mountain where, nearer my God to thee, the grandeur of scenery might be an aid to devotion. In the company of this serious and considerable figure of fun, Boswell walked and talked and was converted. Having attached himself to Williamson, Boswell 'made an obstinate resolve never to eat any flesh, and I was resolved to suffer everything as a martyr to humanity. I looked upon the whole human race with horror.' But the despondency passed, 'I know not how; I think by yielding to received opinions.' It was never clear to Boswell how he shook off the influence of the old Pythagorean or, indeed, his nervous illness. The darkness of depression and doubt remained in the background, nagging his self-confidence and snagging his attempts to be good for something in life.

It was not apparent in the persona he adopted at about this time: at the age of sixteen, a few months short of his seventeenth birthday, he became lively and witty, good-humoured and gay, sociable and high-spirited, noisy and bumptious. He had broadened out, and a natural vigour asserted itself despite the early wilting and languishing. He began to strut and develop his formidable vanity. He discovered that he was attractive to his fellow men and, vitally, to women. The Scots do not, generally, tend to be tall: but in the eighteenth century, a height of five feet six inches, more or less, was not noticeably short. James was a solidly set up young man, with dark hair and black eyes. George Willison painted his portrait in Rome in 1765. The face has a healthy, high colour and the nose sweeps down from a wide brow. The lips, bright and full, are set in the familiar, faintly pursy manner. Of the gorgeousness of his clothes, the full fig of his philosopher-visiting costume, green and red and trimmed with fur and gold lace, there will be occasion to remark later, as he plays variations on his dress which, he claimed, 'affects my feelings as irresistibly as music.'

On his return to Edinburgh, Boswell fell among actors. Mixed with his earlier, pious 'narrow-minded horror' of players had been a lurking 'lively-minded pleasure' which now overwhelmed any scruples about distressing his mother, who had been got to a theatre but once and did not like it, or disturbing his father who suffered no stage-plays to desecrate his library. The attraction of 'painted equipages and powdered ladies' became irresistible. The Edinburgh Presbytery had drawn up a general exhortation that 'all within its bounds discourage the illegal and dangerous entertainments of the stage, and restrain those under their influence from frequenting such seminaries of vice and folly.' In 1756, John Home's tragedy, *Douglas* had been performed to the enthusiastic delight of the laity and the scandal of the Church. It was bad enough that the author, popularly supposed to rival 'Wullie Shakespeare,' was a minister, worse still that he should have enjoyed the support of his reverend colleagues who attended performances and if discovered, could expect to be censured or suspended for their audacious profanity on return to their presbyteries. Not until 1764 was a playhouse licensed in Edinburgh.

In the late 1750s, actors were categorised, without distinction, with beggars and vagrants. Plays were acted, nevertheless, in the Taylor's Hall in the Canongate. To escape legal penalty, they were advertised as performed gratis after a concert of music. To prevent their arrest and detention as vagrants, the learned and literate Lord Somerville established a charming legal fiction that the entire company of players should be employed as his domestic servants. Dutifully, once a year, they would troop to his house to hand him a plate. The amusements of Edinburgh in the early part of the century were neither varied nor lively. Even the most minor infringements of daily decorum, and of the Sabbath in particular, were reprobated and condemned. Where the relaxations of the ungodly gave no offence to the eye, the lively imagination of the pious supplied the scandal. It was a terrible time for such as the devout Mr Robert Wodrow who appealed in vain to the Almighty, 'Lord pity us,' he grieved, 'wickedness is come to a terrible height.'

In the spring and summer of 1758, Boswell was left more or less to his own devices in Edinburgh, when his family closed up the flat in town to return to Auchinleck. In 1754, Alexander Boswell had been elevated to the dignity of a judge of the Court of Session. This had had a tremendous effect on his son who began immediately and inappropriately to refer to his mother, in addressing a letter to her, as the Right Honb^le. My Lady Auchinleck. He is conscious of honours that may accrue to his family, and ultimately to himself, through offices of state and public recognition of worth. But how to set about proving fitness and worth? Not, perhaps, through versifying, though that is delightful and the products of a leisure hour may give pleasure to himself and others through being published.

Better, perhaps, to form suitable attachments. First, of course, there is the question of a wife. In July 1758, he reports to Temple that his affections have centred upon a certain Miss Martha Whyte, the first of many candidates for the place of wife to Mr Boswell. She is suitable to be the partner of his soul. An initial violent passion for his Dulcinea has subsided to 'a rational esteem of her good qualities,' so that if she should not incline to consent to pass her life with him, he can bear it '*aequo animo* and retire into the calm regions of Philosophy.' Her accomplishments are amiable and varied: she dances, sings, plays with equal talent upon several musical instruments, reads the best authors, and has 'a just regard to true piety and religion.' Besides, she is 'extreamly pretty' and has a fortune of £30,000 – but 'Heaven knows that sordid motive is farthest from my mind.' Presumably the comforts of calm Philosophy were called upon, for we hear nothing more of Miss Whyte. There will be others.

In the same letter, Boswell mentions that he has met Temple's surprising acquaintance, Mr Hume the Deist. To the fat, affable philosopher, in his middle forties, the eighteen-year-old Boswell may have been but one more in a steady stream of admirers, but young Mr Boswell had not come to adore: he had come not merely for the entertainment of David Hume's agreeable company but also for 'a great deal of usefull instruction'. To this end, they 'talk a great deal of genius, fine language, improving our style, &c' as gentlemen of wit, learning, and manners will do, but Boswell is disappointed, 'I am afraid, sollid learning is much wore out' and Hume 'has not, perhaps, the most delicate taste' despite his familiarity, through study, with the ancients and history. He is, however, a 'proper person for a young man to cultivate an acquaintance with.'

Another proper person is Sir David Dalrymple, 'my worthy

Maecenas' who is to accompany Lord Auchinleck and Boswell on the North Circuit as Advocate Depute to prosecute cases at Perth, Inverness and Aberdeen. Dalrymple, later to be raised to the bench as Lord Hailes, was thirty-two, a lawyer, antiquarian, and littérateur. His company was 'refined' and his conversation 'agreable and improving'. Johnston, Dalrymple, Hume and, next, Lord Somerville in his sixtieth year, may have supplemented the inadequacies of Auchinleck as a model of ideal behaviour. Professor Pottle regards Somerville as the personification of six of Boswell's 'most passionately held ambitions'. First, he had revived a dormant peerage and thus justified himself as of ancient lineage; second he had been to London as a young man and become known at Court; third he had made two rich marriages; fourth he included poets among his literary acquaintance; fifth he ensured the survival of theatre in Edinburgh; and sixth he maintained private apartments in romantic, historic, royal Holyrood where Boswell was pleased to be entertained and made much of. He had also held a commission in the Dragoons, and Boswell had, at the age of fifteen, earnestly desired to go among the Highlanders who sailed for America in 1756 at the beginning of the Seven Years' War. Auchinleck had put his foot down firmly on that burning martial ambition, but had not extinguished his son's urgent desire to be commissioned.

Despite the near-embarrassment of choice of superior models, Boswell chose rather to emulate the glamorous figure of West Digges, the profligate actor-manager of the Canongate Concert-Hall or Playhouse. Among his theatrical acquaintance Boswell also numbered James Dance, alias Mr Love, who besides giving lessons in elocution to Boswell and Miss Whyte had obligingly taken 'every unsuspected method to lend me his friendly assistance' in fostering Boswell's romantic aspirations towards the heiress. More importantly, he also encouraged his pupil to keep a journal of his trip on the North Circuit, the beginning of a lifelong habit. Pages from this journal, particularly desired by Mr Love, were sent to him 'in sheets, every post'. By Christmas 1758, Boswell could also announce 'a few trifles of my own' in exchange for the receipt of a poem by Temple. He has 'published now and then, the production of a leisure hour, in the magazines'. In August, November, and December, the *Scots Magazine* had been pleased to print his youthful verses. They are not very good: and whatever talent Boswell supposed himself to have for poetry never improved, though he, and they, gained dignity by being published alongside the better works of better poets.

Boswell's reputation as a dramatist suffered a first and fatal blow when he passed off (at the request of the author, Lady Houston) as his own a comedy entitled *The Coquettes, or The Gallant in the Closet* which, in an age when short runs were the rule, was given very short shrift by a hooting audience. It closed on the third night. It was found to be a frank translation of a play by Corneille, and not one of his better ones. Though he had written the Prologue, the responsibility for the play was Lady Houston's, but she refused to take the odium and insisted on retaining her ladylike and modest anonymity. In drawing the curtain over herself, she exposed Boswell to the catcalls and jibes – but, however pained and frustrated he must have felt, Boswell continued to pursue the delights of the theatre which included its 'powdered ladies'. In December 1758, besides leisurely versifying and laboriously studying law, Astronomy, and Roman Antiquities, another attraction was added to his life: an actress named Mrs Cowper joined the Edinburgh theatre to play leading roles. Her leading parts and her person struck Boswell forcefully. He fell in love. Exit Miss Whyte, enter Mrs Cowper of no fortune but her face and her figure. It was a duty and a pleasure for Mr Boswell to sit through her performances as a critic and a lover.

The summer performances of 1759 were reviewed in the press by Boswell, and Mrs Cowper could never have had better notices: her beauty and virtues almost defy adequate description, but the attempt is made – sweet virtue irradiates her face, a blush heightens her colour should an indecent word sully her ear, her stage and public presence are alike the finest, the most agreeable, and the politest, and her talent as an actress is the most perfect in the land. This compensates for one minor flaw – she is not, it is admitted, 'a quick study'. Temple was less impressed: she was perhaps not to his taste and thus he preserved some objectivity as a man and a critic while his friend played the rhapsodic gallant in the public press and, no reason to doubt, in private life.

Love and literature may have been considerable light relief for Boswell, who was applying himself diligently enough to the study of law, but the flighty, distracting company with which his whimsical son was associating began to alarm Lord Auchinleck. To judge by the relative freedom Boswell apparently enjoyed at this time, Auchinleck may have been inclined to relax the reins a bit. In August 1759, some ten weeks before his nineteenth birthday, James became a Freemason, a body noted for its conviviality. His father may have decided that a sufficient crop of oats had been sown and that he should not wait for harvest, because Boswell was suddenly and unexpectedly enrolled as a student at Glasgow University for the academic session 1759–60.

Glasgow was respectably free of theatres, actresses, or indeed any form of entertainment. It was a commercial city, with a fine University graced by the edifying Adam Smith whom Boswell, who at least had the sense to know a good man when he met one, admired. He fell in with his father's decisive plan without excessive complaint and composed his mind to be contented. He led 'quite an academical life' as he wrote to Johnston in January 1760, rarely visiting Auchinleck, though he was still anxious for particulars about the Edinburgh stage. But life was very dull, and diversion was sought. In February, a book of the previous summer's reviews of the Edinburgh stage was published in London. The delights of Mrs Cowper were revived in this *View of the Edinburgh Theatre during the Summer Season, 1759, containing an Exact List of the Several Pieces represented, and Impartial Observations on Each Performance* by 'a Society of Gentlemen'. It is to be hoped that the Society had the grace to giggle over the reference to impartiality when it got the fifty-page pamphlet in its partial hands.

Even in exile, the name of Boswell was kept in the public eye: Francis Gentleman, who had been in Edinburgh as an actor-manager during the 1758–59 theatrical season, gushingly dedicated his adaptation of Southerne's Restoration play *Oroonoko* to James Boswell, Esq., in exchange for a few guineas. It was a common enough practice to extract a generous gift from a patron whose pockets were lightened and importance swelled by associating himself with a work of literature. Whether the dedication settled a debt already owed to Boswell by Gentleman, is uncertain – but Boswell was a glad-handed fellow who also later loaned money to Love and, no doubt, there had been some expense connected with the staging of Lady Houston's piece of plagiarism.

The tergiversations of Boswell's regular and unsuitable conversions to a variety of religious doctrines took a serious turn in Glasgow. Mrs Cowper, though not present in person, was influential in spirit. She was a Roman Catholic, and Boswell, who had some independence of mind was, even so, open to influence. She had introduced him to a priest in Edinburgh who gave Boswell some books with a view to converting him to the Catholic Church. He had already sampled Methodism, Episcopalianism, Pythagoreanism, and the love of ritual and rich tradition was well established in his emotional character. Roman Catholics were barely tolerated in Scotland, and incurred severe penalties for their faith and the practice of it. Conversion was a serious step, but that never worried Boswell.

Had he considered the implications in detail, he would have experienced, perhaps, a momentary alarm: Roman Catholics were debarred by statute from entry into the Church, the Navy, the Army, and the law – though minor posts in the last were open to them, with no opportunity for advancement. They could not stand for Parliament and were not entitled to vote in elections. They could not teach at the Universities, and strictly (though means were found to circumvent the problem), they could not succeed to an estate. Everything to which an able lawyer and a man of ancient lineage could hope to aspire would become impossible. But no matter: Boswell wished to become a monk or priest to which Roman Catholic faith was no impediment, was indeed a prerequisite. 'At eighteen,' he informed Rousseau, 'I became a Catholic. I struggled against paternal affection, ambition, interest.' Lord Auchinleck, on receipt of a letter announcing his son's fixed intention, summoned him to Edinburgh to account

for his improbable and appalling decision. On 1 March 1760
Boswell bolted to London. Many a Scottish landed gentleman
lived in London, a point that did not escape Boswell now, or later
when he used it to justify his enjoyment of the pleasures of
London to Johnson. Despite a reputation for philosophy and a
degree of politeness in its society, Edinburgh in the mid-
eighteenth century was not famed for lightness of heart or laxity of
morals. Philosophy had not corrupted the kirk, and the increasing
ceremoniousness of society implied no degeneration of traditional values. Edinburgh was provincial, and the glittering prospect of London was irresistible. Many a Scotsman found it so:
then, and now. In Boswell's time, there was a general resentment
against the Scots in London. Rallying round the considerable,
weighty, political figure of Lord Bute, they had carved out a
comfortable niche for themselves and wielded authority much as
their recent ancestors had waved their claymores.

For Boswell, London was a haven of religious tolerance, a
source of illicit pleasure since London liberally permitted bawds,
bagnios, and theatres to flourish, and thirdly it was a centre of
patronage where prizes of preferment in the military or politics
were offered for the taking to young men of genius.

Mr D. B. Wyndham Lewis devotes a significant part of his
biography of Boswell, *The Hooded Hawk*, to an examination of
Boswell's impulse and supposed conversion. He is the first to take
it seriously, more as a compliment to Roman Catholicism than to
its youthful adherent and neophyte. The inclination towards the
Roman Catholic Church lasted the rest of Boswell's life and it
cannot briskly be dismissed as a 'youthful prank ... or an
indication of mental disorder' as Macaulay would have it.
Whether Boswell took it, in youth, as seriously as Lewis does as
his biographer, is open to debate. Boswell 'thought more than any
body supposed' but to what effect, or to what depth of understanding, may be more to the point.

'Conversion to the Catholic Church entails, over and beyond
the spiritual metamorphosis involved, certain formalities whereby
the convert seals and proclaims his faith;' remarks Mr Lewis,
'essential instruction beforehand, a simple ceremony of reception

to follow. It seems doubtful whether Boswell ever went to this length, judging by his frequent questions to Johnson on points of Catholic belief. Possibly, like Gibbon and Wilde and others, he did not think instruction necessary.' For all Boswell's later attendance at Mass in Germany, Italy, France and London, Lewis is sceptical that Boswell experienced a 'true change of heart,' a desirable precondition to reception into the Catholic Church. It seems more likely that Boswell's need was less for spiritual comfort than the need to identify more closely with the real object of his desires – closer union with Mrs Cowper. It was an episode he never mentioned to John Johnston, with whom he corresponded and talked intimately, and certainly never revealed to Samuel Johnson except in so far as he quizzed him on points of Catholic doctrine.

The flight to London was attended by rumour: it was said he had eloped with Mrs Cowper, an actress damned by the faint praise of being reputed virtuous among Catholics, her behaviour being the best that might be expected of a Papist. But Mrs Cowper *was* virtuous, and James was alone. He knew, however, where to go and soon picked up allies. His thoughts had dwelled on London where, he assumed, his happiness would centre, and he had at least got there for the first time. It was to be a short visit, but eventful. Immediately he made himself known to Thomas Meighan, who had a Roman Catholic bookshop in Drury Lane, and who was reputed to be a conduit to proselytising priests. The young apostate from the Presbyterianism of his father was directed to the Bavarian Chapel where, enthusiastically, he saw Mass celebrated for the first time. If Boswell was indeed received into the Roman Catholic Church, it was now: and his intention was to retire to a monastery in France.

But that intention could be momentarily postponed, for Boswell was in London 'and had begun to taste its delights –', with the result that the cloth of the priest gave way to the glamour of the gaudy scarlet cloth of the Guards, the cloisters to the Court, and the devotions of the religious to the gossip of the *beau monde*. Here, too, were men of genius with whom to dine and dawdle. Having satisfactorily settled the question of his soul, Boswell turned his attention to satisfying the urgent needs of his body: having found a priest, he now found a pimp and in a room at the Blue Periwig in Southampton Street, near Covent Garden, he experienced 'the melting and transporting rites of love' in the arms of Miss Sally Forrester, a whore.

Since he had some sense of filial obligation and not much money, Boswell told his father where he was. Lord Auchinleck did not immediately rush to London, but appointed the Earl of Eglinton, an Ayrshire neighbour then residing in London, to locate the truant. He was found in the company of Mr Samuel Derrick, a dubious cicerone whom Boswell later referred to as 'a little blackguard pimping dog' but who was for the moment agreeable company, introducing the wide-eyed Boswell to London 'in all its variety of departments, both literary and sportive.' Sportive meaning, at that time, sexual. Opinions vary as to the degree of depravity and disrepute to be attributed to Derrick. Johnson, to whom Derrick had promised Boswell an introduction but failed to make the connection 'of which I was very ambitious,' said of him, 'Derrick may do very well, as long as he can outrun his character; but the moment his character gets up with him, it is all over.' Some years later, Johnson conceded that 'Derrick has now got a character that he need not run away from.' D. B. Wyndham Lewis characterises him as 'a neat, brisk, amiable little butterfly . . . ex-actor, minor poet and playwright,' and in 1761 successor to Beau Nash as Master of Ceremonies at Bath, where he won a reputation as 'a pretty little gentleman, so sweet, so fine, so civil, and polite,' which sits uneasily with Professor Pottle's disparagement of the arbiter of elegance as 'a dingy fifth-rate man of letters, countryman, and friend of Francis Gentleman.'

He was supplanted by the Earl of Eglinton as Boswell's sponsor 'into the circles of the great, the gay, and the ingenious'. Eglinton took Boswell from lodgings and housed him under his own roof just three weeks after arriving in London. Eglinton gave James liberty to indulge every passion that had hitherto been thwarted by his parents, his own doubts about the propriety of his first furtive excesses, and the restrictive moral climate of Scotland. Eglinton, apparently giving him his head, subtly guided Boswell's taste from the ridiculous to the sublime: or, at least, from Roman Cathol-icism, monasticism and low life to military ambitions, libertinage, and the high life of literary, intellectual, and aristocratic conver-sation and acquaintance. From the gloom of superstition, as Boswell himself remarked, Eglinton led him to the other extreme. They went racing at Newmarket, Boswell met the young Duke of York (a youth with whom Boswell would have liked to be on terms of intimacy, were the gulf between them not so great and the Duke but 'simple Ned'), and was introduced to Laurence Sterne, the exciting author of *Tristram Shandy* who made much of Boswell's verse. The experience was so overwhelming as to make a disciple of Boswell and all but wreck his style with Shandy-isms for a while.

Eglinton suggested that Boswell had best attempt to purchase a commission in a Guards regiment and Lord Auchinleck was informed of Boswell's agreement that this was the best of all possible plans. The Seven Years' War was still in progress, but an officer of a regiment of Foot Guards would not be likely to be required to leave London for the inconvenience of battle. The profession of arms was suitable for a gentleman, the clothes were gorgeous, the situation in London was agreeable, and altogether the gay and gregarious life of an officer and a gentleman would suit Mr Boswell very well. Auchinleck immediately came person-ally to London, invoked the influence of the Duke of Argyll, who thought Mr Boswell too fine a boy to 'be shot at for three and sixpence a day' (a prospect equally distasteful to Boswell) and Auchinleck begged his son to return to Edinburgh to consider the matter more closely.

Towards the end of May, three months after his arrival in the full flush of 'an almost enthusiastic notion of the felicity of London,' which had not generally been disappointed, Boswell and Auchinleck returned to Edinburgh. A year later, he is fretting and regretting in a letter to Temple, 'consider this poor fellow hauled away to the town of Edinburgh – obliged to conform to every Scotch custom, or be laughed at, – *"Will you hae some jeel?"* *O fie! O fie!* His flighty imagination quite cramped, and he obliged

to study *Corpus Juris Civilis*, and live in his father's strict family: –
is there any wonder, Sir, that the unlucky dog should be somewhat fretfull? Yoke a Newmarket courser to a dung cart, and I'll
lay my life on't, he'll either caper and kick most confoundedly, or
be as stupid and restive as an old, battered post-horse. Not one in
a hundred can understand this. You do.'

To add to his ills, he had caught a venereal disease. 'I went to a
house of recreation in this place, [Edinburgh] and catch'd a
Tartar, too, with a vengeance.' He is tart with Temple, who has
reprobated him for being 'indelicate in the choice of my female
friends.' Boswell does not condescend to regard 'passing some
hours with an infamous creature' as a *connection*. He drew a firm
line between ladies of virtue and piety, prettiness and fortune,
who might be regarded as material for marriage or elegant
friendship, and the drabs with whom a gentleman might take his
grosser pleasures. In September 1760 he was 'taking a regular
course of Medecines, and keeping within doors, with spare diet,
in order to get effectualy rid of my Indisposition, that troublesom
Companion and bar to my innocent pleasures.'

'Within doors' he would also be cooped up at Auchinleck
House with his father and 'strict family'. An offer of a commission
in a marching regiment was made to him, but turned down. There
was no other course for it, insisted Lord Auchinleck: it must be
the law, and for two years or so he personally instructed his son in
its points and principles. They moved back and forth between
Auchinleck and Edinburgh, according to the legal seasons, and
the life of dissipation and vice in London to which James aspired,
in the opinion of his father, grew more alluring. But wherever
diversion is to be had, James will find it: where there is none, he
will create it.

[2]

The Moth and the Candle

The twentieth century visitor to Auchinleck and its environs will be hard put to it to understand Boswell's eighteenth century enthusiasm for that particular part of Ayrshire. The village itself has little to recommend it: in the mid-1700s it could only have been a huddle of houses in a straight line, and it is not much better than that now. The tourist will readily recognise Boswell's urgent desire to be in London. The pits and bings that have been sunk and raised to disfigure the unromantic landscape of this mining area are, of course, modern. But Ayrshire can be pretty and picturesque, particularly towards the softer, agricultural south and the coast. The climate is temperate, and rather damp. It is more the land of Burns than of Boswell.

The Adamesque Auchinleck House itself is fine, and the grounds that surrounded it inspired Boswell's romantic rapture. Dr Johnson did not think badly of them, though he regretted the passing of the original castle and the later Renaissance mansion that Alexander Boswell's new house had supplanted. The estate had increased with the years and the ambitions of the Boswells: Johnson considered Lord Auchinleck's house of hewn stone 'very stately and durable' though 'I was, however, less delighted with the elegance of the modern mansion, than with the sullen dignity of the old castle.' Auchinleck was a good landlord and, in his own interests, had 'advanced the value of his lands, with great tenderness to his tenants.' This, then, was Ulubrae somewhat distant from London, as its namesake, near the Pontine marshes of Latium, was remote from Rome. Boswell was often at Auchinleck, with his family, from the time of the death of his grandfather in 1749.

There is a certain pride and closeness about the Scots – they do not, generally, care to give any cause for gossip: if a man cannot keep his business to himself, then it should certainly go no further than his immediate family. An eldest son particularly is expected to be a credit to his family, and the Scots have produced some resounding credits as well as the notable scapegraces who naturally attract most attention. Lord Auchinleck had been beaten by his own father and saw no reason not to be severe in turn with his own sons. James concedes that he was beaten physically only once, for lying, a profoundly affecting experience that made it exceedingly difficult for him ever to lie again. Lord Auchinleck announced his judiciously considered domestic decisions in the manner of *obiter dicta*, and he did not expect there to be any appeal, since they were self-evidently for the good of his children. Regular hours, diligent application to study and work, a proper sense of decorum, and an appropriate regard for the dignity of the family name and social position were all expected as a matter of course: Lord Auchinleck, himself a Newmarket courser in youth, had adopted the staid respectability that he hoped to discover and encourage in his sons and particularly in James, his eldest. But even John and David, Boswell's younger brothers, were dismayed by the stern countenance and peremptory manner of their father. They were difficult enough; but James was a sore trial, a 'heedless, dissipated, rattling fellow who might say or do every ridiculous thing,' as he readily admitted. He was in low spirits, but appeared naturally vivacious – a persona he consciously adopted 'to make myself easy.'

A dose of clap, the 'Tartar' he had caught in Edinburgh and confessed to Temple, persuaded him to stay clear of 'the mansions of gross sensuality' for a while, and his creative energies required some outlet: he began to resume literary activities. His facility for versifying was spontaneous and quick: sheer ease of composition probably persuaded him that, since very little effort was required to produce a pleasing poem, he had a natural talent for poetry. Posterity has granted Boswell a permanent fame, but not for poetry which even ardent Boswellphiles are reluctant to quote or publish.

In November 1760 he published, at Edinburgh, 'Observations,

Good or Bad, Stupid or Clever, Serious or Jocular, on Squire
Foote's Dramatic Entertainment entitled *The Minor* by a Genius'.
This threepenny pamphlet set out to review and animadvert upon
a London theatre production which the 'Genius' had had no
opportunity to see, but which had had such a controversial
success in its thirty-five night run that no rattling man of letters
could afford to forbear adding his threepenny-worth to the
debate. In August 1761, Boswell followed up smartly with a
sixpenny pamphlet, ten pages of which were devoted to *An Elegy
on the Death of an Amiable Young Lady* and *An Epistle from Lycidas to
Menalcas*. The greater part of the publication, however, was
fourteen pages of three 'critical recommendatory letters' which
fulsomely, to the point of satire, praised the quality of the author's
efforts. The critical recommendations may not have been
seriously intended: but the poems were quite without irony.

   In the next month, September, a letter by 'A Gentleman of
Scotland to the Earl of *** in London' was published in the *Scots
Magazine*. The 'Gentleman' was instantly identifiable just as, by
association, was the elegant Earl of Eglinton whose raffish tutelage during the three months crash-course in the ways of 'the
great, the gay, and the ingenious' was still pricking Boswell's
imagination. This vivid, indiscreet letter revealed the improbable
intelligence that the author was about to be married, that he had
been the intimate of Laurence Sterne, and that although he was
now irksomely restricted by a strict study of law, he proposed to
continue his study of happiness when his stars fated him to return
to London. In December 1761 he published, anonymously, an
Ode to Tragedy which he dedicated, without compunction, to
himself. He contributed thirty bad poems to an anthology of
'Poems by Scotch Gentlemen', and in March 1762 there
appeared *The Cub at Newmarket*, a humorous narrative poem
recording the author's humiliation when abandoned by Eglinton
at the Jockey Club. This, he considered, was a most important
production and in a letter to the publisher Bowyer, in London,
urged that 'no expense be spared to make it genteel. Let it be done
on large quarto, and a good type. Price one shilling.' Since
Boswell was publishing at his own expense, a shilling may have

seemed on the one hand a bargain price for such a handsome and accomplished publication and on the other a sum calculated at least to defray costs. His devotion to 'simple Ned,' the Duke of York, induced Boswell to dedicate the poem to this royal sprig without permission. Ned was furious, and rounded on Eglinton who in turn berated Boswell sorely for his latest piece of impudence.

In the summer of 1761, Boswell added two friends to his extensive social and literary acquaintance. The first was Andrew Erskine, also twenty-one and a writer of inadequate verse. He accompanied Boswell, in August, to a series of lectures given by the Irish actor Thomas Sheridan (father of Richard Brinsley Sheridan), who had been sponsored by the Select Society of Edinburgh to eliminate Scotticisms from the speech of fashionable Edinburgh. Three hundred gentlemen paid a guinea a head for this opportunity to acquire some gentility of speech – or, at least, to acquire a more perfect knowledge of the English tongue albeit flavoured with Sheridan's Irish brogue. Anything was preferable to the impropriety of Scots corruption of standard English.

Boswell again played his trick of adopting an older man as mentor and substitute father-figure: Sheridan became his confidant and correspondence continued when the sympathetic Sheridan returned to London pursued by letters detailing all Boswell's doubts and perplexities about which he requested advice and direction. A correspondence also arose between Boswell and Erskine, a series of flighty, frivolous letters which were to be published in 1763. In an age when letters were written, Boswell's correspondence was perhaps no more conscious or comprehensive than that of many another busy, sociable man. But it was extensive, extravagant, enlightening, and sometimes erudite. When added to the journals, memoranda, memoirs, pamphlets and poems he also produced, the quantity of words is immense. It is as though nothing became real to Boswell until and unless he had, in some form, recorded or communicated it – revealing himself not only to others but equally to himself.

His amorous adventures, although he had forsworn whores,

were pursued with vigour. He fell readily into the arms of, if not in love with, Mrs Love whose husband owed Boswell £40 and was not allowed to forget it. She was an actress of at least forty, a point not lost on her gallant who referred to her as 'old Canongate' after the theatre in which she played comic parts. Professor Pottle has ingeniously identified two other liaisons at this time: one with an actress called Mrs Brooke who was in Edinburgh during 1761 and 1762, and the other with Jean Heron, wife to a landed gentleman of Dumfries and daughter to the redoubtable Lord Kames with whom Boswell had become intimate for a while. The affair was fraught with difficulties, as he later confided to Rousseau, 'She let me see that she loved me more than she did her husband. She made no difficulty of granting me all. She was a subtle philosopher. She said, "I love my husband as a husband, and you as a lover, each in his own sphere. I perform for him all the duties of a good wife. With you I give myself up to delicious pleasures. We keep our secret. Nature has so made me that I shall never bear children. No one suffers because of our loves. My conscience does not reproach me, and I am sure that God cannot be offended by them."'

This charming philosophy gave Boswell pause for thought, but did not wholly convince. For one thing, Lord Kames had been kind to him, and Mr Heron was amiable. So amiable, indeed, that he had warmly pressed Boswell to make extended visits to Dumfriesshire. Boswell wished to be open, to be rid of his remorse even if the revelation should drive Mr Heron in a frenzy as a cuckold to deprive him of his own life. He consulted with Mrs Heron who reproached Boswell for his miserable weakness. 'What could I do?' Why, nothing but enjoy what must be endured. 'I continued my criminal amour, and the pleasures I tasted formed a counterpoise to my remorse.' But Boswell did not like to lie, even by omission, and he disapproved of adultery. It was attended by too many inhibitions to be satisfying: like the harlots he enjoyed, he preferred pleasure without responsibility – though that may be too harsh a judgement on the whores, who perhaps took little pleasure in their occupation and found themselves saddled with too much responsibility. One certainly did: on 17

August 1762 Boswell wrote to John Johnston, his man of affairs (the pun can be carried too far, perhaps), to request that provision be made for the son, Charles, about to be born to one Peggy Doig in December. Little more is heard of this child, who died while Boswell was in Holland in 1764, though Boswell set aside £10 per annum for his maintenance.

The connection with Peggy Doig (whom Pottle suspects to have been a servant) was made in March 1762, coinciding with a crisis in the relationship between Boswell and his father: Auchinleck spoke seriously of disinheriting James. In law, it is doubtful whether he could have done so, but he was a better lawyer than his son and convinced Boswell that the threat was not only genuine but perfectly possible. He induced James to sign a 'renunciation' of his interests in the family estate: or, at least, vested it in trustees on the ground that James would be personally incompetent to administer it to best advantage. A document of this nature may be drawn up by an exasperated father as a ruse to bring a giddy son to heel, to impress him more forcibly with the likely outcome of his persisting in folly and vice. It may be done in the heat of the moment, without serious or permanent intention to deprive the eldest son of his just inheritance. Auchinleck respected the principle of succession by the nearest male heir as much as James did, so that it can have been no easy matter for Lord Auchinleck to make his decision. He would never have done the thing without the most serious intention and would never have succumbed to a whim or resorted to a ruse. The fornications were less important than the lack of discretion and distaste for a regular life he observed in his son. He should not be allowed to profit from his profligacy nor bring the Boswell name and fortune to ruin. James was granted an allowance of £100 per annum, and though it was an inadequate sum on which to go convincingly to the devil, it was at least an assurance that James would not starve – or, if he did, that it could not be alleged against Auchinleck that he had cut the lad off without a shilling. Boswell himself may have been, for the moment, content to have such a sum in hand.

Almost immediately, Boswell conceived the improbable plan that he should marry the widowed, sexagenarian Duchess of

Douglas, but perhaps he (or she) thought better of it and the idea of obtaining a commission in the Guards again surfaced in his mind, plopping up like a bubble from the depths to burst into his brain. Lord Eglinton was notified that the plan had been resurrected, and Erskine was regaled with Boswell's 'most agreeable reveries'. The letter to Erskine is a dazzling performance as the Boswell brain, seized with an idea, grasps it and runs off with it at top speed: he has no sooner exhausted the felicity of being a Guards officer fêted and petted by ministers of state, the nobility, and elegant women, than he is using the perfection of manners he will acquire in such company to hob nob on terms of equality with 'the learned and ingenious in every science,' and travelling to pick up honours like daisies at every foreign court and being of assistance to his countrymen abroad. Having exhausted these delights, he will return to England to enter the House of Commons, rival Pitt, and be made principal Secretary of State. He will have his own gallant regiment of Guards to throw back a Spanish invasion, marry a fortune, sire men 'of sense and spirit' and women 'of beauty and every amiable perfection'. And this grand personage will be accorded the most prodigious respect, inspiring dedications and statues in his immortal honour. One can see Mr Boswell, his head in the empyrean, sinking back in a graceful curve from this letter, pen thrown aside, the thing accomplished, basking in the glory that is not merely to be visited upon him but which irradiates his being with the glow of the thing having been all but achieved.

The reply from Eglinton is a bumping reminder that Boswell's wings are of wax. Boswell had insisted that the commission be obtained in a battalion based in London, while Eglinton reasonably but irritably reminded Boswell that a soldier would at least be expected to show some readiness to fight if necessary, however much it might inconvenience him, and required Boswell to state his willingness to accept a commission in a battalion on service in Germany. When Boswell was disposed to quibble, Eglinton lost interest. There was no help for it, but to press Lord Auchinleck to use his influence. Boswell's father wrote to the Duke of Queensberry, who replied that there were difficulties but that he would

do what he could. This did not seem very likely to Auchinleck, but
Boswell was clutching at straws. On 30 July 1762, James Boswell
passed the examination in Civil Law, satisfying at least one of the
demands made by his father and perhaps, as a token of approval,
Auchinleck agreed that James should go to London in November
to try his luck in obtaining the desired commission.

Despite his disdain for the grosser, less genteel, style of
Scottish society, Boswell could not resist enjoying the attentions
of its notabilities. He was welcome anywhere, because he contrived with nice judgement to suit his behaviour to the company
he kept. He had a pleasing civility of manners and a grave though
never subservient attention for the likes of Sir David Dalrymple,
and an indefatigable frothiness with younger and less formal
friends for whom he founded the Soaping Club – a regular
Tuesday night assembly of fairly innocent and self-satisfied
libertines among whom could be counted Johnston and Erskine.
The motto of the club was 'Every man soap his own beard,' which
Boswell took to mean 'Let every man indulge his own humour.'

The Soaping Club song which he composed is a piece of happy
self-advertisement in which Boswell congratulates himself on his
ability to talk with ease and grace and set the table in a constant
roar. The company can laugh with him, or at him, just as they
please, as he rattles and prattles, and no offence will be given or
taken. The thing is to be amusing. He is in love with half a score of
women who are in error if they take him too seriously. To put it in
a nutshell, as he did:

> He has all the bright fancy of youth
> With the judgement of forty and five;
> In short, to declare the plain truth,
> There is no better fellow alive.

In 1763, a description of this fine fellow is included in the
'Erskine Correspondence': it describes him very much as he
viewed himself on the eve of his adventure. 'The author of the *Ode
to Tragedy* is a most excellent man: he is of an ancient family in the
west of Scotland, upon which he prides himself not a little. At his

nativity there appeared omens of his future greatness. His parts are bright, and his education has been good. He has travelled in post-chaises miles without number. He is fond of seeing much of the world. He eats of every good dish, especially apple-pie. He drinks old Hock. He has a very fine temper. He is something of an Humourist and a little tinctured with pride. He has a good manly countenance, and he owns himself to be amorous. He has infinite vivacity, yet is observed at times to have a melancholy cast. He is rather fat than lean, rather short than tall, rather young than old. His shoes are neatly made, and he never wears spectacles. The length of his walking stick is not yet ascertained; but we hope soon to favour the Republic of Letters with a solution of this difficulty, as several able mathematicians are employed in its investigation . . .' Boswell, as much as the indeterminate walking stick, is clearly a suitable subject for detailed measurement. Charmingly, he airs his faults as easily as his graces, and adds a few telling particulars – plump, neatly shod, devoted to apple-pie and good wine. Perhaps the echo of Adam Smith's lectures on Rhetoric and Belles-Lettres at Glasgow had come floating back to remind Boswell that we are glad to know that Milton wore latchets instead of buckles in his shoes, and that great men may be evoked through the minutest detail.

He took his ceremonious leave of Edinburgh on Monday 15 November 1762: Lord Auchinleck had paid his debts and assured him of an allowance of £200 a year. He felt 'parental affection was very strong towards me, and I felt a very warm filial regard for them.' This was all to the good, since he would never see his mother again. At ten o'clock in the morning, he entered his chaise, and bowled off towards the Canongate where, at the Cross, 'the cadies and chairmen bowed and seemed to say, "God prosper long our noble Boswell."' Having taken his leave of these respectful representative lieges of Edinburgh, he proceeded to Holyroodhouse where he 'bowed thrice: once to the Palace itself, once to the crown of Scotland above the gate in front, and once to the venerable old Chapel,' after which he bowed three times to Arthur's Seat, 'that lofty romantic mountain on which I have so often strayed in my days of youth, indulged meditation and felt the raptures of a soul filled with ideas of the magnificence of God and his creation.' Having completed this orgy of sentimental patriotism, he perhaps adjusted the fine cocked hat set atop his wig and settled his 'brown coat made in the Court fashion, red vest, corduroy small clothes, and long military boots' in the chaise, checked behind him to see that his servant on horseback was ready for the off, and fixed his black eyes and imagination on the road to London.

On Friday 19 November, he and his travelling companion, a Mr Stewart, 'came upon Highgate hill and had a view of London, I was all life and joy . . . and my soul bounded forth to a certain prospect of happy futurity.' On 20 November, he reported to Johnston, 'At last I am got to this great Metropolis the object of my wishes for so long; the Place where I consider felicity to dwell and age to be a stranger to. I am all in a flutter of joy. I am full of fine wild romantic feeling to find myself realy in LONDON.'

O rare and rarefied James Boswell, possessed of every capacity for life and £200 a year. Likely enough, narrow though his purse might be, he would have it in mind to return to the scene of a triumph of his previous visit, the Drury Lane Theatre where he had excited some attention by giving a lifelike imitation of a lowing cow. Here, he would be sure to see the great actor David Garrick, a friend of Mr Johnson's, who appeared regularly as Hamlet, Romeo, Shylock, and was soon to electrify the town as Lear, gorgeous in white wig, diamond-buckled high-heeled shoes, and a short, regal cape of velvet trimmed with ermine. Later, the delights of fashionable Ranelagh gardens, open to the public and the peerage from May to August, might claim his patronage. Though the elegant suppers in the supper-boxes, close to the music of strings and organ, might be too expensive to enjoy, what could be more delightful than to stroll on a balmy evening by the lake, or around the Rotunda, or to idle by the Chinese Pagoda while deciding which of the ladies of the town, in full fig, to escort through the shrubbery and entice down darkling glades? Boswell was simultaneously robust and romantic in his pleasures.

How to begin to enter upon every felicity? One thing, at least, is clear: he will not miss or minimise a minute of it. Every experience will be grist to the mill, to be ground fine and studied minutely. 'I have therefore determined to keep a daily journal in which I shall set down my various sentiments and my various conduct, which will be not only useful but very agreeable. It will give me a habit of application and improve me in expression; and knowing that I am to record my transactions will make me more careful to do well. Or if I should go wrong, it will assist me in resolutions of doing better.' But the exercise is not all for self-improvement. The follies may be instructive, but that is not to say they may not be enjoyed, and Boswell knows himself to have a capacity for both folly and pleasure, normally followed by remorse and an imposs-ible dedication to reform. It will be a journal remarkably unres-trained and various in content. 'I shall here put down my thoughts on different subjects at different times, the whims that may seize me and the sallies of my luxuriant imagination. I shall mark the anecdotes and the stories that I hear, the instructive or amusing conversations that I am present at, and the various adventures that I may have.' Boswell intends that his journal shall be picaresque.

He also intends that it should be more or less secret, and from the latter part of December 1762 he sends his journal, with a covering letter, to Johnston with the warning, 'I must insist that no Mortal see a word of it. You need not mention it at all.' But parts of it may be too good to waste, 'You may tell any storys or anecdotes you think can entertain from it, and just say you had them from your friend Mr Boswell, at London.' Though Boswell entertains no thought of publication, it would be a pity to lose such a vitally interesting document. 'Let it be carefully deposited at full quarto size and kept clean and safe. Perhaps at the year's end, we may think of binding it up.' Meanwhile, life must be lived if the journal is to be of any interest, and £200 a year, doled out at the rate of £25 every six weeks, is not a great deal after necessary expenses have been deducted. At a rent of forty guineas a year, he takes rooms with a civil servant, Mr Terrie, in Downing Street. The Terries took such a liking to Boswell that this sum was twice reduced – 'I was extremely agreeable to the family.' At length, £43 is left for riotous living, 'which I shall find a very slight allowance.'

He is determined that life should be regular and makes daily notes to remind himself what must be done: this is a symptom of severe anxiety. He is on his own now and must not fail in his designs. For all the swaggering in the London Journal, Boswell is constantly insecure. Wild imaginings and pleasurable fantasies are one thing, real life quite another. 'Be reserved and calm and sustain a consistent character,' he advises himself. His shorthand word for this is the French '*retenu*'. His father will expect discretion. London must fire but also firm his character, 'so when you return to Auchinleck, you'll have dignity.' But, equally, he knows himself to be whimsical even in the most minor activities: on 6 January he takes it into his head 'that between St Paul's and the Exchange and back again, taking the different sides of the street, I would eat a penny Twelfth-cake at every shop where I could get it. This I performed most faithfully.'

Settled in decent lodgings, determined to be *retenu*, but avid for all that London can offer, he is dismayed to find himself associating with fellow-Scots. Lady Betty Macfarlane, Lady Anne Erskine, Captain Erskine (actually Lieutenant Andrew Erskine), and Miss Dempster (the sister of George Dempster, MP, a Scottish crony of Boswell's), meet him at an inn, but 'to tell the plain truth, I was vexed at their coming. For to see just the plain *hamely* Fife family hurt my grand ideas of London.' There is finer game to snare: Boswell had already, warily, called upon Lord Eglinton and received a card of invitation to dine with him. He had looked, in vain, at the Blue Periwig for Miss Sally Forrester, and had dug up the Loves again. As a man of letters, he had called upon Dodsley, his publisher, and dunned him for thirteen shillings owing on *The Cub at Newmarket*, and he had picked up a girl in the Strand 'with intention to enjoy her in armour.' (That is, to protect himself with a prophylactic sheath.) Gratifyingly, 'she wondered at my size, and said that if I ever took a girl's maidenhead, I would make her squeak.' Boswell was vain in many respects, not least about his sexual prowess and the dimensions of his penis. But this time, despite his unhappiness for want of women, 'I gave her a shilling, and . . . resolved to wait cheerfully till I got some safe girl or was liked by a woman of fashion.'

On 27 November, Boswell dined with Eglinton on beefsteaks

at the Beefsteak Club in Covent Garden where the company included the poet Charles Churchill and John Wilkes, the notorious author of the *North Briton*. In the chair was Lord Sandwich. This is, on the face of it, dangerous company for a young man – but Boswell is, he assures Lord Eglinton, no longer the 'raw, curious, volatile, credulous' fellow of his first jaunt to London. '"My Lord," said I, "I am now a little wiser." "Not as much as you think," said he.'

Boswell took this judicious reply in good part, and continued to cultivate respectable as well as disreputable acquaintance. Mr Samuel Johnson is in Boswell's busy mind when he calls on Thomas Sheridan and his excellent, if homely, wife. Derrick having failed to effect an introduction, Boswell is dismayed to find Sheridan, too, a broken reed: he has nothing but abuse for Johnson who resented Sheridan's government pension and had said so. There is a falling-out, before long, between Sheridan and Boswell who had written a Prologue for Mrs Sheridan's play *The Discovery*. Sheridan rejected the Prologue, having weighed it in the balances and found it light:

Boswell: What, is not good?
Sheridan: Indeed, I think it is very bad.

The indifferent qualities of Boswell's prologue were then pointed out to him 'with an insolent bitterness and a clumsy ridicule that hurt me much.' There ensued a dispute about poetry, Sheridan maintaining that excellence was the only criterion, Boswell asserting that since most readers had a mediocre taste, their appreciation would be satisfied by mediocrity 'so that a man of tolerable genius rather gains than loses'.

Being thus made aware of Sheridan's 'bad taste, his insolence, his falsehood, his malevolence in the strongest light,' Boswell determined to break with him, then immediately thought better of it, 'I was entertained in his company, so had better keep in with him.' But things were never so warm again between the two men, however indifferent Boswell might pretend to be as to Sheridan's opinion of him. Mr Boswell took his leave of Mr Sheridan and

looked about for more consoling acquaintance, someone who
would have no reservations about the prodigy who combined 'a
warm heart and a vivacious fancy' even at divine service where,
Mr Boswell was curiously interested to discover, he could simultaneously lay plans for having women, while enjoying 'the most
sincere feelings of religion'. He had his coat and his cocked hat
and a silver-hilted sword that had cost him five guineas. More
than one coat, indeed: in his trunks there must have been the 'full
chocolate suit' he had worn to dance a minuet at the Holyroodhouse Ball to celebrate the Queen's Birthday; he had 'now got a
genteel violet-coloured frock suit,' and, though he coveted 'rich
laced clothes' was satisfied to make do with acquiring 'just a plain
suit of a pink colour, with a gold button'. He had his hair dressed
almost every day, and his shoes regularly wiped.

He was out and about, and alert to amorous adventure: on
4 December he and Erskine encountered several ladies of the
town in the course of a stroll through St James's. 'There was one
in a red cloak and a good buxom person and comely face whom I
marked as a future piece, in case of exigency.' But towards
mid-December, having 'now been in London several weeks
without ever enjoying the delightful sex, although I am surrounded with numbers of free-hearted ladies of all kinds: from
the splendid Madam at fifty guineas a night, down to the civil
nymph with white-thread stockings who tramps along the Strand
and will resign her engaging person to your honour for a pint of
wine and a shilling,' Boswell fell in with Mrs Lewis, an actress he
had met briefly in Edinburgh. She had been playing at Covent
Garden, and an intrigue commenced. Boswell lays siege to the
lady, whom he calls 'Louisa' in his journal, and an appointment
for tea on Thursday, three days hence, is readily agreed upon. On
Thursday, he declares and she agrees that love is a fine passion
not to be controlled by reason. She offers the little fact that a
gentleman had once offered her £50, but ran away, and they laugh
merrily at the joke while Boswell attempts to melt her with looks
of passion. Next day, he discovers her to be a single woman whose
affections are not presently engaged, and on the 18th he talks
freely of love, and, perhaps with the thought of the £50 niggling at

the back of his mind, tells her 'I am here on a very moderate allowance ... and I am obliged to live with great economy.' Louisa, to her credit, 'received this very well.' On 20th December, nevertheless, she prettily accepts the loan of two guineas to disembarrass herself of a dun. Though Boswell has the wit to view the request with some suspicion, he comforts himself with the thought that even should she cost him ten guineas it would be 'but a moderate expense for women during the winter'.

Louisa now is pressed to come across. She dissembles a little, delaying the consummation of Boswell's desire for her, but on 1 January Boswell impatiently begins to make specific advances ('a sweet elevation of the charming petticoat') but Louisa is worried lest someone should burst in upon this scene of libertinage and she appoints Sunday, when her landlady will be at church, as a more auspicious occasion. The next day, he approached with 'a kind of uneasy tremor. I sat down. I toyed with her. Yet I was not inspired by Venus ... Louisa knew not my powers. She might imagine me impotent. I sweated almost with anxiety, which made me worse. She behaved extremely well ... Said she, "People cannot always command their spirits."' Boswell's spirits improved somewhat after a period of 'pressing her alabaster breasts and kissing her delicious lips'. He barred the door, set Louisa a-flutter, and 'was just making a triumphal entry when we heard her landlady coming up'. Louisa flew to prevent her, and begged time to recollect herself before agreeing to meet her paramour in some less risky rendezvous.

She agreed to meet him at an inn, then postponed their tryst. Finally, on 12 January they took a hackney-coach to the Black Lion in Fleet Street where Boswell signed them in as Mr and Mrs Digges before supping and drinking a few glasses and retiring for the night during which, 'Good heavens, what a loose did we give to amorous dalliance! ... A more voluptuous night I never enjoyed. Five times was I fairly lost in supreme rapture.' Louisa gave a demonstration of being mightily impressed, but Boswell pooh-poohed it as normal, 'although in my own mind I was somewhat proud of my performance.' He concludes, this 'Man of Pleasure,' with the satisfactory thought that 'the whole expense was just eighteen shillings'. For the moment he has forgotten the two guineas, but not for long. Six days later, the full price is exacted for his night of rapture. 'Too, too plain was Signor Gonorrhoea.' He is at first disinclined to hold Louisa to blame, but there is no other explanation. 'Am I, who have had safe and elegant intrigues with fine women, become the dupe of a strumpet?'

Louisa, pressed ("Pray, Madam, in what state of health have you been in for some time?" "Sir, you amaze me."), breaks down to confess an infection contracted three years ago, but swears she has been quite well for fifteen months and been with no man other than Boswell. Boswell conveniently forgets his own previous distempers, of which this one may have been but a recrudescence, and writes to demand the return of his two injudicious guineas, 'I neither *paid* it for prostitution, nor *gave* it in charity.' The dunning letter of 3 February has been provoked by a thought, inspired by the discomfort of his malady, that 'the treacherous Louisa deserved to suffer for her depravity,' and he takes an opportunity to abuse her roundly: '. . . long course of disguised wickedness . . . deceit and baseness . . . your corruption both of mind and body . . . unworthiness.' He concludes, 'I want no letters' presumably to forestall any imprecations on his own head, 'Send the money sealed up. I have nothing more to say to you.' Louisa does so, with a dignified and injured wordlessness, and the affair is at an end.

The two guineas is useful: indeed it could ill have been spared. The expense of coming to London and setting up has obliged Mr Boswell to be very canny in his disbursements. Often, for a period of a few weeks, he is obliged to skip a meal or sell some possession. It is not very pleasant, but he suffers it with dignity. He locks up his candles against covetous eyes. There are other disappointments: despite his most sanguine hopes, Mr Boswell is betrayed by the Duke of Queensberry who, in a letter of 26 December, declared that 'a commission in the Guards was a fruitless pursuit. I was quite stupefied and enraged at this. I imagined my father was at the bottom of it. I had multitudes of wild schemes. I thought of enlisting for five years as a soldier in India, of being a private man either in the Horse or Footguards,

&c. At last good sense prevailed, and I resolved to be cheerful and to wait and to ask it of Lady Northumberland.' Boswell had been taken up and made a fuss of by her, but the Duchess could do no more than the Duke of Queensberry, and finally Boswell had to admit that she was cooling in her attempts to get him into the Guards. He turned again to Eglinton, who spoke to Lord Bute, the Prime Minister. Bute replied that influence alone would not be enough: a commission evidently required money in addition to a good word, and Boswell was well aware that Auchinleck would never pay for the pretty red coat his son so ardently desired to affect. Besides, Auchinleck had not bothered to reply to Boswell's letters since February. It was clear that thunder wreathed the brow of the judge and father.

On 10 February 1763 Boswell had applied to Johnston to collect and send 'the copies which I kept of my letters to Erskine. They are in Parcel 1. Amongst some other papers.' The request may have been prompted by a discussion between Boswell and Erskine on 6 February when they had dwelt upon the virtues of flattery and talked with relish on the subject of the profit to be made from publishing books and pamphlets, and the satisfactions of money and fame. At this time, his thoughts were very much on the proper management of money. 'If a man is prodigal, he cannot be truly generous . . . On the other hand, a narrow man has a hard, contracted soul.' He resolves to be a man of economy who knows when to save and when to spend. There is also the question of the journal. It is improving in style, which 'is to sentiment what dress is to the person. The effects of both are very great, and both are acquired and improved by habit.'

The necessity and desirability of obtaining money and fame, and the urge to promote himself as a man of letters are very strong, and on 12 April 1763 'Letters between the Honourable Andrew Erskine and James Boswell' is published, 156 pages of determined frothiness, price three shillings. The effect is very great. Boswell has made no bones about authorship: he writes to Johnston, 'with the utmost boldness . . . we have printed our names at length. The narrow-minded and censorious Scotch rail at us. The goodhumoured jolly English like and praise us. To be sure it is a whimsical enough Experiment. I am affraid only of my Father's displeasure. He will think it terribly imprudent.' The laboriously facetious tone of the collected letters was not the principal cause of Scotch censoriousness – the letters managed to offend almost everyone of note that the two young men had ever met and declared admiration or affection for. Lord Kames, Adam Smith, John Home, Thomas Sheridan, Samuel Derrick, and David Hume were specifically referred to by their full names. Others, including Lady Betty Macfarlane and the Laird of Macfarlane, were, as less celebrated persons, accorded only an initial as Lady B——, Mr M——. They were, nevertheless, perfectly identifiable. The Macfarlane would immediately take offence at being referred to as Mr, Lady Betty was more or less alleged to be lousy, Sheridan was acknowledged *sometimes* to speak sense, Home was granted the dubious accolade of having written *one* good play, (presumably *Douglas* – the others do not, in truth, hold up very well) and Lord Kames was informed that his style was obscure.

Eglinton was appalled by the indiscretion. 'Upon my soul, Jamie, I would not take the direction of you upon any account . . . except you would agree to give over that damned publishing . . . You must get it suppressed, or put an advertisement in the papers denying it. By the Lord, it's a thing Dean Swift could not do – to publish a collection of letters upon nothing.'

Hugh Blair, the blameless man of letters, was sorely distressed. 'I'm really vexed at the publication.' Boswell attempted to mitigate the error. 'O Doctor, I'm sure they are innocent.' Blair perceptively added, 'They are not only innocent, Sir, but very lively . . . It appears to those who do not know you as if you were two vain, forward young men that would be pert and disagreeable and whom one would wish to keep out of the way of.'

Lord Auchinléck, when he heard of the book, was mortified: he took the publication as the latest and most galling attempt by Boswell to discredit him. The joyful reception alleged by Boswell to have been given to the book by the English was largely based on the review that appeared in the *London Chronicle* which recommended the letters 'as a book of true genius, from the authors

of which we may expect many future agreeable productions.'
Boswell basked in the glow of this puff which he had written
himself.

Somehow, Lord Auchinleck had got at Boswell's journal and in
April, pushed to the limits of his temper, he began to talk again of
selling the family estate. Boswell was alarmed and sought the aid
of Sir David Dalrymple, to whom he wrote on 21 May urging him
to talk with Auchinleck and make matters easy. 'Tell him to have
patience with me for a year or two, and I may be what he pleases.'
Auchinleck was bent on Boswell's returning to Scotland to
become a lawyer, but Boswell pleaded, 'I cannot bear control, nor
to hang on like a *young Laird*.' He felt a 'sincere regard and
affection for my father, and am anxious to make him easy . . . It is
not from the fear of being disinherited (which he threatens) that I
am anxious. I am thoughtless enough not to mind that. But my
affection for him makes me very unhappy at the thoughts of
offending him.' Dalrymple's intercession produced a compro-
mise plan: Boswell would go abroad, probably to Utrecht which
his father favoured as a suitable place to study Civil Law, and then
he might be permitted to visit Paris and Germany for a while.
Boswell fell in with this plan, and Auchinleck unbent a little: he
was genuinely fond of James and could moderate his harshness in
the face of true repentance.

Boswell's fancy was not for Utrecht, however: it was not gay,
though better, admittedly, than dull Leyden. 'Pray tell me,' he
begs of Dalrymple, 'if Utrecht be a place of a dull and severe cast,
or if it be a place of decency and chearfull politeness?' He essays,
in a minor key, the faint possibility that he might acquire the
French language better in the country itself, than in Holland, but
there is not much doubt that Utrecht is his fate. Boswell, as ever,
makes the best of it in his imagination: in a letter to Johnston on
30 June he is philosophic about his failure to make anything of an
army career, and admits to a couple of days when depression
rendered him 'indifferent to all pursuits'. But 'I am perswaded
that when I can restrain my flightiness and keep an even external
tenor, that my mind will attain a settled serenity.' Aspirations to
serenity do not yet, however, prevent Boswell's glee. 'You may

figure the many spirited gay ideas which I entertain when I consider that I am now a young man of fortune just going to set out on his travels.' Even Utrecht, that dull prospect, has put on a certain charm, 'I am told I shall have a most beautifull city to live in; very genteel people to be acquainted with; an opportunity of learning the French language, and easy opportunity of jaunting about to the Hague, Roterdam and, in short, up and down all the seven Provinces.' Almost as an afterthought, he mentions the fact that he is to put himself 'on the plan of acquiring a habit of study and application.' But 'too much of that would be bad for me.'

The clouds had cleared somewhat, but it had been a bad time. Boswell had suffered a serious gloom lasting about three weeks, from the last week of April to mid-May. Even London had seemed dull. On 3 May, Boswell walked to the Tower to see John Wilkes taken from there to the Court of Common Pleas to answer for charges implicitly laid in the *North Briton* against the King. By the time Boswell got there, Wilkes was gone but there were prisoners in Newgate to be inspected. The effect was to depress him still more. Newgate lay on his mind 'like a black cloud' and even the soporific of being read to by his barber from Hume's *History* was ineffective. Next day, curiosity 'to see the melancholy spectacle of the executions was so strong that I could not resist it.' Boswell and a friend 'got on a scaffold near the fatal tree' at Tyburn. The sight of a vast crowd of spectators was shocking and threw Boswell into deepest melancholy. For three nights thereafter he could not bear to sleep alone. It had been his first execution, though not his last: Boswell's horrid curiosity in this respect was a sad masochism, a desire to welter in horror and excite his imagination. A hanging affected him deeply, and he was never able to keep away from one.

Boswell's literary acquaintance was not extensive: he waited upon James 'Ossian' Macpherson, a prodigious celebrity, and had struck up an acquaintance with the actor David Garrick after the coolness that had eventuated between himself and Sheridan. Boswell had decided that Derrick was disreputable, and saw no more of him. But he had taken to having tea with the bookseller Tom Davies and his wife. Davies had been apprised, as early as

19 December, of Boswell's wish to meet Mr Samuel Johnson, and Davies had invited him to dine on Christmas Day when 'He and some more men of letters are to be with me.' But, in the event, Johnson had gone to Oxford and the company included merely Mr Dodsley, the publisher, and Mr Oliver Goldsmith, 'a curious, odd, pedantic fellow with some genius'. Boswell had seen 'no warm victuals for four days,' being at that time temporarily short of money, and he tucked in heartily, talking of literary matters with his three companions 'in the way of Geniuses'. Goldsmith having disposed of Shakespeare, Boswell introduced Johnson for Goldsmith to pronounce upon. 'He has exceeding merit. His *Rambler* is a noble work,' replied Goldsmith. Boswell offered the observation that, 'His *Idler* too is very pretty. It is a lighter performance; and he has thrown off the classical fetters very much.' Davies chipped in, 'He is a most entertaining companion. And how can it be otherwise, when he has so much imagination, has read so much, and digested it so well?'

Johnson, at this time, was fifty-four years old. His reputation as a man of letters rested firmly on the essays, reprinted in book form, he had contributed to the periodical magazines, the *Rambler* from 1750 to 1752, and the *Idler* from 1758 to 1760. His style was particularly his own, but was widely imitated. The moral content of the essays assured him of the respect and admiration of his peers, though it was not to the taste of more radical spirits among whom might be counted the dangerous and inflammatory John Wilkes. In the manner of the times, Johnson's prefix described his most notable achievement or the thing for which he was most celebrated: thus, he was known as 'Dictionary Johnson'. Having nailed a number of truths that were generally held to be self-evident in his essays, he turned to fiction and in 1759 produced a novel, *Rasselas* which was enthusiastically received not only by Boswell but by most of his admirers, including Sir John Hawkins who regarded it as a 'specimen of language . . . scarcely to be parallelled; it is written in a style refined to a degree of immaculate purity, and displays the whole force of turgid eloquence.'

Rasselas, which gave Johnson pride of place as an authority on any question relating to Abyssinia, was compared by Boswell to

Voltaire's *Candide* which it ante-dated by a few months, but posterity has preferred the picaresque delights of Voltaire's attack on the philosophy of Leibnitz's 'best of all possible worlds' to Johnson's laboured fable which, in contrast, lacks the liveliness of an imagination adapted for fiction or a tight dramatic form. It would have been incautious for a critic to compare the intentions of Voltaire with those of Johnson: they were very different, Boswell suggests. Voltaire 'meant only by wanton profaneness to obtain a sportive victory over religion ... Johnson meant, by shewing the unsatisfactory nature of things temporal, to direct the hopes of man to things eternal.' But however solemn the intention behind *Rasselas* it had been thrown off, hurriedly and casually, to earn the advance payment of thirty pounds he needed to pay for his mother's funeral.

Johnson took a good deal more pride, and put long and dedicated effort into his Dictionary, published in 1775. The demands of the work stretched to the limit his wide reading and deep scholarship. His aim was to compile 'a dictionary like those compiled by the academies of Italy and France, for the use of those who aspire to exactness of criticism or elegance of style.' The dictionary, in two volumes, amounted to 2300 pages each with the masterful stamp of Johnson. Though he was prone to occasional errors due to 'ignorance, pure ignorance' self-confessed, and acerbities such as the reference to 'oats' being 'a grain, which in England is generally given to horses, but in Scotland supports the people,' Johnson's genius was to imprint upon the dictionary the accumulated experience of a man 'long employed in the study and cultivation of the English language.'

Johnson was known to be sociable, and liked to meet new people constantly. Mr Boswell had put himself once or twice in the way of meeting him but, perhaps oddly, had not chanced to make his acquaintance. At any rate, the desire was there but Boswell had not pursued it with his customary dedication: there had been enough, what with the getting of a commission and women and fame, to occupy his time. But, on 16 May at about seven o'clock in the evening, as Boswell was sitting in the Davies' back parlour behind the shop, Johnson's bulk loomed behind the glass door. 'Look, my Lord, it comes,' cried Davies in a fair imitation of Horatio announcing the dread presence of the ghost of Hamlet's father. He then rushed to Johnson, exclaiming, 'The Scots gentleman is come, Sir; his principal wish is to see you; he is now in the back-parlour.' 'Well, well, I'll see the gentleman,' declared Johnson and rolled forward.

'I was much agitated,' writes Boswell. The cat was out of the bag: Johnson's prejudice against the Scots was notorious. 'I do indeed come from Scotland, but I cannot help it,' cried Boswell. It was an unlucky turn of phrase: 'That, Sir, I find is what a very great many of your countrymen cannot help,' said Johnson, knocking the gnat with his great paw. 'This stroke stunned me a good deal;' admits Boswell, 'and when we had sat down, I felt myself not a little embarrassed, and apprehensive of what might come next.' He had not long to wait. Johnson began grumbling to Davies that Garrick had refused him an order worth three shillings for a seat at a play. Boswell got in quickly, but ill-advisedly, 'O, Sir, I cannot think that Mr Garrick would grudge such a trifle to you.'

The well-intentioned pleasantry bounced round the room, and came back to stun Mr Boswell, already reeling from the first impact of Johnson. 'Sir, I have known David Garrick longer than you have done: and I know no right you have to talk to me on the subject.' Boswell was devastated. 'I now felt myself much mortified, and began to think that the hope which I had so long indulged of obtaining his acquaintance was blasted.' Despite the blows, Boswell persisted. The rough reception counselled caution, and Boswell kept quiet while Johnson pontificated vigorously. At length Boswell felt less discomfiture and essayed a few blameless remarks which Johnson received civilly enough, perhaps regretting the initial bruising. Boswell, he may have observed, was down but not out. Johnson was rough, to be sure, but not ill-natured. When Boswell made to leave, Davies followed him to the door, applying balm to the blows: 'Don't be uneasy. I can see he likes you very well.'

A period of eight days elapsed before Boswell made a further sortie, first having taken the precaution to consult with Davies

this morning with the illustrious
Donaldson. In the evening I went
to Temple's; he brought me ac:
:quainted with a Mr Claxton a
very good sort of a young man tho'
reserved at first. Mr Nicholls was
there too. Our conversation was
sensible & lively. I wish I could
spend my time always in such company.

Monday 16 May.

Temple & his Brother breakfas:
:ted with me. I went to Love's
to try to recover some of the mo:
:ney which he owes me. But alas
a single guinea was all I could
get. He was just going to dinner,
so I stayed & eat a bit, tho' I was
angry at myself afterwards.
I drink tea at Davies's in Russ:
:el Street and about seven came
in the great Mr Samuel John:
:son, whom I have so long wished
to see. Mr Davies introduced
me to him. As I knew his mortal
antipathy at the Scotch, I said

to

Extract from Boswell's journal for 16 May 1763,
in which he records his first meeting with Dr Johnson

to Davies; don't tell where I come
from. However he said From Scotland.
Mr. Johnson said I indeed I come
from Scotland, but I cannot help
it. : Sir replied he. : That I find
is what a very great many of
your countrymen cannot help.
Mr. Johnson is a man of a most
dreadfull appearance. He is a
very big man is troubled with sore
eyes, the Palsy & the King's
evil. He is very slovenly in
his dress & speaks with a
most uncouth voice. Yet his
great knowledge, and strength
of expression command vast
respect and render him very
excellent company. He has
great humour and is a worthy
man. But his dogmatical rough:
ness of manners is disagreable.

who assured him that Johnson would take it as a compliment if Boswell were to call on him at his Chambers in the Temple. On the morning of 24 May, 'after having been enlivened by the witty sallies of Messieurs Thornton, Wilkes, Churchill and Lloyd,' Boswell repaired to the first floor of No 1 Inner-Temple-lane to beard 'the Giant in his den' as Dr Blair had described Johnson. For a moment, the lion looked moth-eaten and tatty, the Giant disturbingly shrunk: for all Johnson's courteous welcome, Boswell was a little shocked. The picture was not elegant, 'his apartment, and furniture, and morning dress were sufficiently uncouth. His brown suit of cloaths looked very rusty; he had on a little old shrivelled unpowdered wig, which was too small for his head; his shirt-neck and knees of his breeches were loose; his black worsted stockings ill drawn up; and he had a pair of unbuckled shoes by way of slippers.' Then the lion began to stalk and roar, 'and all these slovenly particularities were forgotten the moment that he began to talk.' After a while, Boswell rose to follow some other visitors who went away, but Johnson bade Boswell stay. In his best manner, Boswell demurred, 'Sir, I am afraid that I intrude upon you. It is benevolent to allow me to sit and hear you.' Even lions like to be stroked, and Boswell was very sincere. 'Sir, I am obliged to any man who visits me,' said Johnson and Boswell gracefully gave way to gratifying Johnson's wish that he should remain. The time was not wasted.

From the very first, Boswell had noted the conversation in Davies' shop. 'In my note *taken on the very day*, in which I am confident I marked everything material that passed . . . my first interview with Dr Johnson, with all its circumstances, made a strong impression on my mind, and would be registered with particular attention.' This note to the *Life of Johnson* is appended to confound one Arthur Murphy, a young Irishman who claimed, in an *Essay on the Life and Genius of Samuel Johnson, LL D*, to have been present at Boswell's first meeting with Johnson. Boswell strenuously denied that he had been present at the scene which, though Murphy described it in the *Essay*, Boswell dismissed as a derangement of his memory thirty years later.

The conversation on 24 May included animadversions on

madness and the Christian religion which Boswell reproduces in the *Life*, and again, after a while, Boswell rose to take his leave and was again pressed to remain, which he did. The acquaintance 'of which I had been so long ambitious' was on its way to becoming the most valuable friendship of Boswell's life. 'Come to me as often as you can,' smiled Johnson, 'I shall be glad to see you.'

Boswell had not dropped any of his previous acquaintance since meeting Johnson, and indeed it was not until 13 June that he met Johnson again, and then only by chance, in an eating house in the Strand. Creditable acquaintance was inspiring and greatly to be desired, but John Wilkes and others equally claimed his attention. Boswell had been introduced to Wilkes on 24 May by Bonnell Thornton, who had written a favourable review of the Erskine/Boswell *Letters* in the *Public Advertiser*. Wilkes was accompanied by the poet Charles Churchill and the author Robert Lloyd, 'so that I was just got into the middle of the London Geniuses,' crows Boswell in his journal. 'They were high-spirited and boisterous, but were very civil to me.' He was not intimate with them, but their outrageous and uninhibited, roistering profanity excited Boswell and the disrespectful attitude of the *North Briton* confirmed Boswell's peevish dislike of Scotticisms. Wilkes was pleasant, if startlingly ugly, and had already astonished the world of politics and letters. He was exhilarating and fascinatingly dangerous.

Boswell took care to conceal his philanderings and disgraceful friendships from Johnson to whom he began, more and more, to attach himself. On 14 June he called once again, for the third time, on Johnson, and on 25 June he and Johnson passed an evening together at the Mitre Tavern where, as the candles burned low, and the port was poured, and the landlord yawned, Boswell spilled the details of his life to Johnson 'which he listened to with attention.' Boswell confessed that he had been an infidel, but 'I believed the Christian religion; though I might not be clear in many particulars.' This frank declaration pleased Johnson mightily. 'Give me your hand. I have taken a liking to you,' he cried, and assured Boswell that the differences between Papists and Protestants were political rather than religious. Johnson also thought that Lord Auchinleck 'has been wanting to make a man of you at twenty which you will be at thirty.' He enlarged on the felicity of being a Scotch landlord and promised to put Boswell on a plan of study to quiet his anxieties about his state of ignorance. 'Will you really take charge of me?' asked Boswell, wonderingly, and went home after two bottles of port, at about one or two, 'in high exultation'.

Boswell clung to Johnson like a lifebelt and contrived to be pretty constantly in his company until the day of his departure for Holland. To his delight, Johnson announced his intention to accompany Boswell to Harwich to see him off. At Colchester, they spent the night. Here Johnson offered Boswell the illuminating observation on the resemblance he bore to a moth fluttering round a candle, singeing its wings and immolating itself in the fatal fire of dangerous but irresistible foolishness of behaviour. Then, at length, they parted. Johnson had made Boswell say his prayers before embarking on the packet for Helvoetsluys. It was an affecting farewell. 'I hope, Sir,' said Boswell piteously, 'you will not forget me in my absence.' 'Nay, Sir, it is more likely you shall forget me, than that I shall forget you,' soothed Johnson. He turned to go. The shore receded. 'As the vessel put out to sea, I kept my eyes upon him for a considerable time, while he remained rolling his majestic frame in his usual manner; and at last I perceived him walk back into the town, and he disappeared.'

[3]

Boswell and the Philosophers

In London, Boswell had determined to adopt 'Mr Addison's character in sentiment, mixed with a little of the gaiety of Sir Richard Steele, and the manners of Mr Digges.' To the degree that he succeeded in attaining the comportment of this wonderful triumvirate, Boswell probably felt more or less in command of a character appropriate to his aspirations and needs. The models he selected for emulation in Holland were more formidable: Lord Auchinleck, Sir David Dalrymple and Mr Samuel Johnson. Boswell was conscious of his imperfections and shortcomings, but did not doubt for a moment that through rigid adherence to superior models he might, by an act of will, adapt his character so that it might give no offence to those he most wished to please.

In London, Boswell had made intermittent attempts to control himself, to reinforce his finer instincts, but had also recognised that he was liable to be whimsical, to act as a young man. Though he aspired to 'the judgement of forty and five,' he experienced simultaneously all the powerful urgings of two and twenty. When he lapsed from the ideals he had set for himself, or found his character inadequate to command perfect adherence to these standards, he would scourge himself by regretting his fall from grace and become thoroughly depressed.

At Rotterdam, he fell immediately into a profound gloom. He had been none too pleased to leave London, but Holland was a purgatory, much worse than he had thought. For sobriety, it far outstripped Scotland. Boswell travelled to Leyden, from whence he embarked on a sluggish horse-drawn barge, a *Treck Schuyt*, for

Utrecht. He was pulled, ploddingly, through Holland for nine
hours. One dolorous day in Utrecht was enough: he began
running around the streets groaning and weeping and lamenting
his fate. Then he took a slow barge back to Rotterdam where he
began writing frantic letters of appeal to everyone he had left
behind in London.

George Dempster rushed from Paris to Brussels to rally the
despairing Boswell, but they failed to meet: to relieve his misery,
Boswell had taken himself off on a tour of Gouda, Amsterdam,
and Haarlem. Temple wrote back, sympathetically but bracingly,
'imputing my misery to idleness and beseeching me to act a part
worthy of a Man.' Thoughts of Lord Auchinleck, benignly
imagining his son settled and hard at his studies, rose and fell in
Boswell's distracted mind. 'Luckily,' he reflected later, 'I did not
write all the time to my father.' Instead, he wrote to Johnson who
did not reply: but second-hand advice, possibly no different from
the counsel he would have received direct, was to hand in some
copies of the *Rambler*. Boswell read the fortifying articles written
by Johnson and took their exhortations so much to heart that he
returned to Utrecht inspired 'to fix myself down to a regular plan
and to persist with firmness and spirit and combat the foul fiend.'

When Johnson did finally write to Boswell in early December,
some four months after their parting, he addressed his mind to
Boswell's despondency which, by then, had more or less been
shaken off. The letter dished out conventional, sensible advice.
He had not replied to Boswell's bleatings because they had given
'an account so hopeless of the state of your mind, that it hardly
admitted or deserved an answer.' Johnson had little time for
Boswell's morbid introspection. He was kindly in general, but
held firmly to a strict morality. There was much Boswell could
never reveal of his life to Johnson whom he feared (correctly)
would disapprove of Boswellian bawdy. Johnson knew nothing of
his friend's philanderings, and would have been deeply shocked
had Boswell, in his cups, freely admitted his indiscretions.

It was not, in any case, a confessional age as ours is. It was an
age of gossip, certainly, and of libertinage if not of liberty. Men
like Wilkes defied propriety, while others like Walpole missed no

John Wilkes Esq.r

Drawn from the Life and Etch'd in Aquafortis by Will.m Hogarth.

Price 1 Shilling.   Publish'd according to Act of Parliament May 16. 1763.

opportunity to set scandal running after them (and sometimes before) through the drawing rooms of Europe.

John Wilkes MP, in the famous No. 45 issue of the *North Briton*, a periodical devoted to attacking the Prime Minister Lord Bute, the sovereign, and (almost incidentally, since Bute was a North Briton) Scotsmen, had described references to Prussia in a King's Speech as 'an infamous fallacy'. The Government, baited beyond endurance, had issued a general warrant against Wilkes who was arrested on a charge of seditious libel. Wilkes had become notorious for the spiciness and daring of his criticism, political and personal, but if he had gone too far this time, so had Bute and his faction. Wilkes, though committed to the Tower, was released a week later by the Lord Chief Justice to whom Wilkes had appealed that a general warrant was illegal. He at once sued the Government for unlawful arrest, and four years later, in 1767, was awarded general damages of £4000.

But Wilkes had been incautious in a poem, entitled *An Essay on Women*, which had libelled two clerical gentlemen and an aristocrat, and it was denounced by the House of Lords (to whom it had been read by Lord Sandwich) as 'a most scandalous, obscene, and impious libel, a gross profanation of many parts of the Holy Scriptures, and a most wicked and blasphemous attempt to ridicule and vilify the Person of our Most Blessed Saviour.' In view of imminent prosecution, Wilkes retired to Paris from whence he excused his absence in the House of Commons by medical certificates, sent to the Speaker, attesting to wounds sustained in a duel in Hyde Park as a result of which he was unable to travel to England. In early 1764, Wilkes was formally expelled from the House, and his failure to return to stand trial resulted in a sentence of outlawry. The *philosophes* of Paris received Wilkes as a martyr for Liberty and Atheism, and in Paris he remained, supported by the Rockingham Whigs, biding his time. Meanwhile, Wilkes was regarded in England as a champion of Liberty. His talent for social disruption, even at a distance, remained undimmed.

But conventional piety set the norms of proper social behaviour, and lapses were judged more often theologically than psychologically. Johnson, like Boswell, was of the opinion that resolute adherence to a regular pattern of life and work would, given time, improve a man's base nature. He granted that a man might fail, in which case it was as well to recognise the failure and resolve to begin afresh on the path to virtue. He was astute enough, however, to recognise that 'this advice, if you will not take from others, you must take from your own reflections.'

There was no limit to Boswell's reflections: in Holland, they became almost obsessive. He was, to be fair, succeeding tolerably well in his intention to be frugal, diligent, and discreet. Regularly, to reinforce his determination, Boswell consulted a wonderfully elaborate and hortative document he had drawn up for his own instruction and encouragement: an 'Inviolable Plan' which first defined Boswell's station in life and character – prospective '*Laird* of Auchinleck . . . idle, dissipated, absurd, unhappy . . . in danger of utter ruin . . . idleness was your sole disease. The *Rambler* showed you that vacuity, gloom and fretfulness were the causes of your woe.' – and dwelt upon the expectations of others – 'Your worthy father . . . has suffered much from your follies. . . . Your dear mother is anxious to see you do well. All your friends and relations expect that you will be an honour to them and will be useful to them as a lawyer, and make them happy as an agreeable private gentleman.' General rules of proper conduct follow – 'attain habits of study . . . Remember religion and morality. Remember the dignity of human nature.'

The 'Inviolable Plan' is a lengthy and tendentious piece of self-laceration, but it took some courage to write. Boswell had a capacity and appetite for self-humiliation that perhaps compensated for his inability to be humble. He found himself lodgings in Utrecht, a servant, and settled to the Civil Law lectures of the amiable Professor Trotz who delivered his instruction in Latin. On his own, he studied Latin literature and Scots law. He engaged a private tutor to teach him French, and with the intention of improving his Greek he sought the aid of James Rose, a Scot of the family of the Laird of Kilravock, whom he had met through another Scot, the Reverend Robert Brown who was pastor of the English-speaking Presbyterian church in Utrecht.

Boswell struck up a close friendship with these two good men and for a while dined with them daily. To improve his swordsmanship, Boswell engaged a nonagenarian Italian fencing-master, still surprisingly spry.

Boswell was the only British student at Utrecht, and may have felt a little isolated, though he knew his van Sommelsdyck cousins were within reach. As a law student, the period of study at Utrecht was likely to be useful, since the laws of Scotland and Holland were both based on Roman civil law, and the Dutch were great jurisprudentialists. But the age of the wandering student was more or less at an end, though it was easier for German students, say, than British students to change from one university to another at will. Generally, the British student took his courses in one place and in one country, unless instruction was combined with the social desirability of the Grand Tour. Utrecht was not, perhaps, the first choice of students wishing to combine intellectual with aesthetic and social stimulation: to Boswell, and many another, the Northern countries were as disappointingly Puritan as their own home bases, and the urge was to move south. Paris offered more pleasure to philosophers – as Hume could have told Boswell from his own experience – than other capitals, and the tendency was to gravitate to capitals (however provincial) where morals were more lax. Even The Hague would appear brilliant to a student based in Utrecht.

He made constant notes about his behaviour, counselling himself often to be more cautious, but there was really no need. His behaviour was well-nigh blameless, just short of being colourless. He constructed schedules, timed to the hour, to discipline his days and kept lists – letters received, letters sent, money spent, gambling gains and losses; and in characteristic fashion planned his next day the night before. It all added up to a subconscious suspicion that if Boswell did not control life, life would control Boswell. Lists and schedules and memoranda are all symptomatic of a compulsive personality, having much in common with anyone who has ever anxiously arrived at a railway station half an hour or an hour before the train is timed to depart. However, he was realistic enough to allow himself time off for some respectable amusement: he allotted three hours every evening, and gossiped in Latin with a group of Hungarians on Saturday nights. He attended a concert, but the irregularity of this outburst of high spirits alarmed him and he resolved never to go again. Once, he ate a little too heartily of wild duck, and was gloomy about this minor fall from virtue. But as a reward for general good conduct he gave himself three weeks at The Hague in December and fell joyously into a round of parties, theatres, dinners, and dancing. He met some van Sommelsdyck relations, was introduced to the Prince of Orange, and took Episcopal communion on Christmas Day.

This bout of 'brilliant dissipation,' followed by a resumption of academic routine, brought on a period of depression when Boswell returned to Utrecht determined to 'be extremely *retenu*'. On 21 January 1764 he composed one of his daily essays in French on the theme of idleness, a vice to which Boswell considered himself naturally disposed. Only boredom inspires him to seek relief through work, and he illustrates his character as it was once defined for him by an English officer. 'He said that I was like a great stone couched on the slope of a mountain, and while I stayed there I was lumpish and heavy; but when I was once set in motion, I went with amazing velocity, so that it was impossible to stop me until the projectile force being exhausted, I came again to rest.' The lapidary simile pleased Boswell extremely, and perhaps stirred some memory of a desire he had once expressed to be whinstone on the face of a mountain, exposed to the elements, assaulted by them and yet gloriously insensible. It would be agreeable to be such a rock, enduring everything passively, but capable suddenly of tumbling irresistibly to the bottom of a steep slope. How peaceful to have such an unalterable, God-given nature, to have no responsibility other than to be, ungoverned by any demands of the will to reform.

However that may be, a stone would not have fallen in love with a pretty young widow called Madame Geelvinck, possessed of £40,000 a year, nor have been distressed when she returned to The Hague in February. Nor would a stone have fathered a son and been so deeply affected to learn of the boy's death. John Johnston reported the news to Boswell on 1 February. The letter arrived in Utrecht on 8 March, and one month later Boswell replied. 'I had warmed my heart with parental affection. I had formed many agreeable plans for the young Charles. All is now wrapped in darkness. All is gone.' His son's death gave Boswell a convenient and sincere occasion to groan mightily. 'Black Melancholy again took control over me.' Thinking perhaps of his letter to Samuel Johnson, Boswell remarks, 'Melancholy is timorous, and wishes for the Counsel of the wise.' But Johnson had referred timorous Boswell to his own counsel, and Boswell had become acute enough to realise that society can easily become bored by constant morbidity: so, 'I have learned the important art of Reserve. I can chat for whole evenings, without giving a hint of my Malady.' One of the reasons, it may be, that Boswell's melancholy was never too convincing in the eyes of his contemporaries, was that one moment he could be weeping bitterly, while the next he was quite likely to be standing suddenly on a chair giving out with some creditable piece of mimicry or singing a song, hoping to banish gloom through activity.

In February 1764, as the subject of yet another French theme, he discusses how surprised the fashionable and frivolous, who take him at face value as one of themselves, will be when they discover that Mr Boswell is laughing up his scarlet and gold sleeve at them: little do they know that gay and gallant M. Boswell d'Auchinleck is proposing to furnish them with a dictionary, a Scots dictionary, bound to be an excellent work considering the time, effort, and scholarship it will entail. The impulse quickens in his brain, but subsides gracefully. 'I have many other things to do which are more important to me and which I am resolved not to neglect,' explains the lexicographer rather lamely. Among these vital matters is a certain Isabella Agneta Elizabeth van Tuyll van Serooskerken, more conveniently known as Belle de Zuylen (after a family property near Utrecht), or more familiarly and literarily, Zélide.

Boswell had met the twenty-three year old Belle de Zuylen shortly after arriving in Holland, and her name crops up fairly

'La Belle Zuylen: Isabella Agneta Elizabeth van Tuyll van Serroskerken', portrait by Jens Juel

regularly from the end of October, when he fancies himself to be in love with her, until January 1764 when she becomes a permanent fixture in his journal of the period and, for the next four years, in his thoughts. At first, she was no more a pleasing romantic diversion than many another lady, but there was a great deal more to Zélide than first caught Boswell's attention. On

9 November he had written to Temple that he must not think of matrimony 'for some years, especially as I have yet to travel and settle my conduct in life.' But 'I have a strange turn towards marriage,' he immediately adds and there is no shortage of beautiful and amiable ladies in Holland. He regularly plays shuttlecock with the charming Marguerite Kinloch, a relation of the Reverend Mr Brown's wife, and writes a French theme on the subject of an inconvenient tear in his black silk and linen breeches 'between the legs, rather before than behind' which he should like Miss Kinloch to have the goodness to mend. 'She can do it without risk when I have taken them off. Breeches are improper only when they are on my backside. . . . They have been mended by the most famous beauty in the north of Scotland, and even when I had them on. I must admit, however, that it was only in one of the knees.'

The Countess of Nassau, when he is introduced to her, 'is the finest woman upon earth.' She has introduced him into the gay world of Utrecht which has proved more diverting than Boswell had first supposed, and given him a list of hostesses to whom he may pay his respects and thus be registered on their invitation lists of agreeable guests. Boswell's bachelor state, however, is not endangered to any serious degree and certainly not for the moment by Zélide whose vanity is boundless and whose severity is too intimidating for Boswell's taste. She is interesting, nevertheless, and from 25 February they agree to meet regularly – 'at home at least once a week' – and make a pact to be frank with one another. He has begun to like her.

On 17 April, Boswell wrote to Temple about his success in Holland, about his plans for the immediate future, and almost as a postscript introduced Mademoiselle de Zuylen as 'a charming creature' but 'who has only a fortune of £20,000 a year' compared to some (including Mme Geelvinck) who have twice as much. 'But she is a *savante* and a *bel esprit*, and has published some things.' This goes against her in her preferment, 'She is much my superior. One does not like that.' To be superior to Boswell, who gives his high opinion of himself fully in this letter to Temple, – 'I am a worthy, an amiable, and a brilliant man . . . I am forming into a character which may do honour to the ancient family which I am born to represent . . . I can "know myself a Man"!' – is no mean achievement. Zélide, being 'nervish', 'would make a sad wife and propagate wretches.' The opinion of at least one of her victims, crushed at a supper party, was that 'Mademoiselle de Zuylen has a great deal of wit,' but 'she tries too hard to be subtle.' This is attributed to the fact that she has been brought up among the ladies of Geneva, who lack good principles and who 'sometimes sacrifice probity to brilliance'.

Zélide, in short, generally offended male vanity. Though financially and mentally independent, she wished to marry and thus free herself of the irksome restrictions placed by convention upon a young, aristocratic, woman of fortune. A marriage of convenience would suit her very well, and to that end she was negotiating with a worldly Swiss, Constant d'Hermenches, to persuade his friend, the Marquis de Bellegarde, to make her a proposal of marriage. That Bellegarde was a Catholic was a substantial impediment, and that he set a high price on his title was another, but she professed to love and admire him. Mr Boswell was a likely prospect, if her scheme failed. After all, he was behaving extremely well and had a vivacity to match her own.

But Boswell was being doggedly *retenu*: he wished that Zélide might also be more discreet. In a self-portrait, she wrote, 'Too lively and too powerful feelings; too much inner activity with no satisfactory outlet: there is the source of all her misfortunes. If her organism had been less sensitive, Zélide would have had the character of a great man; if she had been less intelligent and rational, she would have been only a weak woman.' As to her beauty, it depended, she said, on whether she was loved by the beholder, or whether she wished to make herself beloved. She allowed that she had a beautiful neck, and made the most of this considerable asset almost to the point of immodesty. She was conscious that her hands were not white. They were larger than fashion or good taste permitted, but so was her height. Her indiscretions resulted from living too much in and for the present: but to plan the future was futile, and in fleeing remorse she seeks diversion. 'Her pleasures are rare, but they are lively. She snatches them, she relishes them eagerly . . . Can you not guess her secret? Zélide is something of a sensualist.'

Like Madame du Châtelet, Voltaire's charming and serious-minded scientific mistress, Zélide had mastered mathematics and Newton. She was a match for Boswell in Latin, but surpassed him in Greek and had a more stylish command of French. A strong independence and originality of mind made Zélide something of a bluestocking in the eyes of her contemporaries. But it was still considered that 'a man who has not half her wit and knowledge may still be above her.' This, when said to Boswell by a critic of Zélide, impressed him and 'I thought it very true, and I thought it was a good thing. For if it were not for that lack [of good sense], Zélide would have an absolute power. She would have unlimited dominion over men, and would overthrow the dignity of the male sex.' It was a very real terror to Boswell, who was jealous of his status as a man and a lover. He could play shuttlecock with a young lady who would blush to see the rent in his breeches, he could flirt agreeably with the waxy and feminine young widow Geelvinck, he could amuse and abuse the sordid Louisas of London, but Boswell had met more than his match in Belle de Zuylen. In matters of the mind, she was incomparably his superior; in self-regard she was as vain as he, and they were both equally gay in their pleasures and sensual in spirit; and she, like Boswell, had 'thought more than any body supposed' but to considerably more effect – she had established her own principles and could be satiric about the absurdities of others. The depth and supposed irresponsibility of her beliefs profoundly shocked Boswell who would have been interested and disputatious had he encountered them in a man. That they should have been held by a woman prepared to defend them against anyone was shocking. Boswell took it upon himself to rebuke her for such impertinence and imprudence.

He had never met anyone like Zélide, and was alternately fascinated and repelled. She ridiculed rank, which was an institution on which Boswell placed great personal value, and declined to accept a revealed religion without which Boswell would have felt himself cut loose in the world without an anchor. Boswell was accustomed to make use of women who did not place too high a value on their virtue or chastity, but to find a woman who could justify such immodesty in intellectual terms, in exactly the same way as she had a rationale for any other departure from the general moral climate of behaviour appropriate to a lady of her station in rank and fortune, was apt to throw Boswell utterly off balance. She discomposed him thoroughly.

Meanwhile, Boswell had written to his father on 20 March and received a reply on 14 April. He had been depressed, and Lord Auchinleck was not unsympathetic. His own father had been melancholic, though 'never troubled with it in Session time' while performing his judicial duties. The lesson to be learned from this would seem to be to 'arm yourself doubly against' despair and despondency. James is not 'to imagine that variety of company and of diversions is the proper cure . . . just the reverse . . . idleness to those who have a vicious turn is the mother of all manner of vice, and to those who have a virtuous turn, it commonly produces melancholy and gloom.' Auchinleck's opinion of his son, from such words, appears to have somewhat moderated and become more kindly. He does not, at any rate, regard Boswell as naturally vicious. There is a good deal of advice as to the most suitable leisure activities – 'on Sunday good old Erasmus and Bishop Latimer are my entertainment and instructors.' Not a rollicking pair, but such literary companions are to be preferred to 'modern polemic writers, essayers, &c,' who pay no heed to the cardinal necessity of producing a literature that will make men useful or give them a desire to be so.

The letter is generally benign. Despite the premonitory advice that 'travelling is a very useless thing,' Auchinleck wishes to know whether James proposes to visit 'some of the German courts or go through Flanders and see Paris.' Introductions can be arranged through Lord Marischal Keith to the Princes of Brunswick and Baden-Durlach and the King of Prussia. Andrew Mitchell, British envoy to Frederick the Great, will treat James kindly at Berlin. Auchinleck's indulgent tone raised Boswell's spirits and prompted a long, exultant letter to Temple (the one introducing

Zélide) and in it Boswell acknowledged that the 'Inviolable Plan' had been a mistake. 'My feeble powers were crushed in attempting to put it into execution. Hence I was thrown into that deplorable state which my dismal letter from Rotterdam informed you of.' But Boswell can properly give himself some credit. 'I was but a distempered creature, who strove to make the best he could of a wretched existence. I had great merit in this. I stood the most grievous shocks.'

Boswell also gives Temple his reactions to his father's proposal that a prompt return to Scotland after the tour of Germany or Flanders and France would be suitable. It is too confined a scheme. 'I shall insist upon being abroad another winter, and so may pursue the following plan.' The gist of his intention is to leave Utrecht in mid-June to tour the Netherlands and the courts of Germany. Towards the end of August, Boswell proposes to be in Berlin and in Baden-Durlach by the end of September. Thereafter, he will go through Switzerland, visit Rousseau and Voltaire, and at length get to Italy, there to pass 'a delicious winter' before crossing the Pyrenees into Spain for a couple of months prior to coming at last to Paris. 'Upon this plan, I cannot expect to be in Britain before the autumn of 1765.'

The rein of continence having been loosed a little, Boswell decided he had been *retenu* quite long enough, or that the habit of reserve was now so strongly ingrained that it would do no harm to temper it with a minor lapse. 'Think if GOD really forbids girls,' he advises himself in a memorandum. His blood quickens, becomes fiery and vivacious, but he still holds to his plan of virtue. Towards the end of April he is still reminding himself to be *retenu*. A letter from his father, dated 15 April, reminds him that 'travelling about from place to place is a thing extremely little improving except where one needs to rub off bashfulness, which is not your case . . .' But a week after reading this advice, a little travel becomes imperative. Boswell gets to Amsterdam for a brief frolic, risking sensual adventures. But his father is right, after all: diversion is no palliative for depression. Work is the thing. Boswell conceives the grand notion to translate Erskine's *Institutes of the Law of Scotland* into Latin: he has already begun. He will show the work to Professor Trotz who will add his own notes, and 'in time I will have a very respectable work.' He will publish. The plan is settled. Think of the labour! Five hundred hours! But work is the only thing. 'When I am busy, melancholy has no chance to enter . . . Act forthwith and be happy!'

The happiness is short-lived: on 22 May 1764, Boswell is again writing to Temple to complain of the clouds which cast darkness on his brain, but on 25 May Boswell gets an explanation of his malady from a physician, Johannes David Hahn, who prescribes women as 'necessary when one had been accustomed, or retention' (presumably of semen, or perhaps merely of animal desire) 'will influence the brain.' Just what the doctor ordered: Boswell immediately 'saw then that irregular coition was not commendable but that it was no dreadful crime, and that as society is now constituted I did little or no harm in taking a girl, especially as my health required it.' Two days later Boswell was at a brothel, but 'hurt to find myself in the sinks of gross debauchery.' He 'danced with a fine lady in laced riding clothes, a true blackguard minuet,' but none of the girls pleased him and he went chastely home disgusted by his adventure.

On 4th June Boswell got himself up in 'a genteel suit of flowered silk' and, on this occasion of King George's birthday, paid his respects to the English Ambassador. It was a good day: there was a letter from Lord Marischal Keith informing Boswell that he was to accompany him to Berlin, and a letter from Auchinleck confirming the arrangement. Boswell's bankers had arranged a credit of £30 a month for him in Berlin. 'Never was man happier than I this morning.' This Lord Marischal was a veteran of the Jacobite rising of 1715 and a staunch supporter of the Stuarts in exile until the 1745 attempt to restore the Young Pretender, Charles Edward Stuart, to the throne. He was not impressed by the family's hopelessness and he engaged himself to serve Frederick the Great of Prussia. As Prussian Ambassador to France and Spain and Governor of Neuchâtel, he had won Frederick's confidence and even succeeded in obtaining a pardon for his offences against the British government and king. Though he had intended to settle on his Scottish estates, Frederick had begged for his return and, in his seventies, this impressive grandee was now on his way back to his Prussian master.

Boswell's leave-taking of Zélide was difficult. On 14 June they met at her music master's and disputed about religion – 'She threw out the common objections against revelation. She was a poetical sceptic.' – in the morning. In the afternoon, he drove out in a chaise to dine with Zélide at Zuylen. They had a long conversation during which they said they were sorry to leave one another; but Boswell, on his way back to Utrecht, reflected that 'our airy speculation is not thinking.' On 17 June, Boswell was back at Zuylen, where Zélide appeared none too pleased to see him – 'Are you back again? We made a touching adieu.' – but gave him a letter which she bade him read only when he was finally ready to leave Utrecht. She accompanied Boswell, Keith, Miss Kinloch, and her mother on the way to Amsterdam, prattling like 'a frantic libertine,' agitatedly speculating about love ('*one* might meet with *un homme aimable* &c, &c, &c, for whom *one* might feel a strong affection, which would probably be lasting, *but* this amiable man might not have the same affection for *one*.') This rigmarole left Boswell in no doubt that she really loved him. 'Poor Zélide!' To Temple, Boswell confessed, 'be assured that I could have this angelic creature for my wife. But she has such an imagination that I pity the man who puts his head in her power. For my part, I choose to be safe.'

On the morning of 18 June, he opened her letter. The reason for Boswell's thinking her to be unhinged was simple: Zélide imagined him to be in love with her. She had noted 'the agitation of a lover. Not all agitations, thank GOD, are infectious . . . If between two good friends one remembers he is a man, the other naturally remembers she is a woman: a few days' absence should be sufficient to enable both to forget it.' Boswell, however, would find such a lack of distinction between the sexes inconceivable. Nothing in his experience had taught him to regard a woman as his intellectual equal, nothing could induce him to be anything other than flirtatious and gallant in his approach to a woman, however mentally distinguished. Zélide was prepared to enjoy a clandestine correspondence, passionless if possible, like her secret negotiations with Constant d'Hermenches, and she asked Boswell to write to her, not often but at length, and spontaneously. 'It will not matter if the end of your letters contradicts the beginning.'

Boswell admired her 'romantic delicacy' but wrote to her firmly, denying that he was *amoureux* but assuring her that he would be her *fidèle ami*. He determined to be frank: to enlighten Zélide was his duty, motivated by 'sincerity or perhaps my extreme simplicity'. Thus, 'I admire your mind. I love your goodness. But I am not in love with you . . . In such circumstances one must not stand on ceremony.' Four days later, Zélide replies in apparent contentment, 'all the better if I have made a mistake . . . As for your peace of mind and my own (as I understood the matter), these were never in danger.' A fortnight or thereabouts elapses before Boswell replies. The letter is as lengthy as Zélide could have hoped for, but after some graceful compliments and moral reflections, Boswell buckles down to business. He begins to reprove the libertine Zélide for her dangerous sentiments. 'No, Zélide, whatever men may do, a woman without virtue is terrible.'

Zélide had written frankly to Boswell, claiming in the first letter that 'I should be well pleased with a husband who would take me as his mistress: I should say to him, "Do not look on faithfulness as a duty: so long as I have more charm, more wit, more gaiety than another . . . in order to please you, you will prefer me out of inclination; that is all I desire; . . . If you wish me to love you always, the only way is to be always lovable."' Boswell was shocked. 'Is a mistress half so agreeable as a wife? . . . I beseech you, never indulge such ideas . . . Respect the institutions of society. If imagination presents gay *caprice*, be amused with it. But let reason reign. Conceal such ideas. Act with wisdom.' With some insight, he continues, 'I would not be married to you to be a king.' Zélide's ungovernable vivacity may be of disservice to her, and her domestic virtues are inadequate to suit her to be the wife of a sensible man. But these are trifles against many stronger reasons why Zélide may not be wife to Mr Boswell: 'I am very certain that if we were married together, it would not be long before we should both be very miserable. My wife must be a character directly opposite to my dear Zélide, except in affection, in honesty, and in good humour.'

Zélide's suggestion that letters might contain contradictions is immediately followed up. Boswell breaks the seal of his reply to Zélide to charge her to be honest with him. 'If you love me, own it . . . If I had pretended a passion for you . . . would you not have gone with me to the world's end?' He has already set out the mode of life that Zélide might be expected to observe as Mrs Boswell. 'Could you submit your inclinations to the opinion, perhaps the *caprice* of a husband? Could you do this with cheerfulness, without losing any of your sweet good humour, without boasting of it? Could you live quietly in the country six months in the year? Could you make yourself agreeable to plain honest neighbours? Could you talk like any other woman, and have your fancy as much at your command as your harpsichord? Could you pass the other six months in a city where there is very good society, though not the high mode? Could you live thus and be content, could you have a great deal of amusement in your own family? Could you give spirits to your husband when he is melancholy? I have known such wives, Zélide. What think you? Could you be such a one? If you can, you may be happy with the sort of man I once described to you.'

Boswell had in fact been describing the blameless Temple as a suitable husband for Zélide in the event that she should become 'a great deal more reasonable, more prudent, more reserved'. But 'I would not begin on that litany of reforms for a man I never saw,' declared Zélide sensibly to d'Hermenches. Boswell's reputation had not preceded him to Holland, and his constant resolution to be *retenu* had so far been successful that, so far as Zélide could be aware, the discreetly sociable Mr Boswell was the genuine article. Boswell, despite the conscious control he still exercised over his character, really felt himself to be a reformed character, a man of probity fit to be ranked with Auchinleck, Dalrymple, and Johnson. This had been confirmed in every particular by his servant, François Mazerac, who had been whimsically ordered by Boswell to list his good and bad points as a master and gentleman. Mazerac had obligingly complied, providing a satisfactory document that, even when critical, flattered by implication of negligence due only to goodness and nobility of heart.

After this letter of 9 July from Boswell to Zélide, a long silence falls between them, but the correspondence in all will last four years: it would be comic, were it not so pompous, remonstrative, and pedantic on Boswell's part. Her contempt for the institutions of society terrified Boswell who, though unconventional himself, flouted decorum thoughtlessly and merely through high spirits. Belle de Zuylen had fully considered convention and found it wanting or absurd: Boswell could never go so far. He aspired to name, fame, fortune, and dignity and required a wife to reinforce his social position. He did not look for intellectual stimulation in a wife or a mistress. Nevertheless, Boswell persevered with Belle de Zuylen: she will reappear as he trips through Germany, Italy, Corsica, France, and finally returns to Scotland. Meanwhile, at seven o'clock on the morning of 18 June 1764, Boswell joined the retinue of Lord Marischal Keith and, attended by a Swiss servant Jacob Hänni, set off for the little gilded courts of Germany and their princelings, leaving Professor Trotz and his Latin lectures mumbling in the dust behind the coach and four that rattled out of the Cathedral Square bound for Berlin. 'In a charming frame, quite blissful,' Boswell abandons pedantry and prepares to be princely, checking his progress at princes as others might at milestones. 'Here now,' after supper and a pretty long conversation with the Duke of Brunswick, 'do I find myself in the very sphere of magnificence. I live with princes and a court is my home.'

Boswell tends to be boring in his euphoric inflation of ego. Romantic conceits flood his soul, and the blood of his ancient lineage flows the more freely through his lairdly veins. He naturally assumes the title of Baron Boswell, and an affable air that charms his new and splendid acquaintances. The only blow is the failure to be introduced to Frederick the Great despite a determination to add this grim scalp to his belt. 'I will let him see that he has before him a man of no common clay,' Boswell writes to Temple. At Charlottenburg, observing the King in the garden, Boswell had felt a powerful impulse to throw himself at the great man's feet. That he did not do so, is a loss to literature and anecdote. It would have made as immortal a story as the account of Fanny Burney being pursued round Kew by King George.

Disappointed, Boswell left Berlin in November ('I am quite out of conceit with monarchy') and trotted off indefatigably to inspect half a dozen or more grandees ever ardently hoping 'to find a prince of merit who might take a real regard for me, and with whose ennobling friendship I might be honoured all my life.' At his last court but one, Boswell thought he had struck gold: the Prince of Baden-Durlach. 'From my earliest years,' wrote Boswell, 'I have respected the great. In the groves of Auchinleck I have indulged pleasing hopes of ambition.' Boswell confessed that he had 'an enthusiastic love of great men' and that he derived 'a kind of glory from it.' A visible token of glory would not come amiss, and Baden-Durlach 'has an order to give. He creates Knights of the Order of Fidelity. They wear a star and a ribbon hanging from their necks.' Boswell is 'determined if possible to gain it.' After all, the Prince 'has seen my merit,' and has favoured Baron Boswell with 'every mark of distinction' – save the one most longed for, and that is frustratingly, tantalisingly just out of reach.

On taking leave of this 'grave, knowing, and worthy prince,' Boswell braces himself to ask the favour. 'I was quite the courtier, for I appeared modest and embarrassed, when in reality I was perfectly unconcerned.' If Boswell were to furnish proof of his being 'a very good gentleman' might he obtain the order? The Prince pauses and replies that he will consider it. 'I am a very old gentleman,' pleads Boswell, 'I am one of your old proud Scots.' It is a pity to refuse such a thing to such a persistent petitioner, and Boswell is asked to provide an attestation of genealogy, and 'we shall see'. The effort was in vain: the researches of Professor Pottle indicate that civil servants failed to forward the Prince's letters to the hopeful Boswell, and concealed the aspirant's letters to the Prince. There is a real possibility that Boswell's wish might have been gratified and the devoutly-desired order conferred if the two men had not been prevented from corresponding. In the event, Boswell's faith in the promises of princes was sorely tried, though he was never convinced of their perfidy.

Older and humbler friends were not neglected. At Wittenberg, Boswell took it into his head to write to Johnson at the tomb of Melancthon. No doubt he envisioned a convenient ledge on which to rest pen and paper but the tomb itself consisted in 'nothing more than two large plates of metal fixed on the floor'. Nothing daunted, 'I laid myself down and wrote in that posture.' A crowd of 'simple beings' gathered round Mr Boswell lying flat on his stomach, earnestly scribbling. 'I dare say they supposed me a little mad.' In the ruin of the church where Luther 'first preached the Reformation' and which housed his tomb directly opposite that of Melancthon, Boswell 'vowed to Mr Johnson an eternal attachment.' The letter, he was sure, would give him satisfaction, but Boswell's last two letters to Johnson had remained unanswered and he determined to retain the letter until Johnson should give him a favourable answer to his others.

The letter congratulates Boswell on his 'solemn enthusiasm of mind' which Johnson so much loves. In consideration of this, Boswell declares 'I vow to thee an eternal attachment. It shall be my study to do what I can to render your life happy, and if you die before me, I shall endeavour to do honour to your memory, and, elevated by the remembrance of you, persist in noble piety.' It was a dignified, sincere letter, perhaps a little too sentimental, romantically and solemnly written in the most ludicrous circumstances. His duty done, dusting himself off, Boswell rose to his feet and resumed his decorous deportment. He had not fallen at the feet of Frederick, but he had had no scruples about sprawling to offer himself to Mr Johnson. With the Order of Fidelity more or less in the bag, Boswell turned his face from princes to philosophers and on 23 November he and Jacob Hänni set out for Switzerland.

Rousseau and Voltaire had long been in Boswell's mind. He had procured introductions from Keith and Constant d'Hermenches, and in Berlin he had induced the British Minister Andrew Mitchell to intercede with Auchinleck on his behalf to let him continue travelling. The letter to Mitchell is a masterpiece of subtle cajolery. Lord Auchinleck had already written to Boswell to renew his opinion that travel did little good, going so far as to suggest that it might do harm. Auchinleck is opposed to the idea of Boswell going to Italy, but Boswell pleads 'I own that the words of the Apostle Paul, "I must see Rome," are strongly *borne in* upon my mind ... I am no libertine and have a moral certainty of suffering no harm in Italy ... I shall be as moderate as possible in my expenses. I do not intend to travel as a *milord anglais*, but merely as a scholar and a man of elegant curiosity.' However it was done, Boswell was granted licence to go to Italy in spite of Mitchell's dry advice to respect his father's wishes. Lord Auchinleck, nice in his judgements, perhaps realised the cause to be sufficiently pleaded and, for the moment, chose to defer the inevitable heavy sentence to be passed on Boswell's return to the jurisdiction of the judge and father.

Rousseau was living frugally and reclusively at Môtiers in the Val de Travers, only a short distance of fifteen miles or so from Neuchâtel where Keith had been Governor. He was fifty-two years old, in indifferent health, and in the full notoriety of his revolutionary views on the sacred subjects of government, education, religion, sexual morals, and family life which had been published in short order over eighteen months during the years 1761–62. Boswell had taken the trouble to read *Émile* and *The New Héloïse*: it was almost a social obligation to do so. Rousseau, the former footman, was the darling of the highest nobility who were enchanted by his distaste for civilised society and his recommendation of the superiority of the unconditioned savage state in his celebrated *Discourse on the Arts and Sciences*.

Attacks on smart society have always been rapturously received by those that constitute its most glittering and sophisticated membership, and Rousseau was a charming novelty. Less enthusiastic was the response by the established authority to the attack on religion, expressed as 'The Creed of a Savoyard Vicar' in *Émile*, and Rousseau, despite assurances of powerful protection, had been obliged to flee from Paris to Switzerland. Hounded out of Berne by pressure from Geneva, Rousseau came to rest on 10 July 1762 in Môtiers, ruled by Frederick of Prussia and governed by Keith. Here, as ever, he was attended by his mistress Thérèse Le Vasseur. Môtiers, besides being relatively safe, was also convenient: here he could work more or less uninterruptedly,

Thérèse fending off inquisitive tourists, and here he could adopt a long, flowing Armenian caftan which was more comfortable than conventional breeches considering his unfortunate urethral complaint. Here, too, were magnificent country prospects, dear to the heart of the 'natural' man and nature mystic.

All in all, Rousseau's situation should have been ideal and more or less permanent, had it not been for his inability to remain inoffensively dormant. But Rousseau had opinions to air and scores to settle. Unknown to Boswell, his travelling companion from Strasbourg to Basle, a Monsieur Boily, was carrying some advance copies of the controversial *Letters Written from the Mountain* to their author, Rousseau, in which he explicitly attacked the city authority of Geneva. This inflammatory bombshell hit the Genevan Council just after Boswell had left Rousseau and just before he arrived in Geneva. But there were other firecrackers being prepared, this time to be thrown under Rousseau's own feet: Voltaire had discovered the rumour that Rousseau and Thérèse had produced five children whom they had immediately given to the Foundling Hospital in Paris. Though poverty had prompted this action, Rousseau later regretted having abandoned his children and he lived with a weight of remorse.

On 27 December, Voltaire published a pamphlet abusing Rousseau for various domestic crimes and Rousseau responded by developing a persecution-mania that frequently rendered him insane. His life thereafter was a nightmare, bolting hither and thither from imaginary persecutors. Boswell, had he arrived a little later at Môtiers, would have missed his final opportunity to bag the genuinely ascetic 'savage philosopher' at the height of his fame and apparently settled to a tranquil life of the mind and spirit. Into this calm before the storm bounced Boswell, innocent and questing, determined to pay respectful homage, and prise a little enlightenment from a great mind. At Môtiers on 3 December 1764, Boswell considers his campaign. If he is not mistaken, there is the very house: white, with green window-boards, where the hermit hides against a constant stream of trippers who come to stare as if he has two heads. The letter Boswell carries from Keith to Rousseau should be sufficient to gain him admission, but

Jean-Jacques Rousseau, portrait by Allan Ramsay

Boswell wishes to be received in his own right, as a man of merit above the vulgar crowd. He decides to write an irresistible letter of self-recommendation. It is, indeed, utterly irresistible, drafted three times and despatched on the very afternoon of his arrival.

Sir: I am a Scots gentleman of ancient family. Now you know my rank. I am twenty-four years old. Now you know my age . . . I present myself, Sir, as a man of singular merit, as a man with a feeling heart, a lively but melancholy spirit . . . I dare to put myself to the test . . . Believe me, you will be glad to have seen me . . . I feel myself moved. I cannot restrain myself. O dear Saint Preux! Enlightened Mentor! Eloquent and amiable Rousseau! I have a presentiment that a truly noble friendship will be born today . . . You will find in me a simplicity that will put you to no trouble, a cordiality that may help you forget your pains. I have much to tell you. Though I am only a young man, I have experienced a variety of existence that will amaze you . . . Open your door, then, Sir, to a man who dares to tell you that he deserves to enter it. Place your confidence in a stranger who is different. You will not regret it . . . I await your reply with impatience.

This astonishing letter had its effect. A card, written by Rousseau, was delivered to Boswell at his inn. 'I am ill, in pain, really in no state to receive visits. Yet I cannot deprive myself of Mr Boswell's, provided that out of consideration for the state of my health, he is willing to make it short.' At Rousseau's door stood the 43-year-old Thérèse, 'a little, lively, neat French girl,' who conducted Boswell into the presence of the wild philosopher, 'a genteel black man in the dress of an Armenian'. Boswell himself had adopted the full fig of 'coat and waistcoat, scarlet with gold lace, buckskin breeches and boots. Above all I wore a greatcoat of green camlet lined with fox-skin fur, with the collar and cuffs of the same fur. I held under my arm a hat with a solid gold lace, at least with the air of being solid.' This gorgeous figure 'with the air of being solid' began the interview politely enough, but was soon holding Rousseau warmly by the hand and thumping the invalid on the back whenever he said anything that touched Boswell more than ordinary. 'I was without restraint.'

At length, Boswell asked the really interesting question, 'Tell me, Sir, do you not find that I answer to the description I gave of myself?' Rousseau replied that it was too early for him to judge, but that all appearances were in Boswell's favour. 'I shall take the honour of returning tomorrow,' said Boswell blandly. 'Oh, as to that, I can't tell,' answered Rousseau warily, 'I am overwhelmed

James Boswell in his finery
painted by George Willison during Boswell's visit to Rome

with visits from idle people . . . each of them believes he is the only one.'

An hour and a half had elapsed before Boswell finally took his leave to rush back to the inn to write a delirious letter to George Dempster in London. 'Dempster, I have been with him. I have been most politely received . . . We have made an agreement . . . he will see me as much as his health permits.' The next day, Boswell was at the door again and at five o'clock was admitted. Rousseau gossiped for a while about the Abbé de Saint-Pierre whom he had discussed in *Émile*, made a rather dreadful Latin pun, and then sent Boswell home, 'Go away.' On the doorstep, Thérèse confirmed her devotion to Rousseau, 'I would not give up my place to be Queen of France.'

The third interview, the next morning, looked like being short. 'My dear Sir, I am sorry not to be able to talk with you as I would wish.' But Boswell 'took care to waive such excuses,' and plunging on 'immediately set conversation a-going' by confessing that he had turned Roman Catholic and had intended to hide himself in a convent in France. Rousseau admitted his own religious conversions and reconversions until stopped by Boswell, who demanded, 'But tell me sincerely, are you a Christian?' Boswell fixed Rousseau with an unsparing eye and the Savoyard Vicar clapped a hand to his breast and declared, 'I say, God the Father, God the Son, God the Holy Ghost' apparently without any quibbling qualification of the formula. Rousseau urged Boswell to begin paying off, little by little, the evil he had done in his life and, having edged his own preoccupations into the conversation, Boswell broached the matter uppermost in his mind, 'Will you, Sir, assume direction of me?' Rousseau replied that he could be responsible only for himself, and saw off his visitor who cried out his intention to come back.

The thing now was to get Rousseau to discuss Mr Boswell in all his infinite complexity and variety of character. Since the philosopher was evidently not inclined to listen to an oral account, Boswell decided to commit a lengthy sketch of his life to writing and, for good measure, to enclose the letters from Zélide since deep philosophy might help to resolve that vexing question of her true character. A suitable appeal might as well preface the package to be submitted for Rousseau's earnest consideration. 'Oh, vouchsafe to preserve a true Scot! My Lord Marischal is old. That illustrious Scottish oak-tree must soon fall. You love that ancient country. Preserve a sapling from it.' Wisely, Boswell played on the wild philosopher's assumption that all virtue flowed from the noble savages of the Highlands, those good, rude men living amid the natural grandeur of loch and ben, crag and glen. 'Tell me if I can be a worthy Scots laird ... O charitable philosopher, I beseech you to help me. My mind is weak but my soul is strong. Kindle that soul, and the sacred fire shall never be extinguished.'

On 14 December, Boswell returned for an answer – but Rousseau was sitting uncomfortably with a urethral probe in position under his Armenian caftan, in no mood or condition to direct Boswell's conduct in life, though he bade Boswell to be back in the afternoon.

Boswell: 'For how long?'

Rousseau: 'A quarter of an hour and no longer.'

Boswell: 'Twenty minutes.'

Rousseau: 'Be off with you! – Ha! Ha!'

On his return, Boswell 'gave myself full scope' and laid his mind open to Monsieur Rousseau. 'When I get to France and Italy, may I not indulge in the gallantries usual to those countries, where the husbands do not resent your making love to their wives?' was but one question to which philosophy provided no answer in this world. On questions as how best to act in this world, Rousseau merely replied, 'One must have a great plan,' and stick to it. The next day, fired with fine spirits, Boswell returned gloriously to dine with Rousseau who subjected him to his critical test of character, 'Do you like cats?' Boswell did not like cats, nor hens either. Nevertheless, Rousseau introduced his cat, and his dog Sultan, and they displayed their tricks while Rousseau sang to them 'with a sweet voice and great taste'.

'Now go away,' insisted Rousseau after some more chatter.

Boswell: 'Not yet. I will leave at three o'clock. I have still five and twenty minutes.'

Rousseau: 'But I can't give you five and twenty minutes.'

Boswell: 'I will give you even more than that.'

Rousseau: 'What! Of my own time? All the kings on earth cannot give me my own time.'

Boswell: 'But if I had stayed till tomorrow I should have had five and twenty minutes, and next day another five and twenty. I am not taking those minutes. I am making you a present of them.'

Rousseau: 'Oh! You are not stealing my money, you are giving it to me.'

This exchange of banter indicates, more than any high-flown debate, the extent to which Boswell could, on the shortest acquaintance, charm and hold the interest of the most redoubtable figures of the age as easily as he could rattle with the humblest. He had even won over Thérèse immediately by the honesty of his face. After a satisfactory leave-taking of embraces and compliments (Boswell: 'You have shown me much goodness. But I deserved it.' Rousseau: 'Yes. You are malicious; but 'tis a pleasant malice, a malice I don't dislike.') Thérèse saw Boswell off, declaring that he had pleased her. 'I have seen strangers enough in the twenty-two years that I have been with Monsieur Rousseau, and I assure you that I have sent many of them packing because I did not like their way of talking.' Boswell promised to send her a garnet necklace from Geneva, and on 22 December he arrived there, at 'the seat of Presbyterianism' to prepare for his second assault on philosophy – it was Voltaire's turn to be bagged.

He, too, was an exile from Paris, living some four miles from Geneva, a quick dash from French soil at Ferney. He lived in some splendour, as if in a constant *levée*, attended by amusing guests and protected by his housekeeper–niece, Madame Denis. Boswell had hoped for some definition of virtue from Rousseau, some oracular word that would be a refuge in perplexity. He anticipated no such directive from the cynical sage of Ferney: the glow of Rousseau, even at the godless gates of the most famous and powerful philosopher in Europe, continued to irradiate Boswell's being. 'I was in true spirits; the earth was covered with snow; I surveyed wild nature with a noble eye.' Summoning up 'all the grand ideas which I have ever entertained of Voltaire,'

Boswell was ushered into 'a very elegant room' by two or three footmen where he was told, despite the letter of introduction from Constant d'Hermenches, that 'Monsieur de Voltaire is very much annoyed at being disturbed. He is abed.' This was a blow, but Boswell waited for a while, being entertained by some of Voltaire's guests, until at last 'Monsieur de Voltaire opened the door of his apartment and stepped forth . . . He received me with

M.ᴿ *VOLTAIRE*.

dignity, and that air of the world which a Frenchman acquires in such perfection.' He was seventy years old, and certainly worldly. Contemporary caricatures could scarcely exaggerate the long nose, the puckered, toothless mouth, the thin, withered, simian body, and brilliant black eyes. Voltaire took a chair, gathered his 'slate-blue, fine frieze greatcoat night-gown' around him, and perhaps adjusted his three-knotted wig. While the patriarch simpered, Boswell presented the 'foolish face of wondering praise'.

They talked of Scotland. Voltaire praised the printing of Glasgow, but dismissed Scottish painting on the ground that it is hard to paint when one's feet are cold. Since he had no teeth against which to place his tongue, Voltaire claimed to be unable to speak English. He complimented David Hume the Deist as 'a true philosopher,' and hobbled off leaving Boswell to make up to Madame Denis at dinner. On Christmas Day, Boswell wrote to her begging to be allowed to sleep a night under her uncle's roof, and was granted permission to visit. On 27 December, Boswell presented himself again at Ferney where 'some sat snug by the fire, some chatted, some sung, some played the guitar, some played at shuttlecock.' It was very dull until, between seven and eight, Voltaire appeared in the drawing room and Boswell placed himself by the magician of the enchanted castle who flew off into high spirits, wittily, extravagantly, forcibly, nonsensically, now humming a ballad, now swearing like a trooper, all with an oddity of style that had made his squibs and shrills the terror and delight of enemies and allies alike.

'At last we came upon religion,' notes Boswell blandly in an account of the scene to Temple before going on to crow his considerable triumph. Voltaire began to rage, while the rest of the company (who had probably heard it all before) went to supper leaving the apostate and the apologist to battle over the Bible that had been laid between them. The heat of the conflict almost overthrew Boswell: the cackling, crackling vehemence of Voltaire's passionate diatribe flew, razor sharp, towards his adversary, fortunately passing, for the most part, high above Boswell's teeming head. 'The daring bursts of his ridicule con-

THE SAVAGE MAN.

A caricature of Rousseau, apostle of nature, with Hume and Voltaire.
A contemporary engraving, based on an original sketch
by James Boswell

founded my understanding.' Voltaire declaimed his heresies on
his feet, dancing on his spindly old pins, shaking himself and
religion in his agitation. Boswell blustered and watched in wonder. Voltaire suddenly sagged and fell back in an easy chair. 'Oh, I
am very sick; my head turns round,' he commented pathetically.
Boswell inspected him, huddled and spent. Voltaire opened an
eye, perhaps to judge the effect of his performance.

   Boswell pounced, mercilessly. 'I demanded of him an honest
confession of his real sentiments.' A little plain speaking, if you
please, Monsieur de Voltaire. Voltaire, exhausted, was candid,
dredging up 'from the bottom of his heart' the gratifying admission of his veneration, his love, of the Supreme Being, and his
entire resignation to the will of Him who is All-wise. He wished to
resemble the Author of Goodness by being good himself.

Though he doubted immortality, his mind was nevertheless tranquil. But Boswell knew a good performance when he saw one: had he not been an acute critic of the theatre? 'I doubted his sincerity. I called to him with emotion, "Are you sincere? are you really sincere?" He answered, "Before God, I am . . . I suffer much. But I suffer with patience and resignation; not as a Christian – but as a man."' That was, at last, good enough for Mr Boswell: leaving the prostrate philosopher, who perhaps cocked a speculative eye over the plump, scarlet-coated back of his triumphant Scotch confessor, Boswell went in to dinner. His visit at Ferney lasted two nights, and Voltaire, pleading illness and exhaustion, consented to receive Boswell only after dinner on the third day just before he was about to leave. They parted amicably, Boswell extracting a promise that Voltaire would reply to his letters.

Boswell was twenty-four years old, and had reason to be gratified by his achievements. The visit to Ferney had been notable by any standards, and Boswell complimented himself generously in his journal. It is not all idle puffing: he does not delude himself when he writes, 'What a singular being do I find myself! . . . am I not well received everywhere? Am I not particularly taken notice of by men of the most distinguished genius? And why? I have neither profound knowledge, strong judgement, nor constant gaiety. But I have a noble soul which still shines forth, a certain degree of knowledge, a multiplicity of ideas of all kinds, an original humour and turn of expression, and, I really believe, a remarkable knowledge of human nature . . . With this I have a pliant ease of manners which must please. I can tune myself so to the tone of any bearable man I am with that he is as much at freedom as with another self, and, till I am gone, cannot imagine me a stranger. Perhaps my talents are such as procure me more happiness than those of a more elevated kind.' Boswell had more than a sympathy with his interlocutors: he had more than a desire to make himself agreeable. In a very real sense, he wished to *be* Johnson or Rousseau or Dalrymple, or any one of a hundred representatives of a desirable virtue. But he was Boswell, ready to take the impress of their seal, and as Boswell he revealed them to themselves, as an *alter ego*, as another self. Boswell was, in short, irresistibly attractive.

[4]

———— ✦ ————

Passion, Pandaemonium and Piety

———— ✦ ————

On the evening of 7 January 1765 Boswell arrived at Turin. He was now fairly in Italy, having been carried across the Alps in an 'Alps machine' – a sort of cord and board chair slung between parallel poles – by six porters who floundered through snow sometimes six feet deep while Mr Boswell, high as a bishop, noted the scenery 'horribly grand'. But despite his best efforts to rouse himself to peaks of sensibility, Boswell never took much interest in scenery and had no words beyond the platitudinous for the inanimate. A long account of Boswell's Italian tour was composed for the attention of Rousseau, but it was apparently never sent. It was dated October 1765, in the month Boswell made his excursion to Corsica, and began well: the traveller carried in his head, across the Alps, 'ideas of the most rigorous morality'. But these were immediately suborned by the charms of beautiful Italian women, so that 'I thought I might allow myself *one* intrigue in Italy, in order to increase my knowledge of the world and give me a contempt for shameless women.' Even to Boswell, this piece of special pleading cannot have sounded convincing.

He was in Italy ostensibly to drink in classical sites and to refine his artistic tastes. There was, too, the pull of the epicentre of the glamorous religion which had shaken his soul – Rome. His education in cold climates had been mainly intellectual: now, in the warmth of the south, it might take a more sentimental turn. Immediately, Boswell presented himself to the Comtesse de St Gilles, 'past fifty and . . . long *hackneyed in the ways of men*,' after which he went to a ball where he danced with the Spanish Ambassador's wife and incredulously learned that, of all the fine women he so admired, he might have any one of them, manners in Turin being so 'openly debauched that adultery was carried on without the least disguise,' marriage being merely the custom in order to perpetuate families. Boswell's shock was perhaps accompanied by a little frisson of delight. The dangerous reputation of Mme de St Gilles as a notorious seducer of young Englishmen, and as the superintendent of every intrigue in Turin, did not prevent Boswell attending her, as one of her cicisbeos, to the opera the next night. There, in a high box, he noticed John Wilkes whom he already knew to be in town. Boswell was filled with 'romantic agitation' and immediately, on returning home, addressed an invitation to Mr Wilkes to dine and discuss the immateriality of the soul. But Wilkes had gone to bed.

To confirm his contempt for corruption, Boswell began to make up unsubtly to Mme de St Gilles: time was short, so 'I thought an oldish lady most proper, as I should have an easy attack. I began throwing out hints at the opera. I sat vis-à-vis to her and pressed her legs with mine, which she took very graciously. I began to lose command of myself. I became quite imprudent.' But more tender game was at hand: Boswell was taken to the box of Countess Burgaretta to be introduced. 'She was a most beautiful woman. Billon [an obliging Frenchman] told me I might have her. My mind was now quite in fermentation. I was a sceptic, but my devotion and love of decency remained. My desire to know the world made me resolve to intrigue a little while in Italy, where the women are so debauched that they are hardly to be considered as moral agents, but as inferior beings.' Billon was easily persuaded to act as Boswell's pimp, and Boswell, now having convinced himself into a state of violent love for Mme Burgaretta, wrote, attempted to visit, and beseeched – in vain. Mme de St Gilles was, astonishingly, no easier meat. Boswell spoke plainly. 'I am young, strong, vigorous. I offer my services as a duty, and I think that the Comtesse de St Gilles will do very well to accept them.' 'But I am not that kind of woman,' she replied to Boswell's bafflement. He thought to take her *en passant*, but consoled himself with the mean thought that she was jealous of

the beautiful Burgaretta. Billon later came up with more accessible women for Boswell's amusement, but they were not always
reliable and Boswell began to be vexed by his lack of success as a
gallant. At the opera again, Boswell began pressing his attentions
on a third Countess, Mme Skarnavis, to the great chagrin of Mme
de St Gilles, and again started writing letters with more energy
than discretion. The flattery and self-congratulation are outrageous, expressed 'without timidity and without restraint'. Ex-
tracts will serve to give the tone of this, and many another, letter of
passion and entreaty:

> You are already aware that I feel for you the strongest of
> passions . . . I adore you, and nothing could avail to weaken that
> adoration . . . you refrained from telling me it would be
> impossible to win your favour . . . use no evasions with a
> romantic lover . . . never have your charms been more worthily
> felt than by me. If you accord me the supreme happiness, you
> will be showing yourself generous to an excellent man . . . You
> are in perfect safety with me. You can rely on my honour in
> every respect . . . Ah! when we abandon ourselves to pleasures
> under the veil of darkness, what transports, what ecstasy will be
> ours! Pardon me, Madame, I am greatly agitated . . . dispose of
> me as you see fit . . . But if I am not disagreeable to you . . . you
> cannot conceive, Madame, how keenly I shall be touched. O
> Love! baneful and delicious madness, I feel you and am your
> slave . . . Have a care, Madame, there is here something
> important at stake. I tremble, but I have hopes.

Madame Skarnavis, when Boswell sent to retrieve his letter,
replied to his valet that she had thrown it in the fire. 'Here was the
extreme of mortification for me. I was quite sunk.' Here, indeed,
was a little additional knowledge of the world – but where were
the shameless women?

This day, the 22 January, was an education. Boswell happened
on an execution, and he pressed close to the gallows. 'The
criminal stood on a ladder, and a priest held a crucifix before his
face. He was tossed over, and hung with his face uncovered,

which was hideous. I stood fixed in attention to this spectacle, thinking that the feelings of horror might destroy those of chagrin.' But Boswell found himself unusually insensible, even when the hangman put his feet on the head of his victim and had him strangled in a minute. Boswell went then to a church and kneeled devotedly before an altar. 'Here then I felt three successive scenes: raging love – gloomy horror – grand devotion.'

This is typical of Boswell in Italy: passion, pandaemonium and piety. In considerable frustration, Boswell abandoned Turin and got to Milan where he dutifully inspected the church and a few lesser ones, noting Latin inscriptions, and visited the Ambrosian library which he forbore to describe since Mr Addison had saved him the trouble. Boswell's perfunctory inspections of pictures and palaces, churches and cathedrals, were very necessary if he were to be able to boast later of having acquired a proper aesthetic appreciation of art, architecture, and all that Italy had to offer. But there is no shred of real interest, no shiver of delight, no acute comment that invariably characterises his encounters with a responsive human being. His notes have been described as resembling a 'bad Baedeker,' and have never engaged the attention of art historians or Boswell's biographers.

At length after a tour of the northern towns of Italy, Boswell came to Rome in mid-February. It was not his principal preoccupation in Italy to interview famous or grand personages, but when they stood more or less in his way he did not attempt a modest detour. In Turin, he had been presented to the King of Sardinia, Charles Emmanuel I, and at Parma he had made use of an introduction from Rousseau to Alexandre Delyre, tutor to the son of the Duke of Parma. Delyre was a sympathetic man, and, best of all, disposed to listen to Boswell's limitless discourses on melancholy. Like anyone else, Delyre discovered himself to have an affection and concern for Boswell. In Rome, Boswell immediately fell in with John Wilkes whom he seized and embraced with enthusiasm. When he was not falling to his knees, rapt with devotion, in a church, Boswell was falling indiscriminately on girls during the remaining days of Carnival just before Lent. He recruited a young French art student, Guillaume Martin, to pimp for him and he resolved to have a girl every day, in the fashion of a Spaniard. He was, for once, fairly surfeited with sex and now and again had to forgo his resolve in order to recover his strength and virility.

He struck up an acquaintance with Nathaniel Dance, the portraitist, and was introduced to Angelica Kauffmann who was then completing her art studies. She was amiable and modest, and Boswell was 'quite in love,' as was Dance. He declared his earnest, near-idolatrous Jacobitism to Wilkes who was inclined to indict George III, the Hanoverian, as being as much a foe to liberty as any Stuart. But Boswell discreetly moderated his fondness for the Pretenders only a week later, when he cut the cloth of his opinion to suit the young Lord Mountstuart, son of Lord Bute who was a favourite of George III. Wilkes had already left for Naples, and on 25 February Boswell set off in pursuit. The journey along the Appian Way was bone-breaking, hot, and slow, but his stay of three weeks in Naples was to be more amusing than any other period of his time in Italy. Rome had not impressed Boswell: its streets, though he had entered upon them 'with full classical enthusiasm,' were 'very little different from those of any other city,' and the Epistle of St Paul to the Romans, an indifferent congregation, 'seemed to me to be just an ancient writing by some ecclesiastical zealot.' It no longer seemed to be the word of God, and Boswell's terror of it abated.

The secular writings and witticisms of Wilkes were more immediately relevant, interesting, and deliciously harrowing. Wilkes, though he professed a dislike for the Scots, was the man. He and Boswell got along famously: his 'lively and energetic sallies on moral questions' aroused Boswell's spirits to 'a not unpleasing agitation'. Wilkes, 'completely serene and gay' possessed a 'resilient spirit' that enabled him to experience 'all the vicissitudes of pleasure and politics without ever having suffered a moment of uneasiness'. This capacity for survival clearly impressed Boswell whose own spirit was wont to faint in adversity, and he was probably minded to learn the trick from Wilkes, from a man who had 'thought much without being gloomy,' and 'done much evil without being a scoundrel.' Such an example of

Lord Mountstuart, son of Lord Bute, portrait by William Hoare

carefree irresponsibility mightily impressed Boswell who could have wished to be a Wilkes who thus confounded all theories of human nature generally, and in particular Boswell's experience of his own character.

At Naples, Boswell ran about unrestrainedly after women. 'My blood was inflamed by the burning climate, and my passions were violent,' he declared in his note to Rousseau, adding, 'I indulged them.' He escaped infection, but made no moral reflections on this interesting point. With Wilkes, his gay, classical friend, old in the ways of indecency, Boswell listened fascinatedly to the story of his libertine life. 'At school and college never read; always among women . . . my father gave me as much money as I pleased. Three or four whores; drunk every night. Sore head morning, then read. I'm capable to sit thirty hours over a table to study. Plan for *North Briton*: grave revolutionary paper seasoned each time with a character from the Court list.' Wilkes took an opportunity to abuse Samuel Johnson as 'an impudent pretender to literature' but admitted that he did not really think so badly of Johnson though he had attacked him in the *North Briton* and, for his pains, had been described by Johnson as a 'retailer of sedition and obscenity'.

Wilkes and Boswell dined, drank, laughed, and ascended Vesuvius together. They were heaved up to the lip of the crater by five men and lay on their bellies to peer down into the sulphurous smoke. The clouds of smoke billowed in their faces, so there was not much to be seen, and in fact they were obliged hastily to retire and bowl back down the slope, up to their knees in ashes, coughing and crowing. At dinner, there was more earnest discussion.

Boswell: 'What shall I do to get life over?'

Wilkes: 'While there's all ancient and modern learning and all arts and sciences, enough for life if three thousand years.'

Boswell: 'Fate and free will?'

Wilkes: 'Let 'em alone.'

Boswell: 'Why keep company with me?'

Wilkes: '[You're an] original genius. But they'll spoil you [in] Paris; lop luxuriances from you.'

Wilkes loved Boswell for what he was: and Boswell found in Wilkes a man who would not care to mess him about in an attempt to 'improve' him. It was an association of equals, and for once Boswell could keep cheerful company without seeking to profit by it, though the paradoxes of Wilkes's character intrigued him as a contrast to his own peculiarities of personality.

At about this time, Boswell received letters from Temple, Lord

Auchinleck, from Monsieur de Zuylen and from Zélide. To
Belle's father, Boswell had intimated a hint of his feelings for
Zélide, 'I do not cease to please myself with the recollection of
Mademoiselle de Zuylen . . . I find her more and more charming.
I begin to retreat from some of my prejudices towards her.' This
cosy correspondence between Boswell and de Zuylen was satisfactory to both, but took no account of Zélide's own contribution
to the debate. She intruded herself forcefully, after Boswell had,
against her express wish, entrusted her father with a letter to be
delivered to her. The letter, written from Geneva on Christmas
Day 1764, contained effusive compliments, gross flattery, and
severe remonstrances for not having written to Boswell. He urged
his virtues upon her consideration, 'I am proud . . . You ought to
be flattered by my attachment . . . A man who has a mind and a
heart like mine is rare. A women with many talents is not so rare
. . . O Zélide! I believed you to be without the weaknesses of your
sex. I had almost come to count upon your heart . . . have I been
mistaken? Tell me the simple truth without reserve.'

So, without reserve, precisely as instructed, Zélide set to her
reply, fiercely berating Boswell for his reproaches and admonish-
ments and unjustified assumptions. Zélide made no bones about
her fury, 'You went on repeating, ringing all the changes possible
on the words, that I was in love with you, that my feelings were
those of love. You would have me admit this, you were determined to hear me say it and say it again. I find this a very strange
whim in a man who does not love me and thinks it incumbent on
him (from motives of delicacy) to tell me so in the most express
and vigorous terms . . . towards the middle of October I got your
second letter. Once more I found myself commanded by you to
confess that I had felt a passionate desire for you. I was shocked
and saddened to find, in a friend whom I had conceived of as a
young and sensible man, the puerile vanity of a fatuous fool,
coupled with the arrogant rigidity of an old Cato . . . There is no
question of love's anxieties, its suspicions, its jealousies or its
transports.'

Zélide relented a little towards the end of this letter, and
waspishly professed the continuance of her friendship '*as if there*

were something rare about a woman with many talents.' She offered
tenderness, esteem, she would even go so far as to extend her
respect, but she omitted any reference to love. A letter from her
father to Boswell confirmed that she would not give up metaphysics, and from Rome, on 23 April, Boswell replied to Monsieur de
Zuylen, 'My imagination presents me with a thousand lots in life
above mine. I try to admire them all without envying them, and I
keep myself as much from the greed of fame as from the greed of
money. I could wish that my intellectual friend Zélide had a little
of this philosophy. She would be happier for it, and (if I may say so
in simple frankness of heart) she would be still more amiable.'
The rest of the letter was an ample ramble around the topics of
family, honour, and self-love, pompous and pious, delivered in
tones of the greatest humility and with all the conviction of a
courtier scraping to a king. Boswell also wrote, at the beginning of
April, to placate Zélide. She had evidently sobered him momentarily, but she had not gone far enough. She had offered the olive
branch of friendship, which Boswell grasped and took to be
evidence of Zélide's notorious fickleness and indecision. She had
not yet seen him off.

During Holy Week, Boswell was again in Rome. On 24 March
he entered upon a six-day crash course in Antiquities and Arts,
conducted by the Scottish antiquary Colin Morison who bundled
his charge up and down the classical sites from the Capitoline hill
to the Forum where Boswell indulged in 'sublime and melancholy
emotions,' then to the Colosseum, the Palatine hill, the Baths of
Diocletian, and enough other monuments to glut even the most
enthusiastic appetite for remnants of the grandeur of the ancient
Romans. Between the scramblings about the ruins of Imperial
splendour, Boswell participated in masses and observed the
gorgeous rituals of Papal Rome. On 13 May, dressed in silks, he
was presented to Pope Clement XIII. To justify the serious
impression that the solemn services of the Roman Catholic
Church had made upon him, Rousseau's 'Savoyard doctrines'
were rallied to Boswell's aid and 'made me see a church even
more catholic than that which I revered: the entire Universe, all
souls being emanations of the Eternal Being.' He fell on his knees

before the elevated Host in St Peter's. 'Let cold beings sneer; I was never more nobly happy than on that day.'

Boswell determined, like any young gentleman on the Grand Tour, to exercise his taste and discrimination as a patron of the arts. He had been reading Robertson's *History of Scotland* and had been gripped by a passage describing the abdication of Mary Queen of Scots. He approached the Scottish painter Gavin Hamilton, whose painting of *Achilles Dragging the Body of Hector at his Chariot Wheels* he had seen on his first visit to Rome. 'Make it full size, and neglect nothing. As I'm to have a picture, don't mind price,' ordered Boswell, Auchinleck's pensioner, in the grand manner. 'I shall not stand for £100 more or less.' Hamilton had the grace to try to beat Boswell down, on the ground that he would make a great deal of money from the print of such an affecting subject as Mary resigning her crown. But Boswell was adamant, 'I am rich enough.' Hamilton offered to do it for £150, but Boswell topped the offer by £50 to £200, and Hamilton made one last try to control this patron determined to be glad-handed, 'You may pay me just as you can, by degrees.' By this time Boswell was also beginning to doubt his own wisdom, 'In Scotland they'll talk against me: "What, is he bespeaking history pictures?"'

Not only history pictures, but a portrait of himself: on 4 May Boswell was to be found sitting at the studio of the young Scots painter George Willison, composing his features in 'a plain, bold, serious attitude'. He had decked himself in his philosopher-baiting outfit, the gorgeousness of which had contrasted so noticeably with Rousseau's old Armenian robe and Voltaire's dressing gown. This picture was a better investment than the Hamilton historical which, when Boswell got it back to Scotland, was found to be disappointing. Even better might have been to sit to Batoni, whom he saw on 18 April, whose portraits of 18th century British tourists hang in mansion, manor, museum and castle to this day. But the busy mind of Baron Boswell (for that was how he had caused himself to be described to the Pope) was preoccupied with Scotland in this city of Jacobites.

He had struck up an acquaintance with Andrew Lumisden who had been private secretary to Charles Edward Stuart twenty years before in the '45 rebellion. He was now secretary to James III and VIII, the Old Pretender, in Rome. Just as Delyre had done, Lumisden formed an affection for Boswell and treated him kindly. He took Boswell on a tour to Tivoli, to gaze upon the supposed site of the Sabine farm where Horace had experienced his happiest moments. Beside the Bandusian fount, Boswell recited Horace's ode to the Fons Bandusiae and thoughtfully picked up a few stones from the sacred, classical site to take back to Lord Auchinleck, that devotee of Horace and Anacreon.

All in all, Boswell was considered rather eccentric by the Scots in Italy: he took little trouble to frequent the company of his countrymen, tried to learn Italian, showed an excessive interest in antiquities, and attempted to enter into the life of the Italians themselves whom he found, sadly, given up to formal, empty, superficial usages. In company, two or three cardinals usually set the tone, and 'the gross flattery, the obvious scheming, the discontents, and the universal ambition of ecclesiastical politicians' disgusted Boswell.

From the beginning of May, Boswell was taking care to cultivate his friendship with Lord Mountstuart, a 'pretty young man . . . Try to be well with Lord Mountstuart.' To Rousseau, Boswell characterised Mountstuart as 'a young nobleman who merits his being of the blood of the ancient kings of Scotland . . . He is handsome, has elegant manners, and a tempestuously noble soul. He has never applied himself earnestly to anything, but he is not without knowledge and has an excellent mind . . . His money is for him in civilised society what physical strength is to a savage . . . He calmly follows his inclinations: when he wishes to study, he reads; when he is indolent he lies on a sofa. Sometimes he speaks in company, sometimes he says nothing. Sometimes his passion for women is very strong, and he pursues them with the greatest liveliness.' Like Boswell, Mountstuart has the defect of 'weak nerves' but suffers less because he is 'a practical philosopher'. Mountstuart liked Boswell, and Boswell liked the noble Lord, who often said to him, 'Boswell, I will teach you how to live.' Boswell thought 'really he did me good' and hoped to profit by the friendship.

Before leaving Rome, there was the inconvenient little matter of a dose of clap to be doctored, but otherwise there was no hindrance to accepting the 21-year-old Mountstuart's suggestion that Boswell should accompany him on the remainder of his tour of Italy. Mountstuart himself was attended by a governor, Lt Colonel James Edmonstone, and a tutor, David Mallet, as befitted such a princely youth. Edmonstone was in his forties, and a thoroughly solid, reliable, decisive, occasionally rough man. Mallet was a Swiss, aged thirty-five, and a scholar. He was a trial to Mountstuart and Boswell, since he took his duties as a tutor rather seriously, and was in turn sorely tried by the indolence, imperiousness, and self-assured manner of his pupil who was abetted by Boswell in his capriciousness. Edmonstone, asserts Boswell, was pleased to have an ally who could help him prevent Lord Mountstuart 'from being tempted by bad company to renew his dissipations,' but his faith in Boswell as an exemplar was misplaced. 'When I heard him [Mountstuart] hold forth on the pleasures of grandeur I began to wish for employment at Court. I thought of his great interest. Insensibly I tried to please him and was afraid of offending him. He soon noticed it, and could not help from profiting a little from it.'

Boswell immediately took offence at Edmonstone's Scottish bluntness, describing it as 'rudely familiar'. Like a chameleon taking on protective colouring, Boswell assumed an imperiousness to match Mountstuart's and rigorously maintained caste as a gentleman of ancient blood to match his companion's. He even jibbed at Mountstuart's familiarity in calling him 'Jamie,' a diminutive he disliked. He was conscious of Mountstuart's importance, and thus all the more sensitive about his own. Mountstuart might be influential as a patron, but Boswell, despite his respect for blood and title, was no man's vassal. It was not in his nature to admit any claim that diminished the rank of a Boswell of Auchinleck. He was conscious that he had begun to fawn on Mountstuart and, writing to Rousseau, admitted his shock. 'What! Boswell, *the man of singular merit!* The friend of Rousseau! Is Boswell so far overcome by vile interest as to depend on the moods of a young Lord? I recollected myself. I made my

Lord realise that I was as proud as ever. I did it too emphatically.'

Boswell, for all his wiles, was never very subtle. It was not really in his nature to feign what he did not feel, or make compromising accommodations. The result, of course, was a thoroughly uncomfortable trip, tense with temper and suffocating with sulks. Besides, compared with Rousseau, Voltaire and Wilkes, with whom 'each glass of wine produced a flash of wit, like gunpowder thrown into the fire – Puff! puff!', the present callow company may have been in truth rather uninspiring. Friday 21 June was a bad day: the party arrived late at Ferrara and violently disputed as to whether it was necessary to stay to look at the city. Grudges from the day before were aired, and Boswell was blamed – 'I laughed at this display of human weakness.' 22 June provoked more human weakness, and quarrels exploded from Padua to Venice. Mallet derogated Boswell as 'a man who had studied little and seen little of the world, who thought he knew a great deal' but who, indeed, had as few ideas as any student Mallet had ever met.

In Venice, Mallet tried to bag one of the better bedrooms, and was damned by Boswell for his impudence. Mountstuart told Boswell he was honest and honourable, but sometimes disagreeable, and that he would be an imperious husband and father. Mallet alleged that Rousseau had laughed at Boswell and that Voltaire would write to any well-recommended, fiery young man and then forget 'that English bugger'. A truce was called between these 'four odd men' for a week, but it was broken by Mallet who described Boswell as 'a man with no system and with false ideas. You have no attachments, no friends of long standing. They were your toadies, not your friends.' Boswell was shocked that 'a wretch could think so of you'. As well he might be: Mallet was merely being rude.

In Venice, Boswell had begun to conduct an intrigue with a Madame Michieli, who permitted him to pull up her petticoat to show 'whole knees &c' and, later, 'Take her on it fair, and ask her to do it with hand,' and 'All other liberties exquisite'. But it was not a satisfactory affair: Mme Michieli was advanced in years, and declared that far from taking on a lover for two weeks, she would not take on even a good cook that she could keep only a fortnight.

To Boswell's ears had come brilliant rumours of Venetian court-esans. His fancy, and much else, was stirred and he went to see them, getting another pox before he was properly cleared of the Roman variety. Mallet thoroughly enjoyed the discomfiture of Boswell and Mountstuart, who had accompanied him, and Edmonstone took them both severely to task.

Under these repeated assaults on his self-esteem, Boswell began to feel 'a libertine and an ignoramus,' bashful and distrust-ful of his abilities. He thought of his father, a terrifying prospect for one who had failed to observe a proper conduct and uniform dignity of character. But on a short tour of the Venetian states, relations temporarily improved and Mountstuart admitted that he esteemed Boswell and would always be his friend, though 'you have a terrible disposition.' At Milan, Mountstuart, Edmonstone, and Mallet left Boswell, though not before further slanging. Boswell first accused Mountstuart of treating him badly, Edmonstone told Boswell plainly that he was 'geck' (silly) to suppose that he could establish a friendship by being familiar. Then they were gone, leaving Boswell bruised and dull and weak.

Mountstuart had been summoned home by his father, Lord Bute, leaving Boswell in a dilemma. He had been in Italy for five months, a month longer than Auchinleck had sanctioned, and Boswell was not yet ready to go home. In the end, he dealt with the problem by omitting to write to his father on the ground that, had Mountstuart not been recalled, he would have continued to jaunt round Italy with him for a while with permission, however grudging, from Auchinleck. Boswell was well aware that he was taking a great deal too much for granted, but the opportunity to see Florence and Siena was not to be resisted. To raise his spirits, Boswell went to Parma to visit Alexandre Delyre who readily inspected the soul that his new friend bared so freely to his judgement. Boswell rested in this 'consolatory refuge for a week and spoke of Rousseau, religion, John Wilkes, and immortality with the amiable atheist, before travelling by way of Bologna and Modena to Florence. Here Boswell found the Florentines (and the Florentine women in particular) 'very proud and very mercenary,' and took lessons on the flute from Dothel, 'one of the best teachers of the flute in Europe'.

He equipped himself with condoms at Florence before setting out for Siena on 24 August. At Siena, he hoped to meet with Porzia Sansedoni, Mountstuart's former mistress. Here Boswell was happy: Sienese society was simple, open, gay, unaffected by artificiality, and free of self-seeking courtliness. They were ready to welcome a well-recommended stranger. The accent of Siena was melodious, civil conditions were peaceable, and Boswell was the only tourist in the city. Since the ladies of Siena were accustomed to 'making love as their inclination suggested,' Boswell 'yielded to custom' and 'allowed myself to become all sensation and immediate feeling.' He gave himself up, 'without self-reproach and in complete serenity, to the charms of irregular love.'

Mountstuart had glowingly described Porzia to Boswell, and in a letter to the lady Boswell declares that the picture he had drawn of her character indicated 'the very person my romantic soul had imagined; and that soul has begun to indulge in hopes that the time is come, at last, to enjoy the felicity of which it believed itself worthy.' The Sansedoni is, however, virtuous though her cavalier does not displease her. She has a lover, an obstacle that Boswell believes to be surmountable for, as Boswell can inform her, Mountstuart 'is incapable of fidelity himself, and does not expect it of you.' Indeed, Mountstuart 'would be generous enough to desire that his friend should possess the happiness he sighs for.' Are they not, both Porzia and Boswell, already united in being part of the same friend? But Porzia must beware: there is another, already gasping for the attentions of Boswell: would it be sensible to drive Boswell into the arms of another who would distract him?

But Porzia Sansedoni kept Boswell's fire at bay, and despite his ingenious conceit that their mutual regard for Mountstuart should bind them together, Boswell had to take his romantic sentiments elsewhere. He had been hedging his bets in any case, on the one hand clamorously besieging the Sansedoni, on the other making advances to young Girolama Piccolomini, the wife of a civic official and sprig of a distinguished Sienese family.

Girolama, or Moma, capitulated with surprising lack of defence. Boswell had not considered Moma (or Momina) too seriously, but it was not difficult to adjust his taste to her charms, to discover virtues he had unaccountably overlooked. He fell utterly in love. Zélide had written to him to announce the likelihood of her marriage to the Marquis de Bellegarde, and Boswell was in the mood to exchange that virago for someone considerably softer. He gave himself up to Momina and after an initial impotence steadily gained virility and swore passion. He was completely happy. Mallet had even written to admit that he had treated Boswell severely, and conceded that he now found some things in Boswell to 'justify and inspire a great deal of esteem and friendship.' There was a motive behind this apparent *volte-face*: Mallet wanted Boswell to find a chest of papers he had lost. Boswell thought lovingly of 'the romantic woods of Auchinleck' where he supposed, should he find himself there, 'my happiness would be complete,' and fantasised future felicity on his native soil where 'I can honour the memory of my worthy ancestors, live happily cultivating my lands, doing good to my tenants, and showing a cordial hospitality to my neighbours. This is how I wish to live when my travels are over.'

But not yet, not yet. His travels are not over. There is the prospect of Corsica, of which Boswell had talked with Rousseau and solicited credentials from the philosopher who held a high opinion of that island. Momina was genuinely grieved to see Boswell leave for Lucca, thence to Pisa, from whence to Leghorn where he arrived on 6 October.

Mr Corsica Boswell

Boswell, in a letter to Rousseau some six months before, had declared his intention of being in Corsica in September 1765. But 'the charms of sweet Siena' detained him longer than they should have done, and not until early morning on 11 October did the adventurer set sail from Leghorn in a Tuscan wine boat. Prudently, to Boswell's mind, they were bound for Capo Corso, held by Corsicans, to avoid the French controlled territory around the port of Bastia. He had furnished himself with ample recommendations: a short but effective letter of introduction from Rousseau; a passport with an impressive red seal issued by Commander Harrison of the British Squadron in the Mediterranean as a talisman against the improbable event of capture and commitment to the galleys for life by Barbary corsairs, who would have sold such a prize as a Mr Boswell to the Turks at Algiers in a minute; and a sheaf of letters from Count Antonio Rivarola, Sardinian consul at Leghorn, who also arranged to have this amiable and ingenious young traveller discreetly watched and reported on for the information of the King of Sardinia. Innocent of this last flattering attention (for, if he had been aware of it, he would have written it up in his notes with a mixture of excited pride and apprehension), Boswell was looking forward to being braced by the hardy air of Corsica after the soft enchantments of Tuscany. He had been assured by Rivarola that the danger from native Corsicans, bristling with arms and peering from behind every second bush ready to leap on travellers at the least provocation, was unfounded, and thus he was free to anticipate the charm of meeting the illustrious Chief, that Corsican Lycurgus, General Pasquale Paoli.

Meanwhile, Boswell had leisure for his pleasurable imaginings. The boat was becalmed and the normal voyage of one day took, tediously, two. At least, the first day was tiresome. He was seasick and confined to a cabin infested with 'mosquitoes and other vermin,' until he was made comfortable on deck by the crew who began to play on the citra, a musical instrument, and sing *Ave Maria* 'with great devotion and some melody' as part of their evening orisons. Some salty conversation developed, Boswell took out his flute, and the acquaintance with his shipmates became genial. From them, he learned, comfortingly, that in Corsica 'I should be treated with the greatest hospitality;' but, with a delicious frisson, that 'if I attempted to debauch any of their women, I might expect instant death.' To elevate his thoughts from such base and dangerous temptation, Boswell took a pull at the oars for several hours and began to relish his approach to an island 'which had acquired an unusual grandeur in my imagination.'

The Corsica towards which he turned his round, rubicund face was a country of alleged revolutionaries and desperadoes who were ungrateful enough to resent four hundred years of cynical exploitation by the Republic of Genoa which claimed governorship over the island and its inhabitants. If the well-founded grievances of the Corsicans had not been enough to incite them to disaffection, their naturally proud and fiercely independent spirit would have chafed under an irksome foreign tyranny. Since 1729, the insurgents had been ruled by a succession of elected Chiefs or Generals, of whom the latest was Pasquale Paoli who had been offered the generalship in exile and had returned to Corsica, at the age of thirty, early in 1755, to assume his reponsibilities as head of state.

For the time being, in 1765, Corsica was partly occupied by French troops, under the command of the Comte de Marboeuf, to whom Genoa had delivered certain Corsican towns after calling on French aid under an existing treaty. The French settled in, but made no moves to arouse Corsican enmity. They paraded, traded, cultivated their gardens, and made token garrisons of their towns, but otherwise excited no serious suspicion that they meant to overrun the island. Britain had no urgent interest in Corsica, considering it militarily and commercially worthless, and paid only lip service to Genoese claims when, under one of the terms of the 1763 peace treaty that concluded the Seven Years' War, it issued a proclamation condemning the Corsicans as rebels and malcontents and forbidding British nationals to provide aid and comfort to Corsica. As it occurred to nobody to do so, whether for commercial or political reasons, the proclamation was wholly successful by default.

There was a general lack of information about Corsica, and no attempt had been made to obtain any. Rousseau had brought Corsica to public attention when, in 1762, he described it in the *Contrat Social* as a little island that would one day astonish Europe. Governments do not care to be astonished, and the claim that Corsica, morally superior among the hopelessly corrupt administrations of Europe, was alone capable of legislation and enlightened political theory, may have cautioned European governments to be wary of such an unusually and dangerously progressive state. It would be wise, too, of Corsicans to be suspicious of apparently ingenuous tourists, and Mr Boswell happened to be the first British visitor to attempt to penetrate into the interior of Corsica and make contact with its General. The proposed visit was considered so unusual that, at Leghorn, Boswell was rumoured to be a plenipotentiary sent by the British court to scout the terrain and sound out the Chief. Boswell took some pains to disabuse everyone of this glamorous and inflated idea of his importance, but the more Mr Boswell protested and persisted in disclaiming any official commission to negotiate with the Corsicans, the more the Italian politicians persevered in affirming it, and 'I was considered as a very close young man.' 'Generously, I therefore allowed them to make a minister of me, till time should undeceive them.' The thought that he might be taken for a spy and instantly hanged, had occurred to Boswell: the letter he solicited from Rousseau was his passport and proof of a purely philosophical interest in the condition of Corsica and the character of its Chief.

Paoli had trained as a professional soldier at Naples and was a

General Pasquale Paoli, portrait by Richard Cosway

man of great literacy and culture. His father, Giacinto Paoli, had
been one of three 'generals of the people' from 1735 to 1738
when he had gracefully surrendered to the French and departed
into exile with his son Pasquale, leaving his second son, the
mystical and fanatical Clemente, to continue active resistance
against the occupying forces. When Gian Pietro Gaffori, who had
been sole general of the island since 1748, was assassinated at the

instigation, and with the connivance, of the Genoese in 1753, Clemente declined the generalship of the nation and it was offered to Pasquale. As General, Paoli was competent militarily, but his true genius lay in political and economic matters. He was primarily a pragmatic theorist who saw far beyond the immediate and limited guerrilla warfare against the French and Genoese, and had begun to reform and liberalise the customs of the Corsicans. By force of his personality he achieved a good deal: he more or less abolished the feudal power of Corsican lords and he encouraged agriculture, shipping, learning, and printing. Vendettas were discouraged, revolts suppressed, dissidents disconcerted or won round to the benefits of Paoli's benign paternalistic dictatorship.

The constitution of Corsica featured a number of democratic principles, and Paoli was less than a king but more than a chief executive or president. Personally, he commanded considerable respect for his character and behaviour which set an example to the state and its citizens of an independence towards which it, and they, were being led. In 1764, an invitation had been addressed to Rousseau by Matteo Buttafoco, a Corsican in the service of the French, urging him to visit Corsica and draw up a constitution in line with his enlightened social principles. Paoli seconded the initiative, but gave the prospect of Rousseau's visit only guarded approval: he was conscious of the prestige Rousseau could confer, but privately he reserved judgement on the extent to which this wild philosopher could be permitted to impose ideas designed to remodel a government and promulgate laws which Paoli was moulding at his own pace and in his own direction of political necessity and desirability. In the event, Rousseau never visited Corsica and did not achieve, in this world, the ideal state.

Boswell immediately introduced himself to Signor Antonio Antonetti at Morsiglia where he was heartily welcomed as a friend of Count Rivarola. The prospect of mountains covered with vines and olives, myrtle, and a variety of aromatic shrubs, was agreeable and refreshing. Armed Corsican peasants lurked in the coverts, now and again rushing out unexpectedly, but a fine passage from Ariosto:

Together through dark woods and winding ways
They walk, nor on their hearts suspicion preys

was comforting, as was the fully armed man who carried the trepid
traveller's baggage. Expecting Corsica to be entirely another
country and culture, Boswell found Signor Antonetti's house a
disappointment. It was Italian in style, and featured a copy of a
Raphael picture about which, in Johnsonian mood, Boswell
mused, 'There was no necessity for its being well done. To see the
thing at all was what surprised me.' He was well-fed, and
well-bedded, and went with the Antonetti family to hear mass in
the parish church. Boswell's youthful enthusiasm for Catholicism
never wholly deserted him, and he bore no insular or Presbyterian
prejudice against the religion of the majority of Christians at that
time. He felt, remarks Mr D. B. Wyndham Lewis, no 'Protestant
obligation to keep his hat on in the presence of the Mother of
God.' The sermon, however, would have been familiar to ears
attuned to the threat of the uncomfortable life to come envisaged
by the most misanthropic Calvinist minister: the text was, 'They
go down alive into the pit,' and after a graphic description of the
horrors of hell, the priest spoke enviously of Saint Catherine of
Siena who 'wished to be laid on the mouth of this dreadful pit, that
she might stop it up, so as no more unhappy souls should fall into
it.' Confessing that he had not the zeal of the holy saint, the priest
concluded with some good practical advice as to how descent into
the inferno might be avoided. Had Lord Auchinleck seen his son
piously noting the lesson in a Catholic church, he would have
given him up as already at one of the gates of hell.

Boswell now struck out for the interior, burdened with his
baggage which was first strapped to an ass but, as the road
climbed and narrowed, later transferred to the back of his
Corsican attendant. There is not much in the way of scenic
description in Boswell's account of his Corsican tour: the most
striking description is of this road which 'was absolutely scrambling along the face of a rock overhanging the sea, upon a path
sometimes not above a foot broad.' This is satisfactory: neat,
brisk, concise, and evocative of the hazard of the trip. Boswell, as

ever, is more interested in people and their diversions than in inanimate objects or panoramas. It is detail that interests the busy mind of Boswell. 'I shall not tire my readers with relating the occurrences of each particular day. It will be much more agreeable to them, to have a free and continued account of what I saw or heard, most worthy of observation.' This enables Boswell to omit anything of inferior interest to the engrossing subject of himself and his meetings with Paoli to which he devotes a disproportionate part of his book.

Rivarola's letters of recommendation were very useful: Signor Antonetti referred Boswell to the Tomasi family at the next village, Pino, where he so far forgot himself as to call for dishes 'with the tone which one uses in calling to the waiters at a tavern.' Signora Tomasi, perhaps harassed but maintaining her temper, 'looked in my face and smiled, saying with much calmness and good nature, "One thing after another, Sir."' Boswell proceeded from village to village, now 'attended by a couple of stout women, who carried my baggage upon their heads,' to the vast amusement of the Corsicans who shrieked with pleasure at the sight. He stopped at convents and retired for the night to his dormitory as though naturally suited to the pious life of a friar. He cannot resist an earnest reflection on the merits of the contemplative life and with no trace of irony recommends a taste of its serenity and peace of mind to fiery men of the world.

By way of Patrimonio, Oletta, and Morato, Boswell came at length to the provincial capital, Corte, where he learned that Paoli was at Sollacarò, some days' journey beyond the mountains, holding a circuit court. At Corte, he was given Paoli's own apartment at the Franciscan convent. Here Boswell was a tourist: he inspected the vineyard and the garden, admired the many beehives, and learned how to smoke out the bees to get at the honey. He joined the friars in the choir, and approved the workmanship of the wooden tabernacle that graced the altar. He saw the castle of Corte, the university, and met members of the supreme council who impressed him as 'solid and sagacious, men of penetration and ability, well calculated to assist the General in forming his political plans, and in turning to the best advantage,

the violence and enterprises of the people.' The visitor, distinguished by many marks of civility, urgently wished to see 'the
unhappy criminals' confined in the castle. There were three: a
man who had murdered his wife, a married woman who had
bribed her servant to strangle a woman of whom she was jealous,
and the servant who excused himself on the ground that he had
acted without understanding. The lady spoke to Boswell 'with
great firmness, and denied her guilt, saying with a contemptuous
smile, as she pointed to her servant, "They can force that creature
to say what they please."' The wife-murderer said he had been
instigated by the devil. Boswell's voracious forensic curiosity was
sated, finally, by getting a close look at the hangman of Corsica
who had been chosen for the post by Paoli himself who had said,
at first sight of his face, 'Behold our hangman.' The General, says
Boswell, had a wonderful talent for physiognomy. This creature,
a Sardinian, was so despised by the Corsicans that they turned
their backs on him and he was obliged to live in a little corner
turret of the castle where he eked out a frugal existence. No
Corsican would have consented to become a hangman, and the
Sardinian's qualifications had been impeccable for, in addition to
the suitability of his face, his grandfather and father before him
had been hangmen.

Before leaving Corte, Boswell remembered that he would need
a passport before setting out for Sollacarò, bushes and brigands
being hazards likely to be met with on the way, and he was
escorted by the Franciscan Prior to the house of the Great
Chancellor who, while the passport was being written out, be-
guiled the moment by reading from some of the minutes of the
'general consulta'. This pleasing diversion was interrupted by a
little boy running in with the great seal of the kingdom with which
the latter-day Cincinnatus impressed the passport. Accompanied
by Corsican guides and a train of mules, Boswell rode and walked
along 'doing just what I saw them do'. When they were hungry, a
few stones thrown into the branches of a chestnut tree would
bring down a shower of nuts, and when they were thirsty what
could be better than to lie down by a stream and put their mouths
to the water. This, surely, was the life of the noble savage, 'the

primitive race of men' who ran free in the woods and wanted for
nothing, subsisting on a nutritious, if monotonous, diet of acorns
and water. The young disciple of Rousseau could not have been
more entranced.

Boswell cut a gorgeous figure as he marched towards Sollacarò: in his portmanteau was a full formal suit of black, and 'he
threaded the *maquis* and toiled up mountains,' declares Professor
Pottle, 'in the effulgence of scarlet and gold.' He habitually wore
riding boots and, as a result, was to suffer most painfully from
ingrowing toenails which plagued him the rest of his life. His
dress, deportment, and retinue marked him as a man of distinction and his ambassadorial status was readily assumed by Corsican villagers who appealed to him on thorny points of theology:
why did the English believe in God, but not in the Pope? 'Because
we are too far off,' was the grave reply, given and received with
satisfaction by both parties. 'I question much whether any of the
learned reasonings of our protestant divines would have had so
good an effect.' At Bastelica, he attracted a large crowd whose
easy manners and natural frankness while complaining of their
miseries and poverty inspired Boswell to hortation. 'I happened at
that time to have an unusual flow of spirits; and as one who finds
himself amongst utter strangers in a distant country has no
timidity, I harangued the men of Bastelica with great fluency. I
expatiated on the bravery of the Corsicans, by which they had
purchased liberty, the most valuable of all possessions, and
rendered themselves glorious over all Europe. Their poverty, I
told them, might be remedied by a proper cultivation of their
island, and by engaging a little in commerce. But I bid them
remember, that they were much happier in their present state
than in a state of refinement and vice, and that therefore they
should beware of luxury.' Touched and impressed, the men of
Bastelica rose to affirm their loyalty to Paoli. 'I could with pleasure
have passed a long time here,' comments the excited orator.

In this mood of confidence, propagandist for Paoli's principles
and Rousseau's philosophy, in a plenipotentiary fantasy, Boswell
at last came within sight of Sollacarò and immediately 'Could not
help being under considerable anxiety.' It was one thing to travel

cheerfully and hopefully, another to arrive at the summit of his ambition to be face to face with a man who had so constantly been represented as something more than human – Boswell's own insignificance began to dawn upon him and he was in a mood to turn tail and bolt. 'These workings of sensibility employed my mind till I rode through the village and came up to the house where he was lodged.' This was no woman to be wooed, no peasant to be impressed, no Wilkes with whom to be witty, and no unresisting Rousseau. By what right did Mr Boswell aspire to a moment of this noble hero's time or interest?

The first fifteen minutes were not encouraging. Boswell's nerve, for once, almost gave way. He had successfully passed the guards and been conducted to an antechamber. Paoli was informed of his presence, and on being shown into Paoli's room, Boswell found himself alone with the General. His quick eyes noted a tall, strong, well-made man, fair complexioned, with a sensible, free, and open face and a manly and noble carriage. Paoli wore a suit of green and gold which, as a sop to the French who paid attention to such things, he had adopted in order that 'a little external elegance might be of use to make the government appear in a more respectable light.' First the letter from Count Rivarola was presented and inspected. Was this sufficient accreditation? Perhaps not. The letter from Rousseau was delivered and read. The reception given to these two documents and their trembling bearer was polite, but very reserved. Remembering Paoli's assessment of the face of the Sardinian who had been instantly given the unsavoury post of public hangman, Boswell offered his face that the Corsican physiognomist might search it to discover an innocent and pleasing character. 'For ten minutes we walked backwards and forwards through the room, hardly saying a word, while he looked at me, with a stedfast, keen and penetrating eye as if he searched my very soul.' It was a severe trial from which Boswell emerged triumphant but still uncharacteristically timid. 'I was much relieved when his reserve wore off and he began to speak more.' A compliment, no doubt carefully rehearsed, was delivered, 'Sir, I am upon my travels, and have lately visited Rome. I am come from seeing the ruins of one brave and free people: I now see the rise of another.' This was received with caution, Paoli drily observing that Corsica was unlikely to extend its empire over half the globe, considering its situation and modern political systems, but conceding that Corsica might be a very happy country. For a moment, Boswell may have felt his compliment, well-meant, to have been too grandiose. At dinner, seated next to Paoli as a mark of honour, and in company with the dozen or so nobles who attended the General, Boswell felt himself 'under some constraint in such a circle of heroes'. Paoli's conversation was all that could be desired. 'I soon perceived that he was a fine classical scholar,' knowledgeable, instructive, entertaining, and fluent in French and Italian. There were plain, substantial dishes, 'avoiding every kind of luxury,' and domestic Corsican wine was served. By the time the company had retired to another room to drink coffee, Boswell's 'timidity wore off. I no longer anxiously thought of myself; my whole attention was employed in listening to the illustrious commander of a nation.'

The awesome Paoli, some years later when in England, gave his own version of Boswell's initial reception to Fanny Burney who recorded it, apparently verbatim, with faintly malicious pleasure. 'He came to my country and he fetched me some letter of recommending him. But I was of the belief that he might be an impostor, and I supposed in my mind he was an espy; for I look away from him, and in a moment I look to him again, and I behold his tablets. Oh, he was to the work of writing down all I say! Indeed I was angry. But soon I discover he was no impostor and no espy; and I only find I was myself the monster he had come to discern. Oh! a very good man; I love him indeed; so cheerful! So gay! So pleasant!' This, very likely, is the impression Boswell made on most people. Their initial reservations and suspicions melt as soon as they realise that gay, gregarious Mr Boswell has no ulterior motive in being so vivacious and self-recommending, that he desires nothing more than the pleasure of the company of the person to whom he has so suddenly and avidly attached himself. Who could resist? Not Rousseau, not Voltaire, not Johnson, not Paoli. Fanny Burney put up an initial resistance, but even she was won over, and only Lord Auchinleck and sober souls with more dignity than discernment failed completely to comprehend and be delighted by the devotion of such a gay, good-natured dog.

Having already practised his prentice pen on Johnson, noting his saws, sayings, and sermons, the illustrious commander was got round by the indefatigable recorder and 'the memoirs and remarkable sayings of Paoli, which I am proud to record', were scribbled down as fast as they came. They have an oratorical ring, a magisterial air, a Roman sonorousness. Fanny Burney liked to allege that Boswell was forever dancing attendance on his heroes with notebook in hand, his eyes hovering on the blessed lips waiting for them to utter some notable nostrum. Boswell himself describes his method. 'From my first setting out on this tour, I wrote down every night what I had observed during the day, throwing together a great deal, that I might afterwards select at leisure.' He had a good memory, was an accomplished mimic, and there is no reason to doubt that he was perfectly capable of storing the style and content of speech in his head for a few minutes or a few hours until he could commit it to paper. Boswell, like cheerfulness, keeps breaking through, to be sure, but his rendering of Pitt, Paoli, or Johnson is sufficiently distinctive in every case to give what may be safely assumed to be an accurate reproduction of their manner and meaning.

Boswell was entrusted to the care of the Abbé Rostini and lodged in the house of Signor Colonna, local lord of the manor. 'Every day I felt myself happier.' Boswell could not be rid of the imputation of being an official envoy, so he began to enjoy the particular attentions that were shown him. 'In the morning I had my chocolate served up upon a silver salver adorned with the arms of Corsica. I dined and supped constantly with the General. I was visited by all the nobility, and whenever I chose to make a little tour, I was attended by a party of guards. I begged of the General not to treat me with so much ceremony; but he insisted upon it.' Boswell capered on a gorgeously caparisoned horse, richly hung with crimson velvet and broad gold lace, while his guards marched alongside. Boswell adored the panoply of greatness, wearing it like a suit of armour, judging the weight and effect it had on his character. He thoroughly enjoyed his magnificence, and 'I allowed myself to indulge a momentary pride in this parade, as I was curious to experience what could really be the pleasure of state and distinction with which mankind are so strangely intoxicated.' He was as liable to be intoxicated by the image of himself as a grandee as by drink. Not so seriously as to make himself wholly absurd, he would joke with friends on return to London that they did not treat him with a proper respect considering his temporary acquaintance with the trappings of greatness: but there was more truth in the jocular complaint than perhaps he ever admitted even most privately to himself.

For the moment, however, Mr Boswell is entirely happy. Paoli takes to him more and more, and constantly solicits his agreeable company. The General had a pretty good grasp of English, though he had obtained what fluency he possessed from some Irish gentlemen at Naples and, for want of practice, during ten years of having no occasion to speak it, his English was adequate but halting. His English library consisted of some broken volumes of the *Spectator* and *Tatler*, Pope's *Essay on Man*, *Gulliver's Travels*, Barclay's *Apology for the Quakers*, and a *History of France* in old English. Boswell was adequately acquainted with French and Italian, and as he and Paoli were both classical scholars they no doubt had recourse to Latin in any extremity of incomprehension.

The talk was generally elevated: it dwelt upon Corsican, Greek and British history, on pride, politics and philosophy, was peppered with Biblical and classical quotation. Art and ornament, evidences for the being and attributes of God, reflections on mortality and the king of Prussia, the advantages of Stoicism over Epicureanism, the benefits of marriage, the intelligence of beasts and the spirit of the Corsicans, all came under scrutiny and were pronounced upon. Somehow or other the talk touched on more personal matters, and it fell upon Paoli, as upon Rousseau, Johnson, Voltaire, and anyone else with the patience to listen, to advise Mr Boswell on the proper conduct of his life as a gentleman, a lover, a being beset by religious and moral doubt, and reluctant lawyer. On Boswell's youthful morbidity, Paoli spoke with the authority of one who has studied metaphysics, 'I know the arguments for fate and free-will, for the materiality and immateriality of the soul, and even the subtile arguments for and against the existence of matter. – but let us leave these disputes to the idle. – I hold always firm one great object. I never feel a moment of despondency.' Paoli, as much as Johnson, refused to indulge Boswell's taste for abstruse speculation.

On the matter of pride, Paoli explained the want of regular Corsican troops by saying that every single Corsican was as a regiment himself. The Corsicans, distinguished for individual bravery, would not be successful in a body. Of himself, he declared, 'I have an unspeakable pride. The approbation of my own heart is enough.' His aim was to accustom each and every Corsican to feel his importance as a member of the state, and national and individual pride were inseparable. Boswell remarks one notable feature of heroes: Paoli rarely laughed, though he permitted himself a frequent placid smile. 'Whether loud laughter in general society be a sign of weakness or rusticity, I cannot say; but I have remarked that real great men, and men of finished behaviour, seldom fall into it.' One can see Mr Boswell automatically pursing his lips as he writes.

Boswell was particularly impressed that Paoli was utterly chaste: though he spoke favourably of marriage as an institution tried by time and found to be the best calculated for the happiness of individuals, and for the good of society, he himself had not the conjugal virtues. 'His arduous and critical situation would not allow him to enjoy domestick felicity. He is wedded to his country, and the Corsicans are his children.' This 'Father of his Country' impressed Boswell as much as any man he was ever to meet: it is a pity that he was not more continuously under the influence of this paragon who could, if anyone, have led the capricious character of Boswell in the paths of righteousness and creditable conduct. Of all Boswell's substitutes for the parochial paternalism of Auchinleck, Paoli was perhaps the most rigorously moral and magnanimous in his person and attitude towards others.

The charms of the peasants were as attractive as the affability of Paoli: Boswell, an advertisement for the gaiety of the British, was all the rage. He dressed up in a Corsican costume, adorned with

S. Wale del.   *J. Miller Sc.*

JAMES BOSWELL Esq.

In the Dress of an Armed Corsican Chief, *as he appear'd at*
Shakespeare's Jubilee, at Stratford upon Avon, September 1769.

Paoli's own pistols, and the interviews with the General were not so frequent or so weighty as to preclude pleasure. Boswell's account of his time in Corsica is heavily slanted towards giving the impression that he was barely beyond the sound of the Chief's voice for six weeks; but the truth is that he enjoyed the longed-for intimacy for about a week, and 'the English ambassadour, as the good peasants and soldiers used to call me, became a great favourite among them.' Boswell strutted and was besieged by Corsicans curious to know every detail about Britain, and its effervescent representative. The German flute was produced and, after its debut, in constant demand. It would have been ridiculous to protest that he did not play very well, so Boswell gave them Italian airs and a repertoire of pretty Scots tunes including *Gilderoy*, the *Lass of Patie's Mill* and *Corn riggs are Bonny*. The 'genuine feelings of nature' of the Corsicans responded so well to 'the pathetick simplicity and pastoral gaiety of the Scots musick' that, encouraged, he gave in to their insistence to have an English song and gratified them with a vocal rendition of *Hearts of Oak* translated into Italian – 'Cuore di quercia, bravo Inglese,' cried the Corsicans. 'It was quite a joyous riot. I fancied myself to be a recruiting sea-officer. I fancied all my chorus of Corsicans aboard the British fleet.' And Admiral Boswell, no doubt, swam into view across his mind's eye, resplendent in gold lace and a cocked hat, the seasickness five miles out of Leghorn quite forgotten.

It was time to take leave of Paoli: ambassador or not, Boswell had 'mentioned to him the scheme of an alliance between Great Britain and Corsica. Paoli with politeness and dignity waived the subject, by saying, "The less assistance we have from allies, the greater our glory." He seemed hurt by our treatment of his country. He mentioned the severe proclamation at the last peace, in which the brave islanders were called the Rebels of Corsica. He said with a conscious pride and proper feeling, "Rebels! I did not expect that from Great Britain."' Paoli also said, however, that he had a respect for the British, which Boswell took to imply a wish to be in friendship with Britain and, quick to enthusiasm as ever, asked what he could do in return for Corsican kindness. 'Only undeceive your court. Tell them what you have seen here. They will be curious to ask you. A man come from Corsica will be like a man come from the Antipodes.'

Paoli was no fool. He had the measure of Boswell. He knew him to be neither spy nor envoy, but a charming chatterbox with the ability to pin some influential ears. As a propagandist, Boswell could not be bettered. Boswell's imagination immediately swelled: he produced a flow of compliments, visions of amity, hands across the seas. He cheered Paoli, who responded in kind with a beautifully allusive piece of history concerning the noble Romans who had selflessly disregarded their own best interests to protect the Jews against Assyrians, leaving Boswell to pick up the allusion to Britain and Corsica. Throughout the visit, he had flattered Boswell and Boswell had lain back with his legs in the air, wriggling with pleasure at being stroked. But though Paoli was a politician, a statesman, he had enjoyed Mr Boswell, and his kindness and affection was by no means a diplomatic courtesy. He had kindled Boswell's enthusiasm, always tinder dry, with his own reverence and love for Corsica and its people. There was nothing indirect about Paoli: there was nothing indirect about James Boswell. Truly, Boswell intended to bring about a positive and beneficial relationship between Britain and Corsica: how he would do it was the only matter as yet not wholly certain, though he had no doubt of his ability to swing the British government behind him. 'Remember that I am your friend, and write to me,' declared and requested Paoli at their parting. He himself would write 'as a friend,' an honour surpassing his role as commander, philosopher or man of letters.

Boswell realised he had been, too briefly, in the presence of greatness. 'From having known intimately so exalted a character, my sentiments of human nature were raised, while, by a sort of contagion, I felt an honest ardour to distinguish myself, and be useful, as far as my situation and abilities would allow; and I was, for the rest of my life, set free from a slavish timidity in the presence of great men, for where shall I find a man greater than Paoli?'

Boswell at least had the wit to know a good man when he met one. The effect was salutary: for the moment he felt himself to be a better man, and confirmed in his constant resolutions to be virtuous. The example and magnetic presence of Paoli had made Boswell more acutely aware of his own shortcomings and doubts – not in the sense of the inadequacy he had felt on the approach to Sollacarò, but in the more positive sense that faults, once recognised, might be mended rather than relished and indulged. But Boswell's waxy mind took the impress of a Paoli as readily as a Wilkes. He could be as easily dignified as debauched. His chameleon quality, by which he could instantly adapt himself to greatness or degradation, was at once a failing and yet, had he acknowledged its potential for strengthening and broadening his character, a valuable asset. It was his principal asset as a journalist and biographer, but even in that aspect he failed to appreciate its worth and, by association, the primary worth of his literary achievements.

Braced by the warmth and evidences of Paoli's regard for him, Boswell set off to return to Corte. The house of Colonna had been as decayed as its lord; wind and rain had penetrated Boswell's bedchamber, and he was suffering from a heavy cold which ended in malaria. Sniffling with a cold and emotion, burning with pride and fever, Boswell was accompanied by an entourage consisting of a Herculean priest who made him laugh; by Jacob Hänni, his Swiss servant, who was heartily sick of Corsica, scanty meals, and hard beds; Jachone, one of Paoli's huge guardian dogs; and by two Corsican guards, one of whom, Ambrosio, 'a strange, iron-coloured, fearless creature' well-acquainted with war, told Boswell how he had shot two men through their heads with one bullet. 'I was sure I needed be under no apprehension; but I don't know how, I desired Ambrosio to march before me that I might see him.' The feverish Boswell, the roaring priest, the alarming Ambrosio, the surly Jacob, and the recalcitrant Jachone: this sorry, ill-assorted troupe came at length to Corte where they were kindly received back by the Franciscans. Boswell was nursed, dosed, and made to feel quite at home at the convent.

Somewhat recovered, Mr Boswell proceeded to Bastia. He need not have avoided the area on first arrival, since a truce was observed between the French and the Corsicans. Paoli had, indeed, recommended Boswell to the Comte de Marboeuf in a letter. The French commander was charming, delighted, and hospitable. Boswell was fairly felled by his ague, and immediately put to bed in de Marboeuf's own house. Books, a physician and lively company were provided. An officer supplied the invalid with as much money as he needed, since the Boswell finances were exhausted by his extended sojourn in Corsica. Within twelve days he was well enough to proceed towards Genoa. The voyage was appalling. Eighteen miles off Cap Corse, the boat was storm bound on the barren rock of Capraia for a week. Franciscan friars took him in, but these men, 'hospitable without cunning,' could not participate with their guest in an informed discussion of the Rousseauistic 'universal creed' upon which Boswell took an opportunity to dilate. They were unable to understand it. Their sequestered life was frugal in the extreme, but they were kind. Jacob berated Boswell, not for the first time, about his stinginess. By the end of the week, Boswell's temper exploded. He suspected the master of the felucca of delay, and flew into a rage which he expressed in Italian, 'You stupid bugger, I won't be ballocksed around any more. I want absolutely to leave tonight. I'll write to M de Marboeuf. Dammit! If it wasn't a sin to tie a man in a sack and drown him, I'd do it to you this minute!' The master got ready to sail, Boswell embarked, and was immediately so sick he had to rush back to the shore. The master's experienced prediction that they should be able to sail at four was borne out when the wind changed, and finally, heaving and wretched, Boswell disembarked at Genoa on 30 November 1765. From first to last, the trip had taken fifty days.

There were letters waiting for him: three from the delightful Girolama Piccolomini, three from the distressed Lord Auchinleck. In August, Auchinleck had sat on the bench for an extended period without urinating. The stoppage of urine had been complete, and he had been seriously ill. He complains about Boswell's reckless ordering of credit at his bankers; about the lack of any address for, or any communication from, his son; he insists upon Boswell's speedy return, 'There is nothing to be learned from travelling in France. I say this from my own experience,' he sends remembrances from Boswell's mother and brothers. At Genoa, however, James Boswell had important matters to attend to. There are paragraphs to be written for the Italian gazettes, informing a curious public as to the progress of Mr Boswell's Corsican experiences and simultaneously arousing and calming improbable speculation. There is the Genoese secretary of state to be seen, who confesses that Mr Boswell has made him tremble; there is the delicious intelligence that he has been continually spied upon by the Genoese; and an interview with the Doge whom Mr Boswell keeps waiting. There are pictures and buildings to be seen, and ingrowing toenails to be attended to. But at last he is able to set out for Paris.

The trip is notable for two instances that point up aspects of Boswell's character. First, the dog Jachone is possessed of a less-than-brilliant intelligence and an evident dislike for his new master. Paoli's advice had been to be firm with the beast, but Boswell's behaviour towards the dog is so appallingly harsh that even he, later, attempts to strike out all reference to it from his notes. Jachone regularly runs away to steal food: he is beaten ferociously and, on one occasion, hanged from a tree. Boswell never again records any instance of conscious or gratuitous cruelty towards man or beast, so we must take this irrational treatment as an aberration. Jacob, against express orders, feeds the dog in secret. Boswell discovers this piece of underhand rebellion, and remonstrates with his servant who has become tiresome but cannot be discharged until Boswell is able to raise enough money to pay him off. For the moment, they are stuck with one another, and they dispute fiercely.

'Jacob said, "I believe, Sir, that you have been badly brought up. You have not the manners of a nobleman. Your heart is too open."' Boswell has already confessed in his own heart that 'I am always studying human nature and making experiments on the lowest characters, so that I am too much in the secret with regard to the weakness of man in reality, and my honest, impetuous disposition cannot take up with that eternal repetition of fictitious minutiae by which unthinking men of fashion preserve a great distinction between master and servant.' The Scots have never been as class-conscious as the English, and the Scottish clan system operated, more or less, on the principle that all men of the clan were, in some degree, brothers and equals. Polite Edinburgh and provincial society observed some distance between master and servant, but it was quite liable to lapse in the most sudden and unexpected manner. Boswell was stung by Jacob's assessment, but readily admitted it to have some foundation. 'I confessed to him that I was two and twenty before I had a servant.'

Said Jacob, 'The son of a gentleman ought to be accustomed early to command a servant, but reasonably, and never to joke with them; because each must live in his state according to his quality. You, Sir, would live just like a peasant. And you force a servant to speak in a way he shouldn't, because you torment him with questions. You want to get to the bottom of things.' Jacob advises Boswell against marrying, in conclusion, and Boswell is forced to admire the good sense, truth, and naturalness of the Swiss. Boswell takes his lessons where he may: whether from philosophers, men of letters, statesmen, or servants.

His route took him through Marseilles, Avignon, by way of a diversion to Nîmes and Montpellier, thence to Paris. At Marseilles, he had diverted himself by composing puffing paragraphs which appeared at intervals in the British press and addressed as though from various Italian cities. The Corsica campaign was on. From Rome, the rumour is that people are curious to know the consequence of Mr Boswell's tour to Corsica: Italian politicians think they can see important reasons for his visit: the Genoese are not a little alarmed. From Florence, speculation grows to the point of improbability. 'Mr B, with some of his friends, has worked out a scheme for getting the Young Chevalier made King of Corsica.' From Genoa, Mr Boswell is reported as a very close man, constantly fussing with a great number of papers. At Turin, the rumour that Mr Boswell is really a desperate adventurer named Macdonald is proposed and immediately denied. On 15 February 1766, the news is broken that Mr Boswell has arrived in London.

Meanwhile, on 12 January 1766, Mr Boswell has arrived in

Paris. Wilkes is there, supported in exile by the Whigs and the French, and they meet on the 19th. Now in no danger of instant death for debauching women, Boswell is directed at his urgent request to Mme Hequet's where he enjoys the elegant Constance. Walpole, too, is in Paris and in spite of '[his] teeth and [his] doors', Boswell penetrated to this cool notability to try to extract some information about the eccentric Theodore, once King of Corsica, but got very little. On 26 January he visited Montigny's, a recommended bordello, but it was 'sad work'. He dined with Wilkes, some notable Scots, and on the evening of 27 January at the Dutch Ambassador's where he spoke of Corsica despite being stunned by grief.

On the morning of the 27th, Boswell had gone to Wilkes's and picked up a copy of the *St James's Chronicle* for 18 January 1776. In it, he read a notice of his mother's death, which had occurred at Edinburgh on 11 January. It took a little time for the full reaction to set in. Boswell's first instinct was to seek diversion to dissipate the sorrow he began to feel: at six, in a fever, he was at Mme Hequet's where Constance was elegant and, no doubt, temporarily consoling. On Tuesday, the 28th, a letter from Lord Auchinleck arrived confirming the news, and Boswell, stupefied, wept in bursts and intermittently prayed 'like most solemn Catholic to saint'. He crooned Italian airs gently in an effort to soothe himself, and roused philosophy to come to his aid. He called on Principal Gordon at the Scots College, a seminary for priests, and there Lord Alford (Sir John Graham) comforted his distress with philosophy. Boswell generously but inappropriately felt a 'strong enthusiasm to comfort Father all his life,' and on 31 January he left for England.

He was accompanied by Thérèse Le Vasseur, Rousseau's mistress, who was in Paris and required to be taken to her master at Chiswick where he had gone a short time before with David Hume. Her one virtue has been supposed to have been utter fidelity to Rousseau. Despite family censorship of the offending passage in Boswell's papers, the memory of Colonel Isham has retrieved this discreditable episode. In letters of thanks to Rousseau, Boswell had playfully disclaimed all designs on the honour of his mistress. It is doubtful whether either Rousseau or Boswell had ever had thoughts raising any such suspicion. Thérèse's views on the matter are not known: but certainly Boswell had charmed her, and had fulfilled her request for a garnet necklace. Whatever the facts, whether she seduced Boswell, or Boswell seduced Thérèse, their journey together to London was enlivened by vigorous, frequent and ignoble misbehaviour. Boswell was proud of his prowess as a lover, but he did not like to be hurried. He was liable to be impotent at first, but steadily gained vitality. Thérèse was not overwhelmed, barely impressed. 'I allow that you are a hardy and vigorous lover, but you have no art. You are young, you can learn. I myself will give you your first lesson in the art of love.' She applied herself to the self-imposed task of instruction with such dedication and vigour that, by the time they had reached Dover, the terrified and delighted Boswell recorded that they had 'done it . . . thirteen times' by 12 February.

That day, Boswell thankfully dumped her on Rousseau at Chiswick. The reunion was excessively demonstrative – 'Quanta oscula!' – and Rousseau hugged the courier to him like a sack. But enough of them: to Fleet Street, to the Mitre Tavern, and Johnson. Boswell was full of his adventures. Johnson and he again supped together a few nights later, and Boswell spoke of his encounters with Wilkes and Rousseau. 'It seems you have kept very good company abroad – Wilkes and Rousseau,' said Johnson disparagingly. 'My dear Sir, you don't call Rousseau bad company?' asked Boswell, prudently putting Wilkes aside for the moment. Johnson did indeed. 'I think him one of the worst of men; a rascal who ought to be hunted out of society as he has been . . . Sir, Rousseau is a very bad man. I would sooner sign a sentence for his transportation than of any felon who has gone from the Old Bailey these many years.' Tentatively, having had Rousseau shot down, Boswell introduced Voltaire. 'Sir, do you think him as bad a man as Voltaire?' Johnson considered it 'difficult to settle the proportion of iniquity between 'em.' Boswell, his scalps snatched from his belt, subsided.

Corsica, in the forefront of Boswell's mind, was a subject that his intimates rapidly tired of. Johnson testily bade Boswell rid his head of Corsica, but that was the last thing he could do: there was a fuss to be made, campaigns to be waged, important persons to be solicited, a book to be written. He had departed as a private gentleman: he returned as a personage – Mr Corsica Boswell. In his full fig of Corsican dress, Mr Boswell visited Pitt on Sunday 23 February to make his addresses on behalf of Paoli and the noble Corsicans. Pitt, at first doubtful of the propriety of his receiving communications from Paoli while out of office and, as a Privy Councillor, obliged to hear nothing from a foreign power that might concern Great Britain without declaring it to the King and Council, advises Boswell to consider the propriety of what he has to say, and, having considered, to proceed. He inquires about the Corsican harbours. 'One or two excellent, with some expense,' is Boswell's answer, and Pitt is informed of the high regard in which Paoli holds Pitt's character, and the hurt he has felt at Pitt's neglect. Pitt affirms his regret that 'in any corner of the world, however distant, or however small, it should be suspected that I could ever be indifferent to the cause of liberty.' On that oblique but satisfactory note, Boswell takes his leave of the gout-ridden statesman.

Early in March, James Boswell boards the fly for Edinburgh, and on his approach to that city counts his distinctions and advantages. 'I am the friend of Johnson and of Paoli, the gallant of Signora –, am looked after by Mr Pitt, and will probably marry Miss Bosville.' This is encouraging – less so is the uncouth accent of the Scots among whom once again he finds himself: they put it on deliberately, is Boswell's sour judgement, simply to annoy him. He resolves to be 'solemnly sworn to the strictest duty' and the prodigal son, in high expectation of the fatted calf awaiting him as a welcome, prepares to meet his father and his future.

[6]

Boswell in Love

From Auchinleck, on 6 May 1766, Boswell wrote to thank Wilkes for the 'humane and kind behaviour' he had shown to Boswell in his distraction at the news of the death of his mother. Wilkes had suggested that Boswell's return from his travels would be 'a new object' to Lord Auchinleck and 'help to compensate for his great misfortune'. Boswell was able to reply that indeed, for once in his life, he had 'been of considerable use' to his father. He had returned home with his usual sanguine resolve to reform and be a creditable young laird. While Boswell had frolicked, Auchinleck had fretted – but Boswell, ever prone to pin his faith in the probable triumph of hope and good intentions over experience, assumed that the past could be bundled up like so many redundant legal documents, tied with red tape, and consigned to a pigeon hole marked 'old history'. His expectation was at least partly realised.

Auchinleck was pleased to see James. He had already expended much of his bitterness and resentment in letters that had pursued Boswell around Europe and, though he was not effusive in his welcome, Boswell knew his father well enough to recognise that the evenings spent sitting with Auchinleck who talked about the family were a tacit but clear indication of affection and a willingness to let bygones discreetly fade – if not quite into forgetfulness then at least into cautious forgiveness dependent on future good behaviour. If Boswell showed himself to be a dutiful and affectionate son, Auchinleck would respond by continuing to be an affectionate father.

The paragraphs in the London papers about Boswell's antics

had distressed Lord Auchinleck, quite as much as a letter from Boswell requesting permission to return home by way of Holland, to make a formal offer for the hand of Belle de Zuylen. The death of his mother had put an end to this plan. In mid-January, Boswell had written to de Zuylen, Zélide's father, confessing that 'I always had a leaning towards marriage with my friend' and that despite a conversation with Zélide's brother during which 'we said every unfavourable thing that could possibly be said of her,' they 'concluded always by contemplating her with admiration and affection.' This being so, Boswell had been a little put out when he had learned that a marriage to Bellegarde had been proposed, but had rallied when it had become clear that Zélide's affections were not too earnestly engaged.

Boswell formally proposed himself as a husband for Zélide: but he hedged the offer around with conditions. 'I should marry her, no doubt, by the forms of the Church. But that would not be enough for me. I should require a clear and express agreement. I should require an oath, taken in your presence, Sir, and before two of her brothers, that she would always remain faithful, that she would never design to see, or have any exchange of letters with, any one of whom her husband and her brothers disapproved; and that without their approbation she would neither publish nor cause to be acted any of her literary compositions; and in conclusion she must promise never to speak against the established religion or customs of the country she might find herself in.' Bound and gagged by these conditions, Zélide's emancipated views on the conduct of women, her metaphysical speculations, her taste for clandestine correspondence, and notorious free thinking and free speech might be curbed so as to make her a fit and genteel consort to Mr Boswell of Auchinleck.

Mr Boswell, for his part, is quite the coming man. 'I am the eldest son of an excellent family, which is not one of the wealthiest but nevertheless well-off, having a rental of £1000 sterling a year. My father is one of the Scots judges, and his profession brings him in as much again; he will consequently be in a position to make me a very respectable settlement if I decide to marry. I have studied the law, and my plan is to practice as an advocate at our

Scottish bar; and after a certain number of years I hope to obtain a position similar to my father's. It is not impossible that I may become a Member of Parliament. But in these days of political corruption, my mind is not set on it. . . . I will enter into an agreement with her [Zélide] to maintain a decent composure, a certain reserve even, before the world. In private, *vive la bagatelle*, let us give full rein to our fantasy, as the most illustrious of the ancients have done. Sir, I am proud, very proud, and it is perhaps to my pride that I owe my best virtues.'

In all fairness, Boswell does not omit to describe his less happy characteristics. In addition to being hypochondriac, when melancholy puts him quite out of temper, he admits, 'My knowledge is very restricted. I have an excess of self-esteem. I cannot apply myself to study. I can nevertheless maintain my energy where my attention is interested. I have no sufficient zest for life. I have the greatest imaginable difficulty in overcoming avarice . . . the low weakness of wishing to make little savings. I should require a prudent wife, a good housekeeper who would attend to everything and leave me in peace.'

This, then, is the frank portrait of Mr Boswell in search of a wife – in search of an amiable, frugal, domestic, undemanding, discreet, and worthy woman who, like Zélide if she put her heart and mind into the effort, might be 'pious, prudent, kind, and tender, while retaining all her charms'. Boswell's paragon is a woman bawdy in the bedroom, discreet in the drawing room, circumspect in society, and canny in the kitchen. The portrait of such a husband and such a wife may stand here as an introduction to a period in Boswell's life when he is anxiously canvassing a lengthy list of more or less likely candidates for the role of helpmeet to James Boswell, man of parts, property, position, and prospects.

It is only with hindsight, and some inkling of Boswell's character, that he appears absurd in his anglings for the hand of Zélide. Monsieur de Zuylen took him seriously and considered Boswell 'a man of birth and intellectual distinction who remains attached to his good principles of religion and virtue; who dares declare his position with firmness and conducts himself accordingly.'

Negotiations with Bellegarde were still proceeding, and de Zuylen was not therefore in a position to present Boswell's proposal to his daughter. The matter again hung fire.

At Auchinleck, Boswell was obliged to study for the examination in Scots Law which, necessarily, he had to pass before being admitted advocate to the Scottish bar. Lord Auchinleck offered to coach his son and a rather dull relation, Claud Boswell of Balmuto. The matter of Zélide had been settled between father and son: Boswell had discussed her with Auchinleck who 'could not bear such a woman' and James, to Temple, admitted 'a *bel esprit* would never do at Auchinleck.' He was, all things considered, 'glad to be off with Zélide,' and on with a pretty chambermaid, Euphemia Bruce, daughter of the gardener at Auchinleck. This intense flirtation relieved Boswell's low spirits. Temple is informed in full. 'I am entirely captivated by her . . . I am mad enough to indulge imaginations of marrying her.'

She is twenty-three years old, and as children she and Boswell had played together, but how she has developed. '. . . a most amiable face, the prettiest foot and ankle . . . perfectly well made, and has a lively, genteel air that is irresistible.' How Boswell haunts her day, 'I take every opportunity of being with her when she is putting on fires or dressing a room . . . I cut my gloves that she may mend them.' His pleasure is innocent: not only does he restrain himself from any bad design, she has sense enough to form no idea of having the young master for a husband. It is idyllic. 'In short, she is better than any lady I know.' He kisses her hand, he ravishes a lock of her hair upon which he fondly dotes. Such a wife she would make. '. . . my dear girl would be grateful for my attachment, would be devoted to me in every respect, would live with me just as a mistress without the disgrace and remorse. After all my feverish joys and pains, I should enjoy calm and permanent bliss in her arms. Was there ever such madness?' Madness it is.

'All this may do for a summer . . . I will rouse my philosophic spirit, and fly from this fascination. I am going to Moffat for a month. Absence will break the enchantment.' On 17 May, almost three weeks later, the infatuation 'is almost like a dream that is past.' Euphemia, if she continues to dust Auchinleck House, may soon find herself polishing round a new ornament to the Boswell drawing-room: a Miss Bosville, the daughter of a Yorkshireman with whom Boswell had dined three or four times a week in London. The name, deriving from the original Boisville, implied a family connection but aside from such a happy coincidence, Elizabeth Bosville was beautiful, black-haired, modest, and her complexion was charming. For a while, she was marked down as a front runner in the stakes for the Boswell hand and heart. But neither absence nor Miss Bosville accounted for the eclipse of the handsome chambermaid: at Moffat, Boswell had met a young woman, separated from her husband and three children. This Mrs Dodds possessed, among other charms, a voice so melodious as quite to reconcile Boswell to her Scots accent. 'This shall be my last irregular connection,' he declared to Temple. 'I shall be attached to the generous woman for ever.'

He had gone to Moffat to try to wash away a few 'scurvy spots' he had acquired in Europe, for rest and recreation (which Mrs Dodds obligingly provided), and to polish up his knowledge of Scots law ('which I now like') for the forthcoming examination in July. Also on his mind was a book he proposed to write about Corsica, rumours of which had preceded him and come to the ears of Thomas Gray, the poet, friend of Temple and the intimate of Horace Walpole. Johnson had not diverted Boswell's mind from the impulse to tell his 'countrymen so much concerning the brave islanders and their glorious leader that all the true lovers of liberty must admire them and be interested for them.' It will be a very personal account. Boswell will 'be obliged to write like an egotist.' Boswell's thought is to publish in the winter, some six months hence.

In July 1766 Boswell passed the examination and presented his legal thesis, written in Latin, titled *De supellectile legata*, On Legacies of Household Furniture. He dedicated the work to Lord Mountstuart, effusively eulogising Bute's cub, and earned a sharp rebuke from Samuel Johnson who demanded to know why Boswell had dedicated his thesis 'to a man whom I know you do not much love'. He had reservations, too, about the purity of

Boswell's Latin, but Boswell spiritedly and learnedly attempted to refute the cavils on that score, defending himself as well as he could and putting up a creditable show. On 29 July he was admitted advocate and was immediately given a guinea cause to plead. In all, before the legal term ended on 10 August, he earned eight guineas from ten causes. It was an auspicious beginning to a busy legal career and, though some of his contemporaries (notably Henry Dundas, who was made Solicitor-General in his mid-twenties) had outstripped him in realising ambition, Boswell had little reason to doubt that, with application, he might expect at least to be raised to the bench as he had claimed in a letter to de Zuylen.

The law, Corsica, and Mrs Dodds amply filled his time for the moment: he was gathering materials for the Corsica book, publishing puffing paragraphs about Corsica in the newspapers to keep public interest whetted, and receiving advice as to content and style from Sir David Dalrymple (now Lord Hailes, as a judge of the Court of Session). He ignored Johnson's advice to mind his own affairs, and leave the Corsicans to theirs. On 18 September 1766, Boswell was writing to William Pitt, Earl of Chatham, to remind him of the conversation they had had about Corsica and to urge him to befriend that 'noble and unfortunate little nation . . . for whom I will be interested while my blood is warm.' The plea was renewed in a further letter, three months later.

Boswell's interest in the law was never jurisprudential: it was never a science or a philosophy to be studied in a dry, legalistic manner. Certainly, he had a grasp of legal principles and accepted cases as they were offered to him like any diurnal advocate obliged to make a living and, generally, he worked hard enough and earned a decent income from the practice of law. At Glasgow, in September 1766, Boswell represented his first criminal client, John Reid, by 'habit and repute a common thief,' who was accused of stealing one hundred and twenty sheep from a Peeblesshire farm and driving them off to Glasgow for sale to a butcher. It was a hanging offence, if proved. Reid admitted previous bad character, but denied that he had, on this occasion, acted in bad faith. His defence was that he had been commissioned by another man to drive the sheep to Glasgow and sell them. Boswell believed him and contrived to have the case heard in Edinburgh where the jury brought in the equivocal Scots verdict of 'not proven' and Reid was released.

While Reid was being held for trial in the Edinburgh Tolbooth, Boswell solicitously provided him with food and rallied him with religion. The sequel to this case occurred in 1774 when Reid was again arrested for sheep-stealing, and Boswell again acted for the defence. The trial took place on 1 August 1774, and the next day the *Edinburgh Advertiser* described Mr James Boswell's summation of the evidence as having been given 'in a very masterly and pathetic manner, which did him great honour both as a lawyer and as one who wished for a free and impartial trial by jury.' The jury retired to Walker's Tavern after reaching a verdict of Guilty against Reid, and Boswell joined them there to enjoy 'the applause which several individuals of the jury now gave me and the general attention with which I was treated.' The company fell to their bottles, which circulated freely, and Boswell got home at about one in the morning after strolling the streets for a while, 'a very bad habit which I have when intoxicated.'

Boswell rose on the morning of 2 August after a bad night's rest: the anxiety of the trial and his debauch afterwards 'made me in a woeful plight and very unwilling to rise.' At two o'clock in the afternoon, the jury formally delivered its verdict on John Reid, and Boswell immediately stood to ask for a delay of sentence to enable him to argue for a lesser punishment than a capital sentence. This was refused by the judges, including Lord Auchinleck, and Reid was ordered to be hanged. Boswell was, to say the least, *distrait*. He had spoken to the best of his powers for his client, thinking himself an Edmund Burke – 'a man who united pleasantry in conversation with abilities in business and powers as an orator.' Boswell had enjoyed the applause of the jury and the compliments of his colleagues. He made strenuous efforts, practical and fantastical, to preserve Reid's life, from legal manoeuvres and private appeals to an extraordinary plan to have an instant tracheotomy performed on Reid after he had been cut down from the gallows in order to resurrect him. He spent long hours with the terrified Reid, had him sit for his portrait, aired his cause in the *London Chronicle*, appealed for a royal reprieve, and finally attended the execution on 21 September 1774 after which he was sunk in gloom. His considerable zeal in the cause of John Reid some thought to be excessive, and that such personal involvement in criminal proceedings might hurt Boswell's character and interest within the legal profession.

Mrs Dodds had followed Boswell from Moffat to Edinburgh and had taken lodgings there. She had enough money of her own not to be a drain on Boswell's purse, and possessed not only a financial independence but also a certain independence of mind. In a letter to Temple on 1 February 1867, Boswell spilled his infatuation. Temple had been presented to the living of Mamhead, near Exeter, towards the end of September 1766, and was living there as priest to his flock in quiet and rectitudinous retirement from London. The lengthy letter begins with congratulations to the Reverend Mr Temple now entered upon the profession of a clergyman which Boswell regards 'in an amiable and respectable light'. He goes on to discuss his relations with Lord Auchinleck, whose character is such that 'he must have his son in a great degree of subjection to him.'

There had been four points of contention between Boswell and Auchinleck as far back as 1 September 1764 when Boswell had written to Sir David Dalrymple to ask him to convey to Auchinleck the conditions under which Boswell proposed to live and breathe on his return to Scotland. They were that Boswell should not be treated as a 'true young laird,' as a lad to be regarded as still under moral, social, and intellectual tutelage; that Boswell should be allowed to worship in the mode of the Church of England; that Boswell should be permitted to maintain his own household; and that Boswell should be indulged in an annual visit to London. Dalrymple gave short shrift to these demands, though he had the decency to comment seriously upon them. In the event, Boswell was obliged to give up his ultimatum and Auchinleck, though taken to task by Boswell for his high-handedness, was unable to give up the paternal authority he had so long striven to exercise over James.

Temple is now regaled with Boswell's reflections on the virtues of matrimony, 'the condition in which true felicity is to be found'. But a 'batchelor' may be happy, and a mistress as good as a wife. 'What a dear *infidel* you have got (from *not faithful*, you know, Boswell). Nothing so convenient as an eloped wife. How are you so lucky in mistresses?' Thus Temple had written to Boswell with a touch of unclerical envy. He is mistaken – 'don't think her unfaithfull. I could not love her if she was.' Mrs Dodds, in her fashion, is virtuous: to all intents and purposes, having been abused and abandoned by her husband whom she no longer loves, she is free and she is sincerely attached to Boswell. She will not take his money, but he has prevailed upon her to permit him to provide a house for her. 'In this manner I am safe and happy and in no danger either of the perils of Venus or of desperate matrimony.' As a man 'coming into great employment,' he can afford the expense: already he has made sixty-five guineas over the winter, and by the end of his first year expects to have cleared above a hundred.

By the end of February, Boswell has cleared eighty guineas, his clerk comes to him every morning at six and in one day Boswell may dictate up to forty folio pages: there is little time for anything else. But the matter of Mrs Dodds is worrying. Prolonged intimate acquaintance has revealed her true colours. 'She is ill-bred, quite a rompish girl. She debases my dignity. She has no refinement.' The great expense of maintaining her in a house and with a maid is awkward enough, but more – the arrangement 'is too much like marriage, or too much a settled plan of licentiousness.' He has learned, too, of her previous amatory entanglements and he is jealous, 'Damn her lewd minx,' he cries. His vivid imagination conjures lascivious scenes in which her former lovers perform with her. He is disgusted to think of it – but, O! 'she is very handsome, very lively, and admirably formed for amorous dalliance . . . Can I do better than keep a dear infidel for my hours of Paphian bliss?'

'This is a curious epistle to a clergyman,' remarks Boswell, possibly imagining Temple nervously adjusting his bands or mentally composing a sermon, and still the gossip flows: David

Hume has quarrelled with Rousseau who has imagined himself also persecuted by Boswell and they have fallen out; Paoli has sent Boswell a sixteen page letter to help with the book about Corsica; Miss Bosville's beauty is too delicate for the air of Scotland – would Temple allow Boswell to marry a Scots lass? ha! ha! ha! – and Mrs Dodds continues to be a sweet torment. On 8 March, the letter continues to roll amply on. Mrs Dodds has left the house complaining that she has been ill used, and has decided to go and board herself in the north of England. But it is a passing storm: she had imagined her lover had doubted her fidelity. 'We renewed our fondness . . . I embraced her with transport.' But there is worse to come. Boswell, that very night, lies like a brute, all night, with a drab and contracts a venereal infection.

In the first of a series of tearful contritions, Boswell plucks up courage to confess. 'I told her how drunk I had been. I told the consequences. I lay down and kist her feet. I said I was unworthy of any other favour . . . I hoped she would consider my being drunk as a fatal accident which I should never again fall into. I called her my friend in whom I had confidence and intreated she would comfort me.' Mrs Dodds rose nobly to the occasion, 'She bid me rise; she took me by the hand. She said she forgave me. She kist me.' All is well. But there is an unsettling postscript, premonitory with hindsight, in which Boswell admits, 'My present misfortune is occasioned by drinking. Since my return to Scotland I have given a great deal too much in to that habit, which still prevails in Scotland. Perhaps the coldness of the Scots requires it. But my fiery blood is turned to madness by it. This will be a warning to me, and from henceforth I will be a perfect man. At least I hope so.'

Mrs Dodds slowly but surely declined in favour, as a new star began to rise over Boswell's horizon. On 1 March, at St Giles's Cathedral, Boswell had noticed Miss Blair of Adamton, a 'handsome, stately woman: good countenance'. On 11 March she appeared again at a tea party where Boswell discovered he 'liked Miss Blair more and more without any fever.' By 18 March, Boswell had consulted with David Hume who counselled him to break with Mrs Dodds lest he acquire the habit of slavery to her

and ruin himself, and on 20 March Boswell wrote to his mistress
to emancipate himself from this Circe, this Laïs, this insensitive
virago. Temple and John Johnston could clear their minds of
anxiety – he was done with Mrs Dodds. 'What a snare have I
escaped!' The chambermaid and the enchantress are in the past:
Miss Blair is of the present. She has an income of £200 to £300 a
year, an agreeable face, a genteel manner, she is 'of a good family,
sensible, good-tempered, cheerful, pious' and is eighteen years
old. Her little estate marches with the lands of Auchinleck, and an
alliance would be a useful extension of the Boswell dominion.
Lord Auchinleck hints, 'I wish you had her.' Miss Blair is a
princess, all things considered.

On 27 March, with a clear mind and a willing heart, Boswell sat
down to begin his Account of Corsica. To Pitt, Earl of Chatham,
he intimated, 'My plan is, first, to give a geographical and physical
description of the Island; secondly, to exhibit a concise view of the
revolutions it has undergone from the earliest times till now;
thirdly, to show the present state of Corsica in every respect; and,
lastly, I subjoin my Journal of a Tour to That Island, in which I
relate a variety of anecdotes and treasure up many memoirs of the
illustrious General of the Corsicans – *memorabilia Paoli*.' In the
event, it was the last of these proposals that has been of the
greatest interest to posterity and, it must be admitted, most
interested Boswell and his contemporaries. Boswell continued
steadily with the writing of the Account of Corsica through to July
when he was sufficiently advanced to be able to submit specimens
of it to Edward Dilly, the London bookseller, who agreed to
publish it and made an offer of one hundred guineas for the
copyright.

Literary and romantic affairs proceeded in tandem. Just as
there were two attachments of the heart to be dealt with, so there
were two literary preoccupations – but it will be as well to dispose
of Princess Blair and Mrs Dodds before considering the *Account
of Corsica* and the pamphlet titled *Dorando*. It had taken five weeks
for Mrs Dodds to reply to Boswell's letter of dismissal as *maîtresse
en titre*; on 27 April she informed him that she was pregnant. 'Half
delighted to obtain what I had wished, and half vexed to think of

the expense,' Boswell was not displeased. He resolved to 'behave with humour and generosity' and invented 'a thousand airy plans' for the little 'black boy' he anticipated, both he and Mrs Dodds being very dark. In December 1767 she bore him a daughter, Sally. 'What a fellow I am!' Boswell had crowed to Temple but, on the birth, had decided that he would not continue the liaison.

By February 1768 he was back in bed with Mrs Dodds who believed herself to be pregnant once more. For a year, Boswell committed not another word about Mrs Dodds to paper, but on 31 March 1769 he sent her a draft of £10 and took steps towards 'managing with economy that unlucky affair.' Professor Pottle believes that Sally died young, otherwise Boswell would have broached the subject of his daughter again, being a naturally affectionate father. Whatever the reason, Mrs Dodds dropped out of his diary and, we must assume, out of Boswell's life.

Meanwhile, from 28 May to 2 June 1767, the Blairs of Adamton and the Boswells of Auchinleck entertained one another amiably to tea, dinner, strolls around the policies, and consolidated their acquaintance, Auchinleck egging on Boswell to make a declaration, Boswell adoring Miss Blair 'in our romantic groves . . . like a divinity' and considering how much at home she looked in the house of Auchinleck. To cap his contentment, Boswell had had a letter from Girolama Piccolomini which had made him cry, and Mrs Dodds was with child. During the first week of June 1767, Temple visited Boswell and was immediately despatched to Adamton to inspect Miss Blair. His instructions were explicit. 'Salute her and her mother; ask to walk. See the place fully; think what improvements should be made . . . Praise me for my good qualities . . . Observe her well. See how amiable. . . . Think of me as the great man at Adamton – quite classical too! Study the mother . . . take notes; perhaps you now fix me for life.'

Temple reported that a 'formal Nabob' had been hovering around Miss Blair. Boswell was unable to put himself between Catherine Blair and this William Fullerton, a surgeon returned from India, since he was fairly felled by a serious dose of clap, 'a just retribution for my licentiousness.' He wrote repeatedly to

Miss Blair, in the manner of fervent flirtatiousness which he had perfected in Italy, but no response issued from Adamton. Boswell turned to Temple to furnish an explanation, but their ingeniously improbable surmises were too subtle: letters had been delayed, or the Princess merely chose not to answer. Boswell wrote, assuming that the Nabob had gained the advantage, to congratulate her on her acceptance of Fullerton, but she replied that Boswell had no occasion to wish her joy. The game was still on.

On 5 November 1767 Mr Boswell is at Adamton, 'sitting in the room with my Princess, who is at this moment a finer woman than ever she appeared to me before.' He has been at Adamton one night, and Princess Blair has insisted on his staying another. 'I am dressed in green and gold.' He is accompanied by a servant, Thomas, 'in a claret-coloured suit with a silver laced hat'. He has arrived in style, in a 'chaise in which I sit alone like Mr Gray.' Despite the conventional courtesies, there is a coolness compounded by a quarrel between them, and 'if she can still remain indifferent as to what has given me much pain, she is not the woman I thought her, and from tomorrow morning shall I be severed from her as a lover.'

Princess Blair refused to own herself in the wrong, and declined to feel guilt. Boswell, reviewing the matter, as usual discovered alternative constructions to put upon a lady's motives, and soon had settled things to his own satisfaction and his love rekindled in an instant. In December, he seized her hand and declared his love. She was at last persuaded of his seriousness, but her reply was discouraging. 'I really have no particular liking for you,' said Princess Blair frankly, 'I like many people as well as you.' The dialogue that followed is one of Boswell's best set-pieces and Temple was allowed to eavesdrop – 'Temple, you must have it in the genuine dialogue.'

Boswell: 'Do you indeed? Well, I cannot help it. I am obliged to you for telling me so in time. I am sorry for it.'

Princess: 'I like Jeanie Maxwell [Duchess of Gordon] better than you.'

Boswell: 'Very well. But do you like no man better than me?'

Princess: 'No.'

Boswell: 'Is it possible that you may like me better than other men?'

Princess: 'I don't know what is possible.'

(By this time I had risen and placed myself by her, and was in real agitation.)

Boswell: 'I'll tell you what, my dear Miss Blair, I love you so much that I am very unhappy. If you cannot love me, I must if possible endeavour to forget you. What would you have me do?'

Princess: 'I really don't know what you should do.'

Boswell: 'It is certainly possible that you *may* love me, and if you shall ever do so I shall be the happiest man in the world. Will you make a fair bargain with me? If you should happen to love me, will you own it?'

Princess: 'Yes.'

Boswell: 'And if you should happen to love another, will you tell me immediately, and help me to make myself easy?'

Princess: 'Yes, I will.'

Boswell: 'Well, you are very good.' (Often squeezing and kissing her fine hand, while she looked at me with those beautiful black eyes.)

Princess: 'I may tell you as a cousin what I would not tell to another man.'

Boswell: 'You may indeed. You are very fond of Auchinleck; that is one good circumstance.'

Princess: 'I confess I am. I wish I liked you as well as I do Auchinleck.'

This exchange is as good as a play, and quite unlike any that Boswell could have seen on the contemporary stage. The timing, the occasional telling stage directions, the demure and devastating candour of Princess Blair and the calculated progress of Boswell, on a knife edge of disaster: it could not be bettered. 'She could give Lord Auchinleck a lesson how to manage me. Temple, what does the girl mean?' wailed Boswell, genuinely at a loss. 'How long must I suffer? What must I do?' Not long, and nothing is the answer. On 8 February, he announces, 'All is over between Miss Blair and me'.

Boswell: 'I would take a good deal of trouble to make myself agreeable to you.'

Miss Blair: 'You need not take the trouble.'

Boswell: 'What then, have I no chance?'

Miss Blair: 'No.'

Now that it was over, Boswell could 'see many faults in her which I did not see before,' and he made a note, 'I must have an Englishwoman . . . perhaps a Howard or some other of the noblest in the kingdom.'

February 1768 saw Boswell's collapse as a lover, but his reputation as an author was about to soar when, on 15 February, Mr Dilly informed him that the *Account of Corsica* was ready for publication and Adam Neill, an Edinburgh printer, was ordered to give out copies of the book in Scotland. It was published on 18 February. On that day he gave a copy of it to Lord Hailes, danced at a ball with the Countess of Crawford, and 'felt my own importance,' though there was an inevitable deflation now that the book was achieved. 'I am positive I had not so high an opinion of myself as other people had. I look back with wonder on the mysterious and respectful notions I used to have of authors.' A few days later he despatched a copy of the *Account of Corsica* to Horace Walpole, begging him to accept, alleging that his meeting with Walpole in Paris had first incited him to undertake the work. Walpole received the book, in spite of his cool reception and dislike of Boswell. To Mr Gray, Walpole wrote, 'Pray read the new account of Corsica; what relates to Paoli will amuse you much. The author, Boswell, is a strange being, and . . . has a rage for knowing anybody that was ever talked of. He forced himself upon me [in Paris] in spite of my teeth and my doors, and I see he has given a foolish account of all he could pick up from me.'

Mr Gray was pleased and strangely moved by the book, particularly by the part relating to Paoli, but 'any fool may write a most valuable book by chance, if he will only tell us what he heard and saw with veracity. Of Mr Boswell's truth I have not the least suspicion, because I am sure he could invent nothing of this kind. The true title of this part of the work is, a Dialogue between a Green Goose and a Hero.'

Lord Auchinleck, says Lewis, confined himself to a grudging growl. Jamie had 'ta'en a toot on a new horn,' and Johnson preserved silence for a month before writing to complain that Boswell had published his letters without his leave. Despite this, 'I shall be glad to see you, and . . . I wish you would empty your head of Corsica, which I think has filled it rather too long.'

Boswell took a month to reply to Johnson's 'short and by no means complimentary' letter. He asked too much. 'Empty my head of Corsica! Empty it of honour, empty it of humanity, empty it of friendship, empty it of piety. No! while I live, Corsica and the cause of it shall ever employ much of my attention, shall ever interest me in the sincerest manner.' That sincerity, apparently ingenuous, had not pleased Walpole and Gray, and inappropriate enthusiasm dismayed Johnson. But David Garrick approved, and the historians Mrs Macaulay and Lord Lyttelton praised Boswell's effort and achievement. Lyttelton's eulogy was un-blushingly incorporated into the third edition in May 1769. The first edition of 3500 copies had sold out in six weeks, the second was published on 1 April and was equally taken up by a public eager to know what all the fuss was about.

Reviews had been gratifyingly long and laudatory, the book had been extracted for publication in newspapers and magazines, it was translated into five languages, and the King himself had read it. Taking a brisk leave of a pretty, lively little girl 'whom accident had thrown in my way a few days before' and whom Boswell characterises as a slave of profligate men, the celebrated author set off for London on 17 March, arriving on the 23rd. His presence was not unexpected: his imminent arrival had been trumpeted in the *London Chronicle* on 1 March, 'James Boswell, Esquire, is expected in town.' On 24 March, *Chronicle* readers were informed that they might find the traveller from Scotland 'at his apartments in Half Moon Street, Piccadilly'. The stringer who had supplied this intelligence was Boswell himself.

From these lodgings he immediately 'sallied forth like a roaring lion after girls' and 'had a neat little lass *in armour*, at a tavern in the Strand.' Afterwards he went to supper, and the next day to one of his favourite diversions – a good hanging. He could never resist, and got as close as possible to the scaffold to drink in every detail and consider how he might behave himself in such cir- cumstances. On this day, Mr Gibson the attorney was to be executed for forgery, and conducted himself very well. He stood, wearing a full suit of black, with the noose round his neck, composedly sucking an orange while the chaplain of Newgate recommended his soul to God and his conscience to repentance. Boswell's passions were not, in this instance, much moved – but the other two, hanged before and after the despatch of Mr Gibson, were more affecting.

Then Boswell ran round all the afternoon, arriving at Messrs Dilly's, the booksellers, at about three, and moving on to Guild- hall where a poll for the election of candidates for London in the General Election was being held. Here Boswell saw Wilkes who came last among the seven candidates, despite the mob roars of 'Wilkes and Liberty'. Boswell proudly displayed his Corsican pistols, and lost the dog that Paoli had given him. He searched, with friends, for about an hour without luck, and went back to Dilly's to drink tea. In the Strand, later, he discovered a Miss Simson to whom he was taken by a tavern girl. Miss Simson was good-natured, but it was the tavern girl who was in luck and Boswell was *armed*. By any standards, a busy day: but not an unusually strenuous day for Boswell who was amiable and sociable and possessed of a strong constitution that survived all this and a good deal more.

The day was not specially remarkable, nor yet particularly full, though Boswell noted its events in some detail. As a day at random, however, it serves to emphasise Boswell's voracious appetite for activity, for noise and sensation, for lights and commotion, for constant stimulation. Samuel Johnson, to a lesser degree, shared Boswell's needs in this respect. Both loved to be in society, Johnson less for the sake of society than the impulse to divorce himself from his own melancholy which was liable to shroud him when he was solitary. Boswell was, then, jaunting about town much as usual, but fully conscious of the change in his status. He was no longer a carriage dog, running at the wheels of the great, the gay, and the ingenious as they bowled gloriously along: he was, in his own right, a considerable celebrity, a public figure, Mr Corsica Boswell. For the moment he was the cynosure, the rage, the none-too-modest recipient of all that literary fame and the admiration of the crowd could bestow. Some years later, looking back on this period, he allowed 'how much Corsica had done for me, how far I had got in the world by having been there. I had got upon a rock in Corsica and jumped into the middle of life.'

From no conscious motive of keeping the book in the public eye, he continued to clamour on behalf of Paoli and Corsica. He got up appeals for money for ordnance: by August 1768 he had raised £700 by private subscription in Scotland and acquired, from the Carron Company, 'a tollerable train of artillery,' for the brave patriots, 'very cheap'. But too late. In May 1768 the Genoese sold their interest in the island of Corsica to the French who prepared to secure the acquisition. Paoli declared his intention to stand to the last against the French, and Boswell anxiously solicited the intervention of the British government on behalf of the Corsicans. The government took the view, cogently paraphrased by Lord Holland, that, 'Foolish as we are, we cannot be so foolish as to go to war because Mr Boswell has been in Corsica.' A year later, the French were in possession of Corte, the Corsican capital, and Paoli, a fugitive, arrived in England in September 1769. He was granted a pension of £1200 a year, and given apartments in Bond Street. The pension, according to Walpole, was awarded at least partly at Boswell's instigation. Subsequent events in Corsica continued to engage Boswell's attention until the end of his life, and contributed to his final disappointment shortly before his death.

But Corsica, for the time being, had made a man of Boswell. To Temple, he boasted, 'I am really the *Great Man* now . . . I give admirable dinners and good claret . . . I set up my chariot. This is enjoying the fruit of my labours, and appearing like the friend of Paoli.' The crescendo reached its climax in September 1769 at the Stratford Shakespeare Jubilee celebrations organised by the actor David Garrick as 'Chief Steward, poet, orator, pageant-master, chorus-leader, Master of Ceremonies'. Boswell was so puffed up by the importance of this event, to which all the

fashionable world flocked but Johnson did not, and the extraordinary spectacle he made there of himself, that neither his
letter to Temple nor his account of the occasion betrays any
sense of the ridiculous.

The Jubilee celebrations were a disaster, borne with much
dignity and fortitude, to rival the pluvious Eglinton Tournament
of the nineteenth century which its chronicler, Lord Cockburn,
equally failed to salt with more than passing irony. In a letter to the
London Magazine of October 1769, Boswell dwelt upon the felicity
of the sodden event which Samuel Foote described with particularly malicious economy, defining the Jubilee as 'a public Invitation, circulated and arranged by Puffing, to go posting without
horses to an obscure borough without representatives, governed
by a Mayor and Aldermen who are no Magistrates; to celebrate a
Poet, whose Works have made him immortal, by an Ode without
Poetry, Musick without Melody, Dinners without victuals, and
lodgings without beds; a Masquerade where half the people
appear bare-faced, a Horse-Race up to the knees in water, and a
gingerbread Amphitheatre which tumbled to pieces as soon as it
was made.' But that, as Mr D. B. Wyndham Lewis observes, is
'pretty Fanny's way'. The reality was a sustained attempt at high
seriousness which descended into a frivol and was washed by a
constant, unremitting downpour of rain into low farce.

At the Masquerade in the Rotunda (approachable only across
duckboards floating on a meadow drowned by the overflowing
Avon), Mr Boswell of Auchinleck made his sensational entrance
'in the dress of an armed Corsican Chief. He entered the
Amphitheatre about twelve o'clock [midnight]. He wore a short
dark-coloured coat of coarse cloth, scarlet waistcoat and
breeches, and black spatterdashes; his cap or bonnet was of black
cloth; on the front of it was embroidered in gold letters *Viva la
Libertà*, and on one side of it was a handsome blue feather and
cockade, so that it had an elegant as well as a warlike appearance.
On the breast of his coat was sewed a Moor's head, the crest of
Corsica, surrounded with branches of laurel. He had also a
cartridge pouch, into which was stuck a stiletto, and on his left
side a pistol was hung upon the belt of his cartridge-pouch. He

had a fusee slung across his shoulder, wore no powder in his hair, but had it plaited at full length with a knot of blue ribbons at the end of it. He had, by way of a staff, a very curious vine, all of one piece, emblematical of the sweet Bard of Avon. He wore no mask, saying it was not proper for a gallant Corsican.'

This remarkable figure, who thus described himself at length, was very naturally the object of 'universal attention'. In the pocket of his Corsican costume, he had a 46-line poem which he proposed to read to the thousand-strong gay throng of the Rotunda. Some say he began to declaim:

> From the rude banks of Golo's rapid Flood,
> Alas! too deeply ting'd with patriot Blood,
> O'er which, dejected, injur'd Freedom bends,
> And sighs indignant o'er all Europe sends,
> Behold a *Corsican*! . . .

Others hold that at this point, or before he had even begun, he was shouted down: the verses were perhaps too didactic, too dull, too affecting, or perhaps just too much for an audience whose appetite for Odes was not omnivorous. Perhaps they had been gratified on that score too long and too often by Garrick himself. Boswell lets no word of this slip, however: he praises his verses as 'well suited to the occasion'.

In March 1768 he learned that Miss Bosville, of whom he had never quite despaired, was engaged to another. While in London, bereft of Miss Bosville, he had had a letter from Zélide suggesting that, if he were serious in his intention to marry her, they should discuss the matter face to face at Utrecht. But Boswell's attention was distracted by the appearance of 'the finest creature that ever was formed: *la belle Irlandaise*,' Mary Ann Boyd. Instantly, Boswell conceived himself 'exceedingly lucky in having escaped the insensible Miss Blair and the furious Zélide . . . figure to yourself, Temple,' he wrote in his usual manner to the dazed priest in August 1768, 'a young lady just sixteen, formed like a Grecian nymph with the sweetest countenance, full of sensibility, accomplished, with a Dublin education, always half the year in the north of Ireland, her father a counsellor-at-law with an estate of £1000 a year and above £10,000 in ready money. Her mother a sensible, well-bred woman. She the darling of her parents, and no other child but her sister.'

Zélide's prospects of becoming Mrs Boswell (had she seriously entertained any such intention) were demolished. The correspondence between Belle de Zuylen and Boswell trailed off and was never resurrected. In the event, she did not marry Bellegarde: she married her brothers' tutor and, as Madame de Charrière, lived a reclusive life at Colombier until she was sparked to the flame of an eight year intimacy with a nephew of Constant d'Hermenches – Benjamin Constant. When this ended in 1794, Belle retreated again into reclusiveness. Childless, married to an emotionally cold husband, attracted in middle age to a much younger man, this remarkable woman, deeply emotional but equally profoundly intellectual, stoical and scornful of emotional and intellectual dishonesty, survived Boswell by ten years.

While agitating for the cause of Corsica, building up a legal practice, dallying with Mrs Dodds, and suing for the hand of Princess Blair, Boswell was seriously diverted by the Douglas Cause. In a series of *pensées* titled *Memorabilia* Boswell considered how he stood in 1767. 'I am a singular man. I have the whim of an Englishman to make me think and act extravagantly, and yet I have the coolness and good sense of a Scotsman to make me sensible of it.' He added, 'I am a weaker man than can well be imagined. My brilliant qualities are like embroidery upon gauze.' Though he enjoyed and rejoiced in his singular talents and achievements, wearing them like badges, he felt an underlying insecurity. There was not, underneath the gaudy show, the solidity to support the pose. It was perhaps the collision of opposites, the ability to be sensible of one extreme while practising its opposite and to resolve to adopt one course of action while acting out the other, that Boswell felt to be his major weakness. Gregory Smith described this uneasy harness of opposing extremes as the 'Caledonian Antisyzgy'. Boswell felt about himself much as he felt about the gold lace on the hat he carried under his arm to visit Rousseau: it had 'the air of being solid' but was in reality bogus.

Boswell was not professionally engaged in the Douglas Cause, but he eagerly threw himself into it as a partisan on the Douglas side. It was the most interesting and important civil trial in eighteenth-century Scotland, and Boswell's activities in the wings of the drama evidence his propensity to give precedence to an enthusiasm of principle over prudence and propriety. The question to be settled was the paternity of the apparent heir to the estate of Archibald, Duke of Douglas, who had died in 1761. The son of the old Duke's sister, said to have been born to that lady when she was fifty, was alleged to have been bought or abducted from the real parents – a glassmaker and a French rope-dancer. If Lady Jane Douglas or her agents had in fact fabricated the evidence said to prove paternity, the Douglas estate would pass to the Duke of Hamilton. Boswell passionately held to 'that great principle of law – *filiation* – on which we all depend,' and maintained that a successful attack on the probability of parentage in this case would discredit the stability of family inheritance, weakening a principle that, in his own case, much concerned him as the prospective Laird of Auchinleck.

Thus he composed the *Dorando* pamphlet, a fictional skit on a more ample, more particular, and more serious work, *The Essence of the Douglas Cause*, which was thought to be an accurate, if lengthy, summation of the case. To supplement these cannons, he fired off a couple of songs first satirising the Hamilton party and then championing the Douglas camp. The Court of Session found against Douglas, but the decision went on appeal to the House of Lords which reversed it, confirming Douglas in possession of his inheritance. The case was the talk of Edinburgh, and Boswell its principal rattle. On 27 February a messenger left London with news of the decision of the House of Lords. He arrived in Edinburgh where, at the Cross, he announced the news and shrieked 'Douglas for ever!' Bonfires were lit, mobs met in the streets, and anyone who did not set a celebratory candle in his window had its glass broken for his omission. Lord Auchinleck, who had voted for Douglas in the Court of Session nevertheless supported his dissenting colleagues by refusing to illuminate his windows, which provocation incited the rioters to attempt to break down his door. Boswell was alleged to have participated in the riot, and Ramsay of Ochtertyre claims that Lord Auchinleck, putting judicial duty before paternal affection, tearfully begged the Lord President to commit James to the Tolbooth. Boswell was called to account before the sheriff for his behaviour on the night of the Douglas riot and explained that he had been at the Cross where he had heard men plotting and speaking disrespectfully of the sheriff as the Lord President's puppy. Nothing came of Boswell's examination, though he boasted later of that famous night and his glorious part in the window-breaking orgy.

In April 1769, Boswell hurried off to Ireland to renew his acquaintance with Mary Ann and to refresh his passion for her. She happened to be a relation of Miss Margaret Montgomerie of Lainshaw, near Stewarton, a cousin and neighbour of the Boswells of Auchinleck. Boswell had known Miss Montgomerie for some years, but she had very little money, possessed no remarkable beauty, was two years older, and so had been insignificant as a candidate to compete with the Misses Bosville, Blair, Boyd, or Belle de Zuylen. Familiarity perhaps had bred an intimacy and ease of manner between them that Boswell did not identify as a romantic affection – he was accustomed to sudden, violent passions and frenzied flirtations that Peggie Montgomerie had not inspired in the Boswell bosom. On 8 August 1768, indeed, she had merrily set her hand to a joking agreement that she should not agree to marry him on pain of banishment from the kingdom. It is the sort of document that rests, for its effect, on the attachment of long standing and a tacit understanding:

> . . . considering that Mr James Boswell, advocate, my cousin, is at present so much in love with me that I might certainly have him for my lawful husband if I choose it, and the said James being of a temper so inconstant that there is reason to fear that he would repent of his choice in a very short time, on which account he is unwilling to trust himself in my company; therefore, I, the said Margaret Montgomerie, hereby agree that in case I am married to the said James Boswell any time this year, or insist upon his promise thereto within the said time to

take place any time thereafter, I shall submit to be banished out of Great Britain during all the days of my life.

Peggie Montgomerie accompanied Boswell to Ireland on the visit to the Boyds. On the way, Boswell got drunk and abused her, for which he was sorry. Four days into the trip, before even reaching the delicious Mary Ann, before even having got the length of Ayr, Boswell 'felt myself in love with another woman than Marianne.' This cryptic reference in his journal for 29 April 1769 is to Miss Montgomerie to whom he instantly appeals. 'I spoke of it to Margaret. She is always my friend and comforter.' For some reason, Boswell pretends that he is referring to someone else entirely and the journal reads very mysteriously. 'My serious passion came into my mind with more force than ever. I imagined that Miss Montgomerie knew the lady's mind, and from some things she said I concluded that the lady was engaged. I was amazingly affected. I cried bitterly, and would not speak to my companion. I, who was on an expedition to court a pretty young lady at Dublin, and had with me a most agreeable companion, was miserable from love of another woman, and would not speak to my companion . . . till Miss Montgomerie by chance discovered the cause of all my misery, and with her usual kindness assured me that I was mistaken. I then enjoyed the most delightful calm after a dismal storm.'

Despite this sudden switch of romantic direction, Boswell and Peggie continued on to Ireland from where he wrote frankly to the bemused Temple: it is the usual debate with himself, discovering virtues where none had been previously apparent, rehearsing the behaviour of the beloved and her paramour. Margaret Montgomerie had been Boswell's confidante through so many misadventures with minxes and mistresses: she has heard it all and borne with it all like the honest, undesigning creature Boswell now perceives her to be. Between flames, she is the woman to whom Boswell has returned to pledge his devotion. Peggie possesses a person that 'is to me the most desirable that I ever saw.' She is 'of a fine, firm, lively temperament, and can never be old.' She would make a good mother for his children. But, on the debit side, 'she would bring neither money nor interest . . . all my gay projects of bringing home some blooming young lady and making an *éclat* with her brilliant fortune would be gone.'

Boswell found himself in a quandary: he could hardly be assiduous in his attentions to Mary Ann in view of his protestations to Peggie, and he informed the Boyds that Lord Auchinleck did not approve of the trip to Ireland: which was true, but hardly the more pressing reason for Boswell's determination to keep distance between himself and Mary Ann. The problem of proximity was partly solved by the rapturous reception he was given in his role as Mr Corsica Boswell: he was taken up by the quality – he dined with the Duke of Leinster and gratified Lord Charlemont. On 12 June 1769 Boswell arrived back in Edinburgh, *sans* Mary Ann Boyd but nevertheless possessed of a mistress. A correspondence developed between Boswell and Peggie who had returned to Lainshaw. The defeat of the Corsicans was on his mind, he was busy at work as an advocate, he was dining with Mountstuart and Andrew Erskine, and intermittently considering the wisdom of his love for Miss Montgomerie: on 25 June Boswell 'lay abed all day and read . . . Strange's *Catalogue of Pictures*.' He 'felt the pleasures of taste to be exquisite. I thought of Margaret. But then, money would enable me to buy pictures, and my Irish connection make a pretty anecdote in my life. So I wavered. But then again, Margaret was like Raphael's mistress; and what real happiness all my life should I have with her! I was just calm.'

The day before, Lord Auchinleck had attempted to talk of marriage with James, but Boswell had been disinclined to discuss the subject. Had he done so, he might have learned sooner than 1 July, when Auchinleck began to throw out sly hints, that the judge was also considering matrimony. His attention had fixed on a Miss Elizabeth Boswell, with whom Boswell had recently been dining and taking tea in company with her brother, and his cousin, Claud. Three years had elapsed since the death of Boswell's mother, and on that score alone he was shocked that the judge should seek to replace his loss. But Auchinleck had been waiting for Boswell to fit himself out with a suitable Scots wife – Miss Blair, for preference – to head the household and increase the

Auchinleck estate: he did not yet know of Boswell's plan to marry Peggie and doubtless had impatiently decided to marry his own nurse/hostess/helpmeet. Miss Boswell, being a spinster and aged forty or more, at least introduced no rival heir and could more than likely be depended upon (in spite of the remarkable precedent of Lady Douglas) to be past child-bearing age. Nevertheless, she threatened to diminish Boswell's inheritance (and indeed, Auchinleck provided handsomely for her on his death): Boswell was frankly appalled. He rushed around his circle of acquaintance discussing his dilemma, spilling his suffering and inflaming his rage. To add to his trials, he had sent an intemperate letter to Peggie accusing her, more or less, of being too frothy in her frankness with other men. The irony of this was that his jealousy and carping had been stimulated by a conversation with Elizabeth Boswell during which he had fully discussed Peggie's faults. An ominous silence was Peggie's response, and Boswell was miserable but prevented by pride from apologising.

At length, Peggie wrote back, with no reproach, and his loving relationship with her was restored. In the meantime, he had been warm with his father, threatening that, if Auchinleck's marriage plans went forward, 'he would be no more troubled with me . . . for I could not think of marriage when he exposed himself at his years and forgot my valuable mother.' To compound his misfortunes, Boswell was ill, possible on account of a recent binge at Bothwell Castle to celebrate the birthday of Archibald Douglas with whom he had become intimate. For a while, Auchinleck and Boswell were not on speaking terms.

On 20 July Boswell formally proposed, in a letter, to Peggie and on the next day, Auchinleck tried to talk to Boswell about marriage again, but 'insensibly he and I fell into our usual bad humour.' On 25 July, Peggie agreed to become Mrs James Boswell. At this point, Boswell had committed himself to cutting himself off from his father, and, as he thought, all he would have to offer Peggie was his reduced allowance of £100 a year. He had said so frankly, offering to combine it with the interest of Peggie's £1000 and to 'live in an agreeable retirement in any part of Europe that you please. But we are to bid adieu for ever to this country. All our happiness is to be our society with each other, and our hopes of a better world.' He admitted that his fancy was romantic and that only love could induce her to consider it.

On 4 August Auchinleck grumpily agreed to the marriage between Boswell and Peggie, though he gave it, at most, six months. At this, Boswell rushed to Lainshaw and formally engaged himself to Peggie Montgomerie, whereafter he referred to her, even before the marriage, as his wife. For better or worse, and he experienced momentary terror, he had finally committed himself as a husband. To confirm that they should have no secrets, Boswell sent her an indiscreet letter from Temple which unblushingly referred frankly to most of Boswell's lapses from grace – his venereal infections, his affairs with women, and his bastards. If she took these disclosures as proof of sincerity, it is to her credit and it would not be the last time she would be called upon to bear with his scandalous revelations. It was perhaps as well for her to become used to them from the beginning.

From the end of August to mid-November, Boswell was in London, ostensibly to restore his health by imbibing a patent medicine known as the Lisbon Diet Drink and to consult with the Dr Kennedy who evangelised it at half a guinea a bottle. He found time for the Stratford Jubilee, Johnson, Paoli, and a visit to Temple in Mamhead. He had written constantly to Peggie, but no date had been set for the wedding. Whether out of spite or for a frolic, Boswell arranged for the banns to be called on 19 November, the same day as those proclaimed for the forthcoming wedding of his father. On 23 November, he wrote to Peggie from Edinburgh to say, two days before his marriage, that he was urgently called to Bothwell Castle and could not refuse. 'So I shall be there tomorrow night. Your gown comes with me. You can soon put it on. Let dinner be late. We shall both dress in white before it. I ever am your faithful and affectionate J.B.'

Scrambling from Bothwell Castle with Archibald Douglas in tow, Boswell arrived in time to marry Margaret Montgomerie at Lainshaw House in the evening of 25 November 1769. On the same day, at Edinburgh, Elizabeth Boswell became Lady Auchinleck.

Boswell and the Bear

Between publication of the *Account of Corsica* and the marriage to Margaret Montgomerie, Boswell was twice in London. The place was irresistible, with or without an excuse to be there. The excuse was generally a gloss on his real reason – the desire to see Samuel Johnson who, in March 1768, happened to be in Oxford. Boswell was anxious to make things easy between them about Corsica: Johnson had, as yet, made no comment on publication of the book, and he was said to be displeased that one of his letters to the author had been included in the text. In fact, Johnson had written to complain only three days before Boswell arrived in Oxford on 26 March, but apparently his delight in seeing Boswell put grudges out of his head. Johnson 'took me all in his arms and kissed me on both sides of the head, and was as cordial as ever I saw him . . . "What," said he, "did you come here on purpose?" "Yes, indeed," said I. This gave him high satisfaction. I told him how I was settled as a lawyer and how I had made two hundred pounds by the law this year. He grumbled and laughed and was wonderfully pleased. "What, Bozzy? Two hundred pounds! A great deal."'

Immediately they became engrossed in a Socratic dialogue in an attempt to resolve Boswell's moral dilemma as to whether pleading a cause he knew to be bad was injurious to the principles of honesty. Johnson gave the view that it was for the judge to determine whether or not the cause was bad. It is difficult to believe that Boswell really was vexed, in any practical sense, by this hoary old question: it is more likely that he employed an apparent disingenuousness to draw out Johnson's considerable talent for the impromptu aphorism. The sprat caught a mackerel. 'Sir, a man will no more carry the artifice of the bar into the common intercourse of society than a man who is paid for tumbling upon his hands will continue tumbling upon his hands when he ought to be walking on his feet.' 'Wonderful force and fancy,' remarks Boswell, though it is not one of Johnson's pithiest apophthegms. It had the effect, too, of immediately quieting Boswell's alleged moral perplexity. Annoyingly, Johnson had not yet spoken of the *Account of Corsica.* The subject lay between them like an illegitimate paternity until Johnson, taking his cue from a reference to voluntary and spontaneous deathbed declarations, animadverted, 'If I praise a man's book without being asked my opinion of it, that is honest praise and may be depended on. But when an author asks me if I like his book and I give him something like praise, it must not be taken as my real opinion.' Boswell had the sense to keep his mouth shut, and 'thought within myself I should not ask him about my book.' In any case, Johnson well knew that his testy letter was already on its way to Scotland.

The undisguised pleasure Johnson took in triumphing over the most modest antagonist is illustrated by an exchange that occurred in the course of a meandering conversation that turned to 'the pleasing system of brutes existing in the other world'. Johnson, writes Boswell, did not like to hear 'any ideas of futurity but what are in the Thirty-Nine Articles'. He 'was out of humour with me, and watched his time to give me a blow. So when I, with a serious, metaphysical, pensive face, ventured to say, "But really, Sir, when we see a very sensible dog, we know not what to think of him," he turned about, and growling with joy replied, "No, Sir; and when we see a very foolish fellow, we don't know what to think of him." Then up he got, bounced along, and stood by the fire, laughing and exulting over me.' It is adolescent stuff, scarcely remarkable for wit, but the scene is vivid, the relationship between Boswell and Johnson perfectly caught in the cosy but competitive repartee and the satisfaction both parties took in their respective roles – the cunning and glee of Johnson, the willing collusion of Boswell unruffled by the cuff he has received as harvest for the seed sown sometimes calculatedly, often carelessly.

Dr Samuel Johnson, painting by James Barry, c. 1777

Boswell took Johnson's opinions more or less as gospel – he might quibble over fine points, but generally he adopted his views from Johnson's moral pronouncements as he took his law from the *obiter dicta* of the judges of the Court of Session. Both were authoritative in their interpretations and powerful in their jurisdictions. On matter of fact, they might be fallible. Johnson's assertion that swallows certainly sleep all the winter might well be true: that they tended to 'conglobulate themselves by flying round and round, and then all in a heap throw themselves under water, and lie in the bed of a river' appeared strange to Boswell, 'I know not if Mr Johnson was well founded in it.' Still, Boswell was not in a position to contradict Johnson's confident natural history, and there was no telling the limits of Johnson's curious knowledge. Classical authors had been no more fantastical in their assertions about the natural world.

The reason for a second visit to London, from 28 August 1769, was ostensibly to effect a cure for Boswell's distemper, to purify his blood from every remain of vicious poison. Boswell, like many of his contemporaries, was credulous about quacks. The medical profession had been prejudiced against Keyser's pills, a nostrum amply certificated by notable persons who had been cured of a 'certain disorder,' and it was no more disposed to credit the efficacy of the Lisbon Diet Drink recommended by Dr Kennedy whom Boswell had come to consult. Mr Woodcock, a perfumer in Red Lion Square, had the profitable monopoly in the supply of this wonderful patent medicine which was said to cure scurvy, leprosy, and general debility, at half a guinea the pint bottle. Though the visit was to consult with Kennedy (since Boswell was in fact feeling ill) and to consort with Johnson, London was in itself a treat. It was Boswell's Ulubrae: walking round St James's Park with a friend, Sir John Pringle, they agreed that the crowds of well-dressed London people contrasted favourably with the people of Edinburgh who had 'a familiarity, an inquisitiveness, a way of looking through one,' that was disagreeable. In Edinburgh, a man 'must be exceedingly reserved, for, if he allows his vivacity to play, the sarcastical rogues will attack him; and should he, with the politeness well known abroad, show his

displeasure, they would raise a hoarse laugh and never mind him.'
How much more pleasant to be incognito in London, careless of
the need to be so *retenu*.

But Boswell was scarcely unknown, and minded merely the
vulgarity and provincialism of Scotland. London was full of
amusement which, if it were fully to be enjoyed, did not demand
excessive discretion. There was Davies the bookseller to crack
with, Mr Dilly to dine with, easy girls to dally with, and a Jubilee to
savour. Johnson, on this occasion, was at Brighton with his friends
Mr and Mrs Thrale. On 11 September, Boswell received a letter
from him giving the long-desired criticism of the *Account of
Corsica*, until now withheld on the ground that though his opinion
would have given Boswell pleasure it would also have too much
excited his vanity. Johnson thought the *History* of Corsica deriva-
tive, but the *Journal* appended to it was a different matter: it had
arisen out of Boswell's own experience and observation, and
expressed images which had operated strongly upon the author
and which impressed themselves strongly upon the readers. 'I
know not whether I could name any narrative by which curiosity is
better excited or better gratified.' Johnson went on to congratulate Boswell on his forthcoming marriage. 'I have always loved
and valued you, and shall love you and value you still more as you
become more regular and useful: effect which a happy marriage
will hardly fail to produce.' It is a letter of grumpy but sincere
affection, a remarkable testimony of the advance Boswell had
made behind Johnson's guard and the extent to which Johnson
had responded to Boswell's unaffected idolatry.

Boswell continued indefatigably to pursue his acquaintance in
London. Kennedy was dismissed as a 'gaping babbler' but his
Diet Drink (an innocuous decoction) was proving efficacious; he
again encountered Sheridan's 'astonishing vanity' which made
Boswell goggle, but 'his knowledge and talents pleased me.' He
assiduously kept up a journal, but despaired of pinning every
detail, 'I observe continually how imperfectly, upon most occasions, words preserve our ideas . . . In description we omit
insensibly many little touches which give life to objects. With how
small a speck does a painter give life to an eye!' How, then, to

portray on the page 'the vivid glances of Garrick's features,' or the look in the eye and the tone of voice of his beloved Peggie, which have 'engaged my soul in an angelic manner'? Boswell finds himself 'ready to write unintelligibly when I attempt to give any kind of idea of such subjects.' Unconsciously, he had mostly given up any attempt to render character through description. His ear was always better than his eye, and though he will obligingly provide a description of Johnson's appearance (or his own) his true genius is the evocation of a personality through speech and the occasional telling verb or adjective descriptive of behaviour.

Boswell's reception by Paoli's *valet de chambre* – Paoli had not long been in London – when he called at the General's apartments in Old Bond Street on 22 September 1769, precisely catches the excited tone of the meeting without a word of description save a perfunctory reference to clothing. The *valet*, on hearing the name Boswell 'gave a jump, catched hold of my hand and kissed it, and clapped his hand several times upon my shoulders ... Then he ran upstairs before me like an Italian harlequin, being a very little fellow, and, opening the door of the General's bedchamber, called out, "Mr Boswell". I heard the General give a shout before I saw him. When I entered he was in his night-gown and night-cap. He ran to me, took me all in his arms, and held me there for some time.' This rapturous reception prefaced a continuous association with Paoli for the rest of Boswell's visit to London. He took rooms near Paoli, got himself up in some fine new clothes, borrowed a sword from Dilly, and threw himself into social life, appearing 'to due advantage'. He introduced Paoli to Johnson and David Garrick, drove with the General in his coach around town, and when he was not talking he was listening. 'I was filled with admiration whenever the General spoke. I said that after every sentence spoken by him I felt an inclination to sing *Te Deum*.' It was Sollacarò all over again. This Elysium was further populated by Johnson on his return from Brighton four weeks after Boswell's arrival from Scotland. On 30 September, Boswell dined with Johnson at the Mitre and the bear danced obligingly enough to the prod of his tormentor: he did not take seriously the question of general warrants which the case of

John Wilkes had brought prominently to the fore. Johnson was not convinced that the public cared much one way or the other. Rousseau was uncompromisingly mauled, London was praised, Scotland was condemned as a desert, and second marriages were approved as a compliment to the first.

On 6 October Boswell was invited by Mr and Mrs Thrale to their 'charming villa' at Streatham. In the *Life*, Boswell comments, 'I had last year the pleasure of seeing Mrs Thrale at Dr Johnson's for a short while in a morning, and had conversation enough with her to admire her talents and to show her that I was as Johnsonian as herself.' Boswell had first been introduced to Mrs Thrale in 1768 by Johnson, but not until then had he an inkling of Johnson's attachment to the Thrale family. Henry Thrale was a well-to-do brewer, an exceedingly amiable man, who had married Miss Hester Salusbury in October 1763 and taken his bride to the villa at Streatham where Hester Thrale led a more restricted social and intellectual life than she might have wished for. Henry Thrale and her mother, Mrs Salusbury, persuaded Mrs Thrale not to enter London society, and to give up riding. She turned to reading and writing as diversions, and on 9 January 1765, when Boswell was in Turin dancing attendance on Mme de St Gilles, Johnson was lured to dinner at Streatham Park.

He was delighted by his host and hostess, and praised Mrs Thrale's verses, entering into a minor literary collaboration with her. In time, he became a regular and welcome visitor. Boswell, being absent in Europe, knew nothing of this development in Johnson's social life. Johnson's infrequent letters to Boswell gave not a hint of his new pleasures. It became clear to Boswell that Mrs Thrale interested and very much pleased Johnson, and Boswell was capable of jealousy: or, at least, of possessiveness. He was received with great cordiality at Streatham Park, though more as an intimate of Johnson's than on his own merits, and a letter from Boswell to Mrs Thrale, dated 5 September 1769, refers to her as a 'generous rival'.

The relationship between Johnson and the Thrales prospered, he became almost a fixture in the family and was accorded every consideration. Mrs Thrale began to note his saws and sayings, first in a book entitled *Miscellany* and later in six blank quarto books, calf-bound, entitled *Thraliana*. On 4 April 1781, Henry Thrale died after a long illness, and gossip soon circulated the opinion that rich, pretty Mrs Thrale might well marry Dr Johnson. Boswell did nothing to dampen the gossip, and indeed composed his scurrilous epithalamium concerning Mrs Thrale and Dr Johnson which he delightedly sang on various occasions.

Mrs Thrale's affections centred, however, on Gabriel Piozzi, an Italian singing master, who had been engaged to teach music to one of the Thrale daughters. To say the least, the match was not approved by society or, worse, by Johnson who felt neglected and abused and flatly refused to give his blessing to Mrs Thrale's determination to marry Piozzi. He broke utterly with his former friend, and after 15 July 1784 Johnson neither corresponded with, nor saw, Mrs Thrale again.

The relations between Boswell and Mrs Thrale, when as Mrs Piozzi she published her book about Johnson and edited a collection of his letters, became more than strained: they became frankly antagonistic. The detailed account of this long-running feud and tragi-comedy of misunderstanding is given by Mary Hyde in *The Impossible Friendship*. Neither lost any opportunity to abuse or subtly indict the other for faithlessness and bitterly recriminated in print and in private. Boswell was not only jealous, he was never able to form a platonic friendship with an intelligent woman. Mrs Thrale was perhaps also jealous of Boswell, and both liked to be a centre of attention. Both idolised Johnson, and both regarded him largely as a private, personal pleasure, though his public fame made him all the more desirable. In truth, Mrs Thrale and Boswell did not like one another, and the degree to which they were obliged to tolerate one another's existence during Johnson's lifetime probably exacerbated their later enmity. The wretchedness of her parting with Johnson partly inspired her to seek a little 'Fame' by attempting his biography and thereby to give society some proof of his affection for her. That she and Boswell found themselves in competition after Johnson's death, as they had been during his life, was inevitable. That Mrs Thrale and Boswell misunderstood one another on occasions, is certain. That the misunderstandings multiplied and ossified was due to mutual perversity that reflected credit on neither protagonist.

Though rushing about town much as usual, Boswell had his worries. By 16 October he had been put to the knife by a surgeon, Duncan Forbes, to relieve his unspecified ailment, and in a letter to John Johnston he confessed, 'My father's strange scheme [of marriage to Miss Boswell] still alarms me.' Lord Auchinleck was grumbling about Boswell's jaunts to London and, in a letter to Peggie on 2 October, Boswell hinted at the possibility that he might have to give up all expectation of inheriting Auchinleck. Then, too, Johnson was occasionally irritable. Boswell reported to Garrick a sally Johnson had made against him at the Thrales on 6 October, and Garrick's irritation had moved Boswell to observe 'that Johnson at times spared none of his friends.' Boswell had borne with attacks on his own enthusiasms: Johnson had decried the Corsicans, though Paoli himself impressed Johnson when, later, they were introduced by Boswell. On 16 October Johnson more or less damned Boswell as a dunce, and on 26 October he lost his temper entirely, advising Boswell to get his head fumigated. Boswell, despite being knocked down with the butt end of Johnson's pistol, continued incautiously to press Johnson with questions until, for his pains, it was made plain enough that Johnson had been pushed to the limit of endurance and Boswell was ordered to 'give us no more of this.'

Johnson went so far as to forbid Boswell to see him next day, and Boswell 'went home exceedingly uneasy. All the harsh observations which I had ever heard made upon his character crowded into my mind; and I seemed to myself like the man who had put his head into a lion's mouth a great many times with perfect safety, but at last had it bit off.' The next morning, nevertheless, Boswell sent round a note admitting that he might have been wrong and that he intended to call and stay five minutes. 'You are in my mind since last night surrounded with cloud and storm. Let me have a glimpse of sunshine, and go about my affairs in serenity and cheerfulness.' In these words, Boswell pursued Johnson like a lover attempting to patch up a tiff. The note had evidently softened Dr Johnson, who treated Boswell kindly and, when Boswell made to go, stopped him at the staircase 'and smiling said, "Get you gone – *in*."'

All was well, and Boswell stayed 'some time longer'. As a mark of their fondness for Boswell, Johnson and Paoli were both induced to sign their names as witnesses on 31 October 1769 to Boswell's marriage contract before he returned to Scotland. Boswell spent the night of 9 November with Johnson at Streatham and, as once before when Boswell was about to set out on a great adventure, Johnson companionably accompanied him to the point of departure – in this case, a post-chaise in London – talking of marriage, the proper form of service, and the appropriate expectations marriage might afford to the bride and groom. 'Do not expect more from life, than life will afford. You may often find yourself out of humour, and you may often think your wife not studious enough to please you; and yet you may have reason to consider yourself as upon the whole very happily married.'

Had Boswell been on better terms with his father, Peggie might have lodged at Auchinleck, paying periodic visits to Edinburgh to be with her husband while he went about his day-to-day legal business. She preferred the country to the town; but Lord Auchinleck had accepted her grudgingly as a daughter-in-law, and Boswell had not at all accepted Elizabeth Boswell as his stepmother. Relations were, to put it mildly, strained. Mr and Mrs James Boswell set up house in the Cowgate in Edinburgh, but moved soon after, in May 1770, to better quarters in the Canongate at Chessel's Buildings, a new and fashionable residential development. In February, Lord Auchinleck had been ill but by the time Boswell wrote to Temple on 19 June, the old judge seemed to be quite recovered. 'My father is come to town and never looked better in his life. Honest man, he really is, I believe, very fond of me; and we are at present on very good terms. I behave with prudence towards the person [Elizabeth Boswell] who has occasioned so much uneasiness. I do not as yet see any appearance of her multiplying.'

Boswell was applying himself with vigour and industry to the

practice of law, and had been admitted to practice also at the Bar
of the General Assembly of the Church of Scotland which added
to the scope of his advocacy. Peggie was pregnant, and the
admirable house in the Canongate was being decorated, the
Boswells submitting to considerable temporary inconvenience 'in
order to have a future elegance'. Boswell was wholly uxorious,
sober, and busy as a husband, companion and lawyer. It was
generally such an unremarkable life that he scarcely bothered to
note it at all.

On 28 August 1770, Peggie Boswell was delivered of a son.
The child lived only two hours. Boswell sent the next day for
Johnston to come and comfort him, and on 1 September he wrote
to Temple to urge him to visit him at Edinburgh, 'I have much
need of your comfort.' Peggie had been very ill, and in real
danger, for the two days of the birth and both she and Boswell
were greatly distressed by the death of the first legitimate Boswell
heir. To Temple, Boswell wrote, 'I grant you there is no *reason* for
our having an affection for an infant which, as it is not properly a
rational being, can have no qualities to engage us; yet Nature has
given us such an instinctive fondness, that being deprived of an
infant gives us real distress . . . because every parent annexes to
his child a number of most agreable hopes; and therefore, when
he is bereft of his child, he is deprived of all those hopes. This to a
man of a warm imagination is no small loss.' Boswell supported
his view with the example of Adam Fergusson who, though he had
maintained that till a child was four years old it was no better than
a cabbage, was nevertheless much affected by grief when one of
his own children died soon after birth.

Temple arrived at Edinburgh in the third week of September,
and Peggie was well enough to receive him in her new drawing
room. He stayed a week, and was mightily impressed by Boswell's
wife who had paid such particular and tender attentions to his
comfort. 'If you are not the happiest of mortals, it will be your own
fault. Never did I see such a command of temper, such amiable
sensibility. It is absolutely cruelty to give that woman the least
room for uneasiness. Depend upon it, you will always be in the
wrong; she loves you too well ever to give you unnecessary pain.

Continue to love her, to respect her, and thank God daily for having given you, for preserving to you, so excellent a wife.'

Boswell was perfectly well aware of his good fortune. He replied to Temple, 'I am fully sensible of my happiness in being married to so excellent a woman, so sensible a mistress of a family, so agreable a companion, so affectionate and peculiarly proper helpmate for me. I own I am not so much on my guard against fits of passion or gloom as I ought to be; but that is really owing to her great goodness ... I shall endeavour to be better. Upon the whole, I do believe I make her very happy.' Marital relations, it would appear, were not entirely without storms, but they can have been little other than minor skirmishes mainly due, we may take it, to Boswell's recurrent depressions.

The Boswells 'flitted' again early in 1771 to David Hume's former home, a smallish flat in James's Court in the Lawnmarket, not far from Parliament House where the Court of Session held its deliberations and passed its judgements. Peggie liked the flat, and in May 1771 Boswell was busy with no less than five causes at the Bar of the General Assembly, speaking for and against Patronage which he personally considered was inconsistent with libertarian principles. But as an advocate, 'I am to have no opinion. I am only to speak in the person of others. So that the Judgements of the assembly do not affect me.' At this point, in a letter to Johnston, he broke into verse:

> But let them say or let them do
> It's aw ane to me
> If I but get into my pouch
> A braw swingeing fee etc.

Boswell had evidently got over the scruples of conscience which Johnson and a steady stream of guineas had relieved.

Boswell had been on a circuit with his father, and Peggie had been to see her sister in the country in late May, and in August the Boswells went South for a week's jaunt to see friends and look, as tourists, at the sights. In September and October, Boswell went alone to Auchinleck to see his father and recover his health which had been impaired by a 'complaint' which Boswell does not identify. The Scottish passion for planting had not passed Lord Auchinleck by, and Boswell was roped in to help with the pruning of the young trees which so fascinated the landowners of the time. He had come, also, to get Lord Auchinleck to instruct him on Scottish election law and the time was thus passed agreeably and usefully. It was probably, too, an opportunity for father and son to re-establish amicable relations; but Peggie, though she had visited Auchinleck in October 1770, was perhaps not yet wholly *persona grata*, and Boswell missed her greatly. More likely, Peggie herself did not wish to forgive or forget the coldness with which Boswell's father had taken the news of her proposed marriage to James and she would not put up with mere tolerance now she was married.

In 1769, Boswell had bought an interest in the *London Magazine* amounting to one-sixth of the ownership, and though necessarily confined to Edinburgh he nevertheless continued to support his investment by contributing some articles, mostly on theatrical topics including a three-part essay *On the Profession of a Player* in August 1770. He followed this up with an introduction to an edition of Shakespeare which the publisher had dedicated to Garrick with whom Boswell kept in touch by letter. He had been neglectful of London friends and admitted, in a letter that broke a silence of eighteen months between himself and Johnson, 'I can now fully understand those intervals of silence in your correspondence with me, which have often given me anxiety and uneasiness.'

The year of 1771 had been notable for one great event: General Paoli visited Scotland and, from 3 to 11 September, Boswell had the unalloyed joy of escorting his old friend hither and thither from East to West, paying a visit of two days to Auchinleck. To Garrick, Boswell wrote, 'you may figure the joy of my worthy father and me at seeing the Corsican Hero in our romantick groves.' Sir Walter Scott claimed that the worthy Auchinleck viewed Paoli as 'a land loupin' scoundrel of a Corsican' and perhaps was less affected by the honour of a visit than his son. It was possibly not an auspicious time to tell Lord Auchinleck that he might expect to be rejoiced, in the foreseeable future, by a visit from Dr Johnson, who was still flattering Boswell 'with hopes of seeing him among the rocks of Scotland.' Paoli returned to Edinburgh, doubtless impressed with the iron politeness that stiffened the long face of Lord Auchinleck, and spent the night before his departure from Scotland at Boswell's flat.

On 3 March 1772, Boswell wrote to Johnson, preparing an excuse to visit him in London. Since he would not write, Boswell, like Mahomet, must come to the mountain. To drink fully from the 'Fountain of Wisdom,' it 'must be approached at it's source, to partake fully of it's virtues.' Boswell intended to be in London in the spring to 'fix our voyage to the Hebrides or at least our journey through the highlands of Scotland.' In any event, Boswell was obliged to be in London to appear for a client in an appeal from the Court of Session in the House of Lords, on 14 April. At the beginning of March, Peggie had suffered a miscarriage and Boswell had been seriously concerned for her health. But on 14 March he set out for London.

Though he lost the appeal, Boswell considered that his appearance before the House of Lords had done him some credit. Lord Mansfield had complimented him on his presentation of the case, and the notice taken of him was useful, for Boswell had got it into his head that he would like to build up a practice as an English barrister. 'My views in coming to London this spring were: to refresh my mind in the variety and spirit of the metropolis, the conversation of my revered friend Mr Samuel Johnson and that of other men of genius and learning; to try if I could to get something for myself, or be of service to any of my friends by means of the Duke of Queensberry, Lord Mountstuart, or Douglas; to be employed in Scotch appeals in the house of Lords, and also to see how the land might lie for me at the English bar.'

Perhaps the order in which Boswell placed these objectives was their proper order of importance. Immediately on arrival in London, Boswell called at Paoli's magnificent apartments where he was asked to stay, but declined on the ground that he did not wish to give Grub Street writers any opportunity to abuse Paoli by 'saying that he was pensioned by British generosity and kept a

Scotsman gratis in his house.' Instead, Boswell found lodging
with Mr Dilly. A short walk along the Strand was enough to shake
Boswell's faith in his conversion to sobriety: a variety of fine girls,
all inviting him to amorous intercourse, set him to 'indulging
speculations about polygamy and the concubines of the patriarchs
and the harmlessness of temporary likings unconnected with
mental attachment.' Since his 'ideas naturally run into their old
channels, which were pretty deeply worn . . . I resolved never
again to come to London without bringing my wife along with
me.'

On 21 March 1772, Boswell found Johnson at home in his
dusty, shabby study at Johnson's Court, Fleet Street. The intimacy of their association is fully recorded in the *Life* which details
every scrap of conversation from then until Boswell's departure
for Scotland on 10 May. The journal for this, and other periods,
provided ample first-hand material which Boswell reproduced
more or less verbatim in the biography he was later to write. The
journal groans like a banqueting table with a spread of good
things, laid with more generosity than elegance, the fare rich
without being heavy. Not a crumb is wasted or overlooked, swept
up as soon as dropped. When Boswell was not with Johnson, he
was with Dempster, Paoli, General Oglethorpe, David Garrick,
Samuel Foote, Lord Mansfield, Lord Mountstuart, any number
of Scotsmen making good in another country, Oliver Goldsmith,
and Bennet Langton – the great, the gay, and the ingenious,
endlessly discussing, gossiping, and disputing.

At the centre of it all is Boswell: fluttering moth-like from one
candle to another, occasionally singeing his wings when he
presses too close to Johnson's flame and sets it guttering. Boswell:
'Would not you, Sir, now, allow a man oppressed with care to
drink and make himself merry?' Johnson: 'Yes; if he sat next to
you.' This broadside hit Boswell amidships, and Langton murmured, 'I saw that you would bring something upon yourself.' But
Boswell bobbed up again, 'I know Mr Johnson so well and delight
in his grand explosions, even when directed against myself, so
much that I am not at all hurt.' Johnson was not a universal
favourite. Boswell's attachment to him was deep and largely

undisturbed except on occasions when, having been abused, he naturally felt a momentary resentment. Johnson was clumsy in his affections, and terrible in his prejudices. He did not generally bear grudges. He displayed a willingness to repair friendships that had become strained, but which, if his gruff overture was rejected, he abandoned as a bad job. Johnson might fairly fell a man with a random blow, but he expected him to get up again for another round rather than to run off in a fright or a temper, to nurse his knuckles and complain.

To the likes of Wilkes and David Hume, Johnson in his moral aspect was, says D. B. Wyndham Lewis, 'a figure of fun, a bigoted old fool, a reactionary, a clerical, a *cabotin*, what the intelligentsia today would naturally label a fascist, since Johnson often went into a church without the intention of burning it down; a type who believed, talked, and practised the kind of obsolete nonsense no man of intelligence who admitted Progress could possibly endure.' Boswell had ample opportunity to compare Johnson with John Wilkes and Hume, neither of whom he regarded as substitute father and mentor. Boswell was not a full-fledged rake, nor a true libertarian. He took his wicked pleasures remorsefully, and was too conscious of his dignity as a laird and as a man to tolerate any threats to his position. Johnson was comforting, a rock in which to find a niche. Johnson was the ideal father, craggy where the smooth slopes of the lofty and inaccessible Lord Auchinleck allowed few footholds. The traditional virtues appealed to Boswell, but he was no fool and Johnson helped to supply the moral and intellectual example and strength against which Boswell could test his own beliefs.

Boswell had an acute sense of what was proper, and on this visit he was behaving admirably. He found the girls of the Strand distasteful, he was not excessive in drink, and he was keeping the best of company. On 20 April, he and Dilly attended the Lord Mayor's dinner and ball at the Mansion House. Many more tickets had been given out than there were places in the hall, so the guests had to battle for their dinner. Boswell bagged some food and a bottle each of champagne and burgundy. The band played, toasts were cried, and who should be at Boswell's shoulder but wicked John Wilkes. Clutching his bottle and little Mr Dilly against the press of the crowd, Boswell decided to introduce himself again to Wilkes, whom he had avoided since their last meeting in Paris. 'Don't sit by me, or it will be in the *Public Advertiser* tomorrow,' said Wilkes, and then suggested that Boswell was becoming the gravest of grave mortals since he had not come to see Wilkes when he was occupying a comfortable billet in the King's Bench Prison on a charge of seditious and criminal libel.

Boswell had, indeed, kept clear of Wilkes as a popular hero and martyr and an association with him, even now, would be dangerous. 'I do assure you I am glad to meet with you,' said Boswell, 'but I cannot come to see you. I am a Scotch laird and a Scotch lawyer and a Scotch married man. It would not be decent.' But Wilkes was out of prison, his fine of £1000 having been paid by his friends, and he had been three times elected Member of Parliament for Middlesex though the Commons refused to have him. Now he was an Alderman of the City of London, elected by rich merchants who had their own reasons for opposing the Court of George III. 'The Devil Wilkes' would, in time, become Lord Mayor himself and take his seat in Parliament, by which time Boswell would think it safe to know him.

Boswell returned to Scotland in the expectation that Dr Johnson would be ready to make the trip to Scotland in the autumn, but his health did not permit the visit, and he wrote to confirm his intention to 'take the ramble' in some other year. Peggie had mostly recovered from her miscarriage, and Boswell kept himself busy with a little journalism and a good deal of legal work. But a streak of dissatisfaction began to appear: he became more heavily involved in Masonic activities, began to drink more heavily, and acquired a taste for gambling late into the night – whist was a favourite game. His wife was pregnant again, and once at least after 'too much wine' Boswell resorted to a prostitute. He became naturally anxious about the consequences, and confessed to Peggie who sensibly sent for a doctor to put his mind at rest. 'She is my best friend, and the most generous heart,' he discovered anew.

On 15 March 1773, Peggie gave birth to a daughter, Veronica. This event coincided with the first night of Goldsmith's comedy *She Stoops to Conquer*, and Boswell wrote to congratulate Goldsmith and to describe his daughter as a 'fine, healthy, lively child and, I flatter myself, shall be blessed with the cheerfulness of your comic muse. She has nothing of that wretched whining and crying which we see children so often have; nothing of the *comédie 'larmoyante*. I hope she shall live to be an agreeable companion and to diffuse gaiety over the days of her father, which are sometimes a little cloudy.' On 30 March 1773, Boswell set out again for London on what he had come to think of as his annual spring jaunt. On 3 April he was again with Johnson, who declared, 'I'm glad you're come,' and as if without interruption the talk began to flow.

To his surprise, Boswell was bidden to dinner with Johnson on Easter Day. 'I never supposed that he had a dinner at his house; for I had not then heard of any one of his friends having been entertained at his table.' But Johnson said he generally had a pie on a Sunday, so Boswell readily accepted and was interested to find that everything was in good order, even to the extent of knives and forks. 'We had a very good soup, a boiled leg of lamb and spinach, a veal pie, an excellent rice pudding, pickled walnuts and onions, porter and port wine.' Johnson joked over the lamb, and was altogether amiable and, as usual, instructive. On this occasion, Boswell was determined to have some facts, and 'I asked him if he could tell when he was born, when he came to London and such things.' Johnson said he might have them for twopence and that he hoped Boswell might know a good deal more before he began to write the *Life*. The idea of being Johnson's biographer had been in Boswell's head for some time: he had written of it, in passing, in a letter to Garrick in September 1772, when he mentioned that he had been storing materials towards such a project. Johnson gratified his wish by giving Boswell 'many circumstances which I wrote down when I went home,' and which he subsequently used in the *Life*.

The *Life* relates that Boswell and Johnson were together on 30 April to dine with the Hon. Topham Beauclerk, Lord

A literary party at Sir Joshua Reynolds': those present are
Boswell, Johnson, Reynolds, Burke, Garrick, Paoli, Warton
and Goldsmith. Engraving by W. Walker after James E.
Doyle

Charlemont, Sir Joshua Reynolds, and 'some more members of
the LITERARY CLUB, whom he had obligingly invited to meet me,
as I was this evening to be balloted for as candidate for admission
into that distinguished society.' He had been proposed by
Johnson, and supported by Beauclerk. From the *Life*, it might
be supposed that Boswell's election was a mere matter of form.
On the contrary, it had taken as much doorstepping and self-
recommendation as might be necessary to be elected to Parliament or to acquire a peerage. Goldsmith, and possibly Garrick,
who found Mr Boswell resistible, were informed by Johnson that
if his candidate were blackballed they might be sure that they
would get none of their own men elected. For an hour, Boswell sat

in anxious suspense waiting for news which finally came in the coach that Beauclerk sent to carry Boswell to the Turk's Head where he was received by 'such a society as can seldom be found: Mr Edmund Burke, Dr Nugent, Mr (now Sir William) Jones . . . Mr Garrick, Dr Goldsmith, and the company with whom I had dined.' Johnson delivered a humorous lecture on Boswell's duties as a good member of the Club, to which many members would have added a profound 'Amen'. The Club had been established nine years, and it was no small honour to be made a member.

During his prayerful, suspenseful hour Boswell had been kept company by Lady Diana Beauclerk, Topham Beauclerk's wife who had been divorced from Viscount Bolingbroke by Act of Parliament. On 7 May, at breakfast with the Thrales, Johnson had been provoked by Boswell's enthusiasm for her charms and damned her as 'a whore, and there's an end on't.' That same evening, at dinner at Mr Dilly's, Johnson had fallen out with Goldsmith who had tired of Johnson's endless and effortless oratory that afforded no opportunity for him to break in and display his own. Later, at the Club, Johnson made an apology and Goldsmith placidly returned the compliment 'so at once the difference was over, and they were on as easy terms as usual, and Goldsmith rattled away.' On 10 May, Boswell had the rare opportunity to describe Dr Johnson's roaring, rolling midnight laughter at Temple Bar which relieved Boswell's sadness at having to take his leave to return to Scotland. He left not only with the Doctor's peals ringing in his ears, but also the envy and jealousy of Goldsmith who, on hearing that Johnson proposed at last to make the trip to Scotland, warned that 'he would be a dead weight for me to carry, and that I should never be able to lug him along through the Highlands and Hebrides.'

Johnson arrived at Boyd's Inn in the Canongate on the evening of 14 August 1773, and lodged for three days with the Boswells. It had taken a good deal of effort to get Johnson into Scotland. Since their first meeting in 1763 Boswell had been pressing, off and on, for the visit and he had urged any number of eminent Scotsmen to reinforce the invitation and dwell upon the advantages of his great presence in their midst. The Court of Session had risen for the summer vacation, and Boswell was free, ready, and panting to escort his distinguished guest on a tour of an ancient and romantic land. Mrs Boswell had brewed a pot of tea ready for his arrival, and 'insisted that, to show all respect to the sage, she would give up her own bedchamber to him and take a worse.' Peggie knew her place, and knew that this enormous, slovenly creature was her rival. 'I have seen many a bear led by a man,' she sniffed, 'I have never before seen a man led by a bear.' She had a good mind, but she was never able to make out quite what the Doctor was on about when he rumbled, as it seemed, interminably, in the intervals when he was not supping tea or lying humped in her best bed until midday or stumping about the streets arm in arm with James.

Johnson was not insensitive to Peggie Boswell's dismay. She did not care for him, that was plain enough, though she preserved a poker-faced politeness. She kept the tea flowing, gave up her bed, and presented him with a pot of marmalade, but that was the limit of her amiability. She was not generous, but she did her duty as a gentlewoman and, perforce, hostess. The little flat probably seemed, for the first time, too small. The baby, for all that she was a quiet little thing at birth, at four months would be no less demanding than the great, overgrown sexagenarian Doctor who was none too clean and kept the household up till all hours in a roar as tourists anxious to catch sight of a great man marched over her carpets, burned her candles, swilled her tea, and disturbed her routine. It was as though the great brute had brought all the racket of London with him.

Johnson was not an attractive man to those who did not love him. A plain portrait of him by Boswell at the time of his visit describes Johnson's habitual 'full suit of plain brown clothes, with twisted hair-buttons of the same colour, a large bushy greyish wig, a plain shirt, black worsted stockings, and silver buckles.' His 'very wide brown cloth great-coat, with pockets . . . might almost have held the two volumes of his folio Dictionary.' He supplemented this outfit, when travelling, with boots and a 'large English oak stick'. Johnson was sixty-four years old, and the next

Walking up the High Street, Edinburgh.
'Dr Johnson and I walked arm in arm up the High Street to
my house in James's Court. It was a dusky night, I could not
prevent his being assailed by the evening effluvia of Edinburgh. As we marched along he grumbled in my ear, "I
smell you in the dark."'
Drawing by Thomas Rowlandson

'ninety-four days were never passed by any man in a more
vigorous exertion,' remarked Boswell, tugging him away from
Peggie's kettle and the cordiality of Edinburgh company which
had, indeed, begun to disorder even Johnson. To Mrs Thrale, he
wrote 'there was such a conflux of company that I could scarcely
support the tumult.'

On the morning of 18 August, Boswell and Johnson left Peggie

Wit and Wisdom making preparations for dinner.
'We gave him as good a dinner as we could. Our Scotch
wild-fowl or grouse were then abundant, and quite in
season; and so far as wisdom and wit can be aided by
administering agreeable sensations to the palate, my wife
took care that our great guest should not be deficient.'

Drawing by Thomas Rowlandson

to count her spoons and the cost of the visit in terms of meat, tea,
puddings and port, candles and spotted linen. Johnson had
abandoned to her care 'a pretty full and curious Diary of his Life'
which, to Boswell's disgust, Peggie had not bothered to open but
had simply tidied away into a drawer together with the pair of
pistols, gunpowder, and a quantity of bullets with which Johnson
had equipped himself to travel into savage parts but had been
persuaded to relinquish. The travellers were accompanied by

Boswell's servant, a Bohemian called Joseph Ritter, a well-set-up man over six feet in height. They had equipped themselves with a map of Scotland, a Bible, and a copy of *Ogden on Prayer* which Boswell stuffed in a pocket. Peggie 'did not seem quite easy when we left her,' remarks Boswell – she was perhaps undecided whether the explosive little Diary and the pistols and ammunition in her drawer were any less dangerous than the exciting effect of their owner on her husband – 'but away we went!'

Boswell's account of the trip, *The Journal of a Tour to the Hebrides*, was not published until October 1785, some ten years after publication of Johnson's *Journey to the Western Islands of Scotland* and ten months after Johnson's death in December 1784. Two weeks into the trip, Johnson first conceived the thought of writing a book about his adventure and began to take notes of a kind no doubt very different from those that Boswell was continually scribbling and showing to him. On 19 September Johnson came into Boswell's room to read his friend's Journal, 'which he has done all along. He often before said, "I take great delight in reading it." Today he said, "You improve: it grows better and better . . . It might be printed, were the subject fit for printing."' This was no caution on the quality of the writing, but perhaps an indirect warning about attempting to publish. The Doctor had his own plans, and in 1775, though he allowed Boswell to 'write out a supplement to his Journey,' was less inclined to permit it to appear in print simultaneously with his own observations on Scottish travel and topography. 'Between ourselves,' Boswell confided to Temple, 'he is not apt to encourage one to *share* reputation with himself.'

It is absurd to attempt to compare the two books, except to regard them as companion volumes, each supplementing the other. Johnson's effort is now and again damned as dull, and Boswell's elevated as more entertaining and accessible – but both, by very different standards, are invaluable. D. B. Wyndham Lewis acutely remarked that the difference between the two books may be that 'one esteems Johnson's, but one loves Boswell's.'

The travellers struck north for St Andrews, crossing the Firth

Dr Johnson in a Highland hut

of Forth. At Leith, Johnson disparaged Scottish trade, and at St Andrews he abused John Knox. Here, too, he took an opportunity to survey some 'sorrowful scenes' that did not, however, disturb his appetite at dinner with the professors of the University. Boswell's apprehension about the consequences of introducing Johnson to the eccentric, noble judge Lord Monboddo was overcome by his curiosity to see them together and, having travelled over a wild moor in pelting rain, Johnson quoting Macbeth, they arrived at Monboddo, 'a wretched place, wild and naked, with a poor old house' the hospitality of which Monboddo was, nevertheless, proud to offer to his guests. Boswell immediately panicked when Johnson, hardly over the threshold, began to cast doubt on the wisdom of the ancients, since Monboddo held that Greek art and philosophy formed the highest point of civilisation. However, they agreed on the merits of Homer and the complete extinction of learning in contemporary Scotland. The dinner was frugal, in accord with Monboddo's rustic and antique simplicity: he regarded a boiled egg as the acme of the culinary art and often used to say, 'Show me any of your French cooks who can make a dish like this.' Boswell does not record that the subject of men being born with tails was touched upon on this occasion, though Johnson was certainly aware of Monboddo's earnest belief in the phenomenon.

At Aberdeen, the travellers met some more professors and dined with Sir Alexander Gordon who provided as much Scotch broth as Johnson could sup and the next day, says Boswell blandly, 'We spoke of Fingal.' Indeed, who was not speaking of 'Fingal' and, by implication, James 'Ossian' Macpherson, the supposed translator of ancient Celtic poetry. Johnson took his opportunity to state his position which was that Macpherson should deposit the manuscript for professorial inspection and informed judgement. Should he not care to do so, 'he gives the best reason to doubt; considering too, how much is against it *a priori*.' The Doctor and Macpherson came near to actual physical blows when, on his return to London, Johnson took care to include some unpleasant passages, offensive charges, and injurious statements in his *Journey to the Hebrides*, renewing his disbelief that the Ossianic poems were authentic products of a Caledonian Homer. Johnson's reputation had hurried on before him: at Ellon, their landlady proposed to ask the Doctor's diagnosis of a lump on her young son's throat, but far from being disappointed that Johnson was 'only a very learned man,' declared that she had heard him to be 'the greatest man in England except Lord Mansfield.' Her discrimination pleased Johnson mightily.

But it was not Johnson who pronounced the 'Open Sesame' that caused every door in Scotland to be flung wide for their entrance: he was interested to discover the power of Boswell's name that earned them the politest and most generous hospitality from one end of Scotland to the other. By 30 August they were obliged to take to 'equitation' and they were now fairly in the Highlands, where habitation was ruder than they had yet experienced. They stopped by the side of Loch Ness to view the hut of an old woman and converse with her. The sight of Boswell and

Johnson terrified her and she gabbled in the Gaelic to their guide that 'she was afraid we wanted to go to bed to her.' Johnson was vastly amused, imagining the story she would tell. 'She'll say, "there came a wicked young fellow, a wild dog, who I believe would have ravished me, had there not been with him a grave old gentleman who repressed him . . ."' Boswell fell in with the joke, replying, 'No, sir, she'll say, "There was a terrible ruffian who would have forced me, had it not been for a civil decent young man who, I take it, was an angel sent from heaven to protect me."' The ancient beldam then produced a bottle of whisky, demanded snuff, and declared that she was as happy as any woman in Scotland. Boswell gave her sixpence, and she sent her inoffensive guests away with an earful of Erse prayers.

At Glenelg, the inn could provide neither meat nor drink, and the only bed was a quantity of hay. Johnson buttoned himself tightly into his greatcoat and slept in that, but with more gentility Boswell spread a sheet and blanketed himself with his clothes. It was a bad night: Boswell 'slept ill,' fretting about a quarrel he had had with Dr Johnson that day. Johnson had had enough of being jolted about on horseback and had taken umbrage at being briefly abandoned by Boswell who, without disclosing his good intentions, had gone ahead to make arrangements for bed and board. He had been recalled 'with a tremendous shout' by Johnson in a terrific rage which developed into a threat to break off the friendship directly on return to Edinburgh. But the next day they contrived to mend matters between them, and got into a boat bound for Skye, where it rained a good deal.

The intention was to proceed to Rasay, piloted by that model of a Highland gentleman, Mr Malcolm Macleod, sixty-two years old, who was agreeably dressed in a pair of brogues, tartan hose nearly to his knees, 'a purple comblet kilt, – a black waistcoat, – a short green cloth coat bound with gold cord, – a yellowish bushy wig, – a large blue bonnet with a gold thread button.' The boat was rowed by four muscular, half-naked Highlanders, 'something between a wild Indian and an English tar.' Johnson got up in the stern 'like a magnificent Triton,' Macleod and the crew broke into an Erse song which they roared and chorused against the wind that lashed the sea. 'Naval musick is very ancient,' observed the Doctor interested in such an example of 'proceleusmatick song' and reflecting what a shudder would animate a London tea table at the news that he had 'crossed the Atlantick in an open boat.' 'We are contending with seas!' shouted Boswell excitedly. 'Not much,' replied Johnson phlegmatically, determined not to be overawed by the 'Atlantick' which, in its ferment and rage, swept overboard a pair of his spurs. But he was no doubt glad to be landed safely and entertained that night at a *ceilidh* where the laird of Rasay had the carpet rolled up and a fiddler imported for dancing. While Rasay danced and Malcolm Macleod 'bounded like a roe,' Johnson sat on the sidelines now meditating, now smiling, now dipping into a book, but mainly talking against the noise of the ball and the subsequent supper of twenty dishes spread plentifully and elegantly on two tables.

At Kingsburgh, Johnson and Boswell visited Flora Macdonald, 'a little woman, of a genteel appearance, and uncommonly mild and well-bred.' Johnson had not much more than Boswell to say about the heroine of the '45 and perhaps they were both a little disappointed not to find a more spirited woman. At Corrichatachin, Boswell got tremendously drunk, getting to bed at five o'clock after a good carouse and waking at noon the next day with a 'severe head-ach,' terrified that Johnson would abuse him for conduct inconsistent with that which 'I ought to maintain, while the companion of the *Rambler.*' Sure enough, Johnson came into Boswell's room with the words, 'What, drunk yet?' But he did not sound angry, and when several of the previous night's accomplices in drunkenness had also come to see him and pass round a brandy bottle, Johnson joked, 'Ay, fill him drunk again. Do it in the morning that we may laugh at him all day. It is a poor thing for a fellow to get drunk at night, and sculk to bed, and let his friends have no sport.' A dram or two of brandy cured the headache, and Boswell went to Johnson's room where he took up a Prayer-book, opened it, and appositely found the line, 'And be not drunk with wine, wherein there is excess.' 'Some,' remarks Boswell, 'would have taken this as a divine interposition.'

The weather was dreadful, obliging them to remain in Skye

until 3 October when Joseph Ritter reported that the wind was
still contrary, and Johnson quipped, 'A wind, or not a wind? that is
the question,' which Boswell laboriously explains as an example
of the Doctor's habit of amusing himself 'at times with a little play
of words, or rather of sentences.' However, the herring boats
were ready to sail for Mull and the travellers hurried aboard.
Words, for once, failed Johnson who was seasick, while Boswell
paraded himself on deck and 'exulted in being a stout seaman,
while Dr Johnson was quite in a state of annihilation.' Boswell had
the grace to admit, 'I was soon humbled,' and was sick. The rain
poured, night fell, the wind beat at the boat and its shivering crew,
and the sea boiled. Buffeted by wind and waves, they were in some
danger. Boswell was frankly terrified. Piety was a comfort, but to
relieve his mind further he begged for something to do. He was
given a rope to hold and ordered to await the command to pull it.
Boswell gripped the rope grimly, firm at his post, lashed by wind
and rain, waiting for an instruction that never came, since the rope
was merely attached to the top of the mast and served no purpose
of navigation.

Johnson, meantime, was lying below deck 'quiet and unconcerned . . . and having got free from sickness, was satisfied . . . He
was lying in philosophick tranquillity, with a greyhound of Col's at
his back, keeping him warm.' It was not possible to make a landing
until morning, when the boat was forced into the island of Col
where Boswell and Johnson were taken in at a farmhouse where
there was a welcome peat fire, tea, and some books, and so the day
passed pleasantly enough. They were stranded on Col until 14
October when the storms abated sufficiently for them to reach
Tobermory.

At Inveraray, Boswell got them invited to dinner by the Duke of
Argyll whom Boswell regarded with the same veneration as a
bishop might look upon a holy relic. Even Johnson, who was not
easily overawed but paid due respect to title and ancient lineage,
egged Boswell to make his presence known to the Duke who had
always treated Boswell with civility. The Duchess was a different
matter: she was a partisan of the Hamiltons, having been the wife
of the Duke of Hamilton before being widowed and marrying the

Duke of Argyll, and on the day that Boswell went to wangle an invitation to dinner, she thoroughly snubbed him over the teacups. The next day they were civilly received by the Duke and sat down to dinner. What then possessed Boswell to get to his feet to offer a toast to the Duchess, is inconceivable. But he did, and gave the toast not once but twice. The Duchess paid no attention to Boswell, but took pains with Dr Johnson to whom, at one point, she said, 'I know *nothing* about Mr Boswell.' The reaction of Boswell, who complacently records his humiliation, dotting the i's and crossing the t's, is a self-satisfied nod in acknowledgement of the Duchess's beauty and the observation that, if he had to be strangled, it was at least done with a silken cord.

Finally, on 30 October, Boswell and Johnson set out for Ayrshire and on 2 November they arrived at Auchinleck. Johnson had already been primed to avoid three burning issues – Whiggism, Presbyterianism and Sir John Pringle. Sir John, an intimate of Lord Auchinleck's, was Boswell's godfather and, for most of his life, a valued mentor. The old man had regularly advised James, intervened between Auchinleck and Boswell to smooth over difficulties, and Boswell had not only sought Pringle's opinions but had a considerable respect for them when given. From 1748, Sir John had practised as a physician in London, and in 1774 was appointed to attend as physician to the King. He was a Scotsman, having been born in 1707 at Stitchel, Kelso, and was made a baronet in 1766. In the *Life* Boswell refers to Pringle as 'mine own friend and my Father's friend' and though he had wished to establish an acquaintance between Pringle and Johnson Pringle had demurred, saying, 'It is not in friendship as in mathematicks, where two things, each equal to a third, are equal between themselves. You agree with Johnson as a middle quality, and you agree with me as a middle quality; but Johnson and I should not agree.'

'The repulsion,' Boswell acknowledged, 'was equally strong on the part of Johnson: who, I know not from what cause, unless his being a Scotchman, had formed a very erroneous opinion of Sir John.' Lord Auchinleck, on the contrary, agreed very well with Sir John: no doubt they took comfort in one another's opinions. As a

Highland Dance on the top of Dun-Can.

'Old Mr Malcolm McCleod, who had obligingly promised
to accompany me, was at my bedside between five and six. I
sprang up immediately, and he and I, attended by two other
gentlemen, traversed the country during the whole of this
day. Though we had passed over not less than four-and-
twenty miles of very rugged ground, and had a Highland
dance on the top of Dun-Can, the highest mountain on the
island, we returned in the evening not at all fatigued, and
piqued ourselves at not being outdone at the nightly ball by
our less active friends who had remained at home.'

matter of particular courtesy, Johnson agreed to be circumspect.
Lord Auchinleck, says Boswell indulgently, 'had not much leisure
to be informed of Dr Johnson's great merits by reading his works,'
and was therefore imperfectly informed about the guest he had
kindly invited under his roof. Besides, Lord Auchinleck was
accustomed to being treated with due deference to 'his age, his

The Recovery, after a severe drunken frolic at
Corrichatachin.
'I awaked at noon, with a severe headache; I was much vexed
I should have been guilty of such a riot and afraid of a
reproof from Dr. Johnson. About one he came into my room
and accosted me, "What, drunk yet!"'

office, and his character' and did not suffer kindly any diminution
of the respect to which he had attained. In short, he did not take
well to a rival. Auchinleck's Whig and Presbyterian principles
were utterly at odds with Johnson's Tory and Church of England
convictions.

The literary distinctions of Dr Johnson had passed Lord
Auchinleck by, but he recognised a fellow enthusiast for Horace,
Anacreon and Greek Lyric poets, and Johnson was glad to see a
decent library. The first day Auchinleck passed in the company of
the 'Jacobite fellow,' as he had disparagingly referred to Johnson
when he had had occasion to speak of him in the past, was

Scottifying the Palate at Leith.
'I bought some speldings, fish salted and dried in a particular manner, being dipped in the sea and dried in the sun, and
eaten by the Scots by way of relish. He had never seen them,
though they are sold in London. I insisted on Scottifying his
palate, but he was very reluctant. With difficulty I prevailed
with him. He did not like it.'

congenial enough. On the second day, like the first, it rained
incessantly, thus confirming Johnson's sour view of Scottish
weather, and conversation was less easy. When asked perfectly
civilly how he had liked the Highlands, Johnson irritably replied,
'Who *can* like the Highlands? – I like the inhabitants very

well,' which abruptly terminated the polite inquisition. Lord Auchinleck spoke favourably of an author whom Johnson privately damned as a 'coxcomb'.

On the third day, the rain stopped. Johnson was rushed out to enjoy the 'romantick groves' of Auchinleck where Boswell felt most keenly the illustriousness of his ancestry. Johnson was treated to a lengthy genealogy of the Boswells, right back to that Thomas Boswell who had gloriously fallen with James IV at Flodden, and Boswell 'did not omit to mention what I was sure my friend would not think lightly of, my relation to the Royal Personage, whose liberality, on his accession to the throne, had given him comfort and independence.' Boswell, coyly, refers to the king who had granted Johnson a pension. Johnson was pleased to see some sizeable trees – he had the curious notion that there was scarcely a tree to be seen in the length and breadth of Scotland – but was less delighted by Boswell's fancy to erect a monument to his memory among the groves and 'scenes which, in my mind, were all classical.' Johnson could never bear to be reminded so directly of his mortality, and brushed aside Boswell's misguided pleasantry with the words, 'Sir, I hope to see your grand-children.'

On the fourth or fifth day, Boswell's memory is uncertain, Lord Auchinleck and Johnson were blamelessly inspecting a collection of medals, including a coin of Oliver Cromwell which unfortunately 'introduced Charles the First and Toryism.' The two elderly gentlemen became warm, they became hot, and soon they became violent. Boswell stood by, agonised, as Johnson and Lord Auchinleck fought to defend their principles and lost their considerable tempers. Boswell draws a hurried, apologetic curtain across the scene, opening it only to let out one chink of light and a puff of smoke from the roiling and moiling. 'Sir, I defy you to name one theological work of merit written by a Presbyterian minister in Scotland,' we may assume Johnson to have thundered. The challenge only momentarily flummoxed Auchinleck who snatched at a title he had once seen in a catalogue and flung it down with a bold air of knowing what he was talking about. 'Pray, sir, have you read Mr Durham's excellent commentary on the

Galatians?' 'No, sir,' said Johnson. Neither had Lord Auchinleck, but that did not stop him. Acknowledging a disadvantage did not stop Johnson. While Auchinleck was taking advantage of his temporary edge, and congratulating himself on having scored, Johnson came crashing back with a retort that made even Boswell close his eyes and ears in holy dread and forbear to mention in cold print. Though 'Whiggism and Presbyterianism, Toryism and Episcopacy, were terribly buffeted,' Boswell is able to record at least that Sir John Pringle, 'never having been mentioned, escaped without a bruise.'

Lord Auchinleck, like his daughter-in-law, decided that he'd been entertaining nothing less than a bear in brown clothes and a grey wig. He called him 'Ursa Major,' and is said to have dismissed the disputatious Doctor as 'a dominie, an auld dominie that kept a schule and ca'ad it an Academy!' But, with the grim politeness that was expected of him, Lord Auchinleck was coolly civil to Johnson over the next few days and with gentlemanly reserve and noble *politesse* attended his shambling, peering antagonist to the post-chaise that was to take him and James to Edinburgh, where they arrived on 9 November. There, the round of entertainment recommenced until Johnson, almost exhausted, protested, 'Sir, we have been harassed by invitations,' though he immediately added, 'but how much worse would it have been, if we had been neglected.' On 22 November, Johnson being in the mood 'to be again in the great theatre of life and animated exertion' set out for London, leaving Boswell flattered and perhaps just a little flat after one of the few wholly happy stretches of his life. 'Would you lose the recollection of this for five hundred pounds?' Johnson had asked him. 'Sir, I would not,' had been Boswell's sincere response. But nobody asked Peggie what she would have thought of five hundred pounds and the chance to have missed the Doctor.

[8]

The Hypochondriack

Johnson's departure left Peggie scraping at the candle wax which her guest had showered over her carpets, and Boswell 'long in a state of languor'. The Doctor's presence and demands had kept his mind and spirits constantly stretched and at a high pitch for three months. He had to recoup his energy, though the Winter Session of the Court of Session was now in progress and he was in demand as an advocate. Without having to work too hard to get it, he cleared 150 guineas and appeared several times for the defence in criminal trials. Immediately on return to London, Johnson began pressing ahead with his *Journey to the Western Islands* and harried Boswell with requests for information about Scottish life and customs which, earnestly and industriously attended to, occupied much of Boswell's time.

On 9 April Boswell learned of Oliver Goldsmith's death, which greatly shook him and prompted long letters to Bennet Langton and David Garrick, sympathising with the Literary Club and its particular members in their common loss. It was much in Boswell's mind that he would not be able to be in London for his usual spring visit. There were other unsettling matters buzzing in the Boswell brain: he found himself in opposition to his father on the subject of feudal principle which had been put in question by the choice of Sir Adam Fergusson as the candidate supported by a bloc of Ayrshire landholders for election to Parliament. It was a complicated political issue which Boswell felt to be a threat to 'the old families of the County' from *parvenus* who could not claim a lengthy, distinguished ancestry.

Lord Auchinleck promised his interest to Fergusson while

Boswell was agitating for the Auchinleck interest to be committed to the re-election of the noble David Kennedy, younger brother of the Earl of Cassillis, who was also championed by the Earls of Loudon and Eglinton. It was irrelevant, apparently, that Boswell only the year before had scornfully dismissed Kennedy as 'totally incapable of the business of legislation.' The principle was the thing at stake – the nobility, interests, and views of the aristocratic patrons should be maintained through their right and privilege to nominate and elect the candidate, no matter whether Fergusson might have the edge on Kennedy for ability to govern, or make a more competent contribution to the legislative process. Besides, Boswell himself cherished hopes that he himself might at some future date stand for election in the 'old interest' and with the approval of the 'noble association'. Lord Auchinleck's turnabout to support the upstart faction dismayed Boswell not only politically but personally. Auchinleck, through striking at principle, had struck indirectly at his son.

Temple wrote to reassure Boswell, 'Nothing but your own conduct can prevent your succession to the estate and influence of your family. But was ever anything so imprudent, so disrespectful, as to engage your interest without your father's approbation?' Boswell had rashly promised what he could not deliver. Lord Auchinleck was still the laird and had ceded none of his power to his heir. In truth, Boswell was hopelessly reactionary in his support of the feudal principle. Auchinleck was perhaps content to have an opportunity to slap down his son: he was simmering with rage about the ill-advisedness of Boswell's undistinguished marriage, about his improper jaunts to London, and his incomprehensible friendship with Johnson. That he had spent months 'going over Scotland with a *brute*' was the near-fatal straw: luckily he had not yet been apprised of Boswell's wish to set up a practice at the English bar and quit Scotland entirely to live wholly in London. An additional distraction was Peggie's pregnancy. On 20 May she bore him a second daughter, who was named Euphemia, after Boswell's mother.

The Journal from 14 June 1774 records social engagements and legal business and discussions. On 21 June Boswell confessed that, at supper at Sir George Preston's, he became 'outrageously intoxicated and *would* drink a great deal of strong port negus, which made me worse. After I got home, I was very ill; not sick, but like to suffocate – a dangerous state – and my wife was much alarmed.' The next day, he found it difficult to plead a cause distinctly in the Court of Session. A letter from Johnson on 25 June recalled to mind the felicity of London and Boswell found it hard that he should not be there. On 6 July after a period of pretty constant dining out, he decided, 'Social dinners and the practice of law are really incompatible. I must restrain myself from them.' But on 9 July he got thoroughly drunk after a riotous dinner with friends and the next morning 'was, as it were, half boiled with last night's debauch, and I was vexed to think of having given my valuable spouse so much uneasiness.' Peggie was so annoyed that she threatened not to give Boswell a letter that had arrived from Johnson, on the ground that the Doctor would not have written it, had he known what state Boswell would be in when it arrived. 'She thus made me think how shocking it was that a letter from Mr Samuel Johnson should find me drunk.'

On 22 July 'I drank near three bottles of hock . . . I got home about three in the morning.' He found Peggie sitting up waiting for him, but she could get no sense out of him and even the next morning Boswell was 'still quite giddy with liquor,' but contrived spiritedly and spiritously to conduct his legal business. It was not uncommon to be a three-bottle-a-day man in London or Edinburgh, and Boswell was at least in that league, and on 30 July he recorded that his 'head was inflamed and confused considerably.' He met his drinking companion of the previous evening, who was not much better. 'He had struggled to attend his business, but it would not do. Peter Murray told me he had seen him this morning come out of a dram-shop in the Back-Stairs, in all his formalities of large wig and cravat. He had been trying to settle his stomach. In some countries such an officer of the Crown as Solicitor-General being seen in such a state would be thought shocking. Such are our manners in Scotland that it is nothing at all.'

So far, Boswell took the example of himself and Henry

Dundas, the Solicitor-General, pretty much as the norm. The occasional self-disgust he felt at his failure to be *retenu* (though he had given up that particular piece of advice to himself) was not sufficient to alarm him or set himself seriously to be more moderate. The business of trying to get the sheep-stealer John Reid acquitted and comforting him in his agony on conviction was making Boswell anxious and, in the moments when he was not over-excited, depressed. On Sunday 18 September, Boswell awoke insensible of the events of the night before. 'It gave me much concern to be informed by my dear wife that I had been quite outrageous in my drunkenness the night before; that I had cursed her in a shocking manner and even thrown a candlestick with a lighted candle at her.' He was profoundly shocked. 'I considered that, since drinking has so violent an effect on me, there is no knowing what dreadful crime I may commit. I therefore most firmly resolved to be sober. I was very ill to-day.'

The Reid case, and all the others for which Boswell had pleaded, had taken its toll on his spirits. The civil causes for which he was engaged were given routine and competent attention, but a criminal trial and the human emotions and desperate circumstances of it fired his imagination; he threw himself into the defence with a zeal and a personal involvement that amounted almost to obsession. The narrow, dull ways of Edinburgh did not delight him, though from his Journal it would appear that he dined out, drank tea, disputed and drowned his drouth with cronies, and took advantage of such good society as the city had to offer. But he longed for London. A moment of calm was greatly to be savoured and treasured, but immediately the itch to be up and doing and going about was upon him it could not be resisted. He drank to alleviate his depression and to escape the claustrophobia that the stuffiness of provincialism caused him to feel, until the drinking became habitual and he formed a dependence on drink as upon a drug. Drink inflamed and excited his spirits artificially, since his need for excitement and stimulation could not be satisfied by other means. An alternative – though more often a companion – to drinking was gambling, and the frequency of late-night whist sessions increased, as did his gambling losses. He resolved to chance no more than a shilling a game.

Boswell had been in trouble before about incautious letters, paragraphs, and articles contributed to newspapers, magazines, or published as pamphlets and books. He had not only caused offence to others, but also had damaged his own reputation as a man to be respected and taken seriously. Boswell had published a paper anonymously, identifying himself only as 'A Royalist,' in the *London Chronicle*. It had, in the course of comment on the case of John Reid, cast a damaging aspersion on the Lord Justice-Clerk whose son had taken it much to heart as an insult to the honour of his father. He demanded an apology or the satisfaction of a duel. Boswell was confounded by the challenge, and Peggie went nearly off her head with panic. She counselled flight to a foreign country to avoid the fury of the offended nineteen-year-old boy.

Boswell consulted his own wavering resolution and decided, 'if it really should be necessary to fight, I could do it.' Lord Auchinleck would look after Peggie and the children should he fall honourably at the hands of the callow youth. To deny authorship would not, Boswell decided after taking advice, be merely dishonourable – there was a fair chance of being caught out in the lie. Peggie fainted. Boswell penned a suitable apology. The son of the Lord Justice-Clerk did not, ominously, reply. On taking further thought and counsel, Boswell comfortingly came to the conclusion that the quarrel properly lay between himself and the Lord Justice-Clerk who was less likely to take to arms than his hothead son, and that to fight the son would be as demeaning as to fight the Lord Justice-Clerk's footman.

It took the intervention of an uncle, after an alarming late-night banging on the Boswell door and an abrupt demand that Boswell should meet the lad, to explain that his nephew was 'a thinking, metaphysical fellow' prone to think himself always in the right and liable to bear grudges. The adolescent metaphysician and the portly advocate, weak with relief but putting on a faintly pompous air of rectitude, were induced to shake hands and to exchange easy words settling the matter. But the Boswells had had some bad moments. Domestic relations, when these alarms and

excursions were past, settled into a routine. Sexual relations between Boswell and his wife were, to judge by cryptic marks in
his journal, infrequent. On 5 March 1775 Peggie complained
that Boswell spoke only childish nonsense to her and was never
rational. Boswell admitted that he did adopt a tone of 'puerile
jocularity' partly attributable to indolence, partly 'because my
wife, though she has excellent sense and a cheerful temper, has
not sentiments congenial with mine. She has no superstition, no
enthusiasm, no vanity.'

Though Peggie was admittedly 'sensible, amiable, and all that I
could wish,' she was 'averse to hymeneal rites'. Boswell told her
frankly that he must have 'a concubine,' and Peggy sensibly and
amiably answered that Boswell might go to whom he pleased.
Though Boswell, since the beginning of March, had 'not insisted
on my conjugal privilege,' he was still unsure whether Peggie
really meant what she had said and, besides, the old question still
recurred: though 'our Saviour did not prohibit concubinage, yet
the strain of the New Testament seems to be against it.' Boswell
was inclined to interpret scripture liberally and reflected that the
Old Testament patriarchs contrived to be devout while trafficking
with harlots. But he was still unable to make himself easy about
resorting to prostitutes.

A week after having been given licence, more or less, by Peggie
to take to the privileges of promiscuity, Boswell was in London.
On the way, he visited his brother John at Newcastle where he
found him in a sorry state, quite deranged, fancying that he
sometimes saw ghosts and wishing to be reassured that James
himself was not merely a delusion visited upon him by God. 'I am
confined and have lost my senses, and I am surely dying,' said
John and cried a little. Boswell, with the tears streaming down his
cheeks, felt his heart melt with pity. He gave his brother three
shillings and some oranges, and dined with the physician in
charge of St Luke's House where John was cared for along with
others 'all pretty much disordered'.

At Doncaster, Boswell's mind was running in the usual rut of
reflection on the perplexing example of the pious but apparently
promiscuous patriarchs of the Old Testament, and the licence

given by Luther and Melancthon to the Elector of Hesse to have two wives simultaneously. He could not readily imagine the latter-day divines of Edinburgh granting such a dispensation for an elector of Ayrshire. Johnson greeted Boswell warmly on his arrival in London. Some of the novelty had worn off, and Boswell found himself more accustomed to being in London. He hobnobbed familiarly with the distinguished members of the Literary Club, took up old acquaintance with Paoli, and was rather disgusted to find that in his absence an interloping Scot, a 'coarse and noisy' man called Fordyce, had gained admittance to the Club. Boswell went about a good deal, drinking and dining and talking volubly though not always sensibly. He justified his nonsense as manure for the mind.

Now that his classical friend John Wilkes was more or less respectable as Lord Mayor of London, Boswell felt it was safe to know him again. Tucking little Mr Dilly in the crook of his arm, Boswell set out to pay his respects to his hospitable Lordship, so grand but still so gay and disrespectful. Now and again, Boswell got drunk, and at dinner with Sir John Pringle he mentioned his 'love of a dram,' remarking that 'people thought of a dram when I appeared as when a goose appears.' Boswell travelled from London to Mamhead, eight miles south of Exeter, to spend a week with Temple and his wife from 23 to 30 April. Here at his friend's instigation Boswell took an oath, under a venerable yew tree, that he would be sober: or, at least, took a pledge to drink no more than six glasses at a time. On return to London, filled with the most solemn resolve to behave with sobriety and discretion, he began to eat the necessary dinners at the Inner Temple. It was a first step towards admission to the English bar for the 34-year-old Boswell.

He was back in Edinburgh by the beginning of June 1775, and immediately jolted back to the depressing reality of 'the unpleasing tone, the rude familiarity, the barren conversation of those whom I found here, in comparison with what I had left.' He could not, by mid-August, 'remember any portion of my existence flatter than these two months . . . Dr Samuel Johnson being on a jaunt in different parts of England, I had not a single letter from

him during this Session; so that my mind wanted its great SUN
. . . My father's coldness to me, the unsettled state of our family
affairs, and the poor opinion which I had of the profession of a
lawyer in Scotland, which consumed my life in the mean time,
sunk my spirits woefully; and for some of the last weeks of the
session I was depressed with black melancholy.' Nevertheless,
Boswell worked dutifully and earned 118 guineas and one pound
in fees. He was attracted physically to a 'handsome gay widow,'
Mrs Grant of Ballindalloch, who revived youthful memories of
Boswell's associations with actresses; but after a while, like Mrs
Dodds, she talked in an ill-bred manner which disgusted Boswell
and caused him to become indifferent. He had more or less
persuaded himself that while he might permit himself to be
physically seduced by a woman other than his wife, his affections
should not be distracted from his family.

On 9 October, Peggy bore their first son, Alexander. He was
named after Lord Auchinleck, and Boswell 'indulged some
imaginations that he might perhaps be a great man.' It was
something to have produced a legitimate male heir at last. To
Temple, he wrote, 'You know, my dearest friend, of what importance this is to me; of what importance it is to the Family of
Auchinleck which, you may be well convinced, is my supreme
object in this world.' It was a thought, too, that Peggie's achievement might put her in better favour with Lord Auchinleck who
had been near-rudely offhand with her, and blamed her not only
for want of fortune but for failing to keep her husband under
marital control. Since she evidently could not provide all that
James desired at home, he was liable to go extravagantly to
London and consort with a brute who merely encouraged him
in wilful misconduct and filled his head with inappropriate
speculations.

A letter of 6 November to Temple is remarkable for one
observation: Boswell wrote, 'Dr Johnson has said nothing to me of
my *Remarks* during my journey with him, which I wish to write.
Shall I task myself to write so much of them a week, and send to
you for revisal? If I do not publish them now, they will be good
materials for my *Life of Dr Johnson*.' These 'Remarks' were

criticisms or amendments sent by Boswell to Johnson on publication of the *Journey to the Western Isles* in the hope that they
might be useful in the preparation of a second edition. Johnson
had permitted Boswell to write a 'Supplement' to his account of
the Scottish jaunt, but was reluctant that Boswell's observations
should be published with his own. By the close of 1775, however,
Boswell is evidently fired with the idea of writing Dr Johnson's
biography and, certainly, his Journals detailing his encounters
with Johnson are very ample.

During his visit to London in the spring, he had discovered that
the Thrale family was keeping a book of Johnsoniana 'in which all
Mr Johnson's sayings and all that they can collect about him is put
down.' Boswell's immediate reaction was to 'try to get this
Thralian miscellany, to assist me in writing Mr Johnson's life, if
Mrs Thrale does not intend to do it herself. I suppose there will be
many written.' However much he might not like to think so,
Johnson was a figure of immense public interest and not the
private property of James Boswell. On leaving London, Boswell
left his Hebrides Journal with Mrs Thrale, with the intention that
she should read it. His motives may have been mixed. He shared
with Mrs Thrale a deep love for Johnson, and she would genuinely be interested to read an account of Johnson's adventures. At
the same time, Boswell would prove, by an account of his intimacy
with their mutual friend, that his claims to Johnson's attention
were at least equal to her own. Thus generosity mingled with
jealousy, and, it may be assumed, some pride: Johnson's
friendship was something to be proud of, and to be able to give
evidence of that sincere mutual attachment was a bonus – Boswell
loved an audience that could be relied upon to applaud his
performances.

Boswell was already uneasily aware that Mrs Thrale and he
might be rivals not only as prospective biographers, jealously
guarding materials, but as competitors for Johnson's full attention. In mid-October, writing to Bennet Langton, Boswell with
apparent innocence refers to Johnson's excursion to Paris with
Mrs Thrale, taking care to say that he himself had frequently
wished Johnson would visit the Continent, and that Langton had

perhaps the best claim to have been Johnson's escort and to have profited from the jewels that would inevitably drop from the Johnsonian lips. Boswell goes on to remind Langton, not quite incidentally, that he had been instrumental in persuading Johnson to the Highlands so very recently. It is not a conscious dig at the pretensions of the Thrales – but it comes fairly close, as Boswell's subconscious alarm begins to ripple the surface of his complacent confidence in Johnson's undivided affection.

Unconscious as much as conscious anxieties may account for Boswell's bad temper in late 1775. He drank, bounced, fell into fits of rage, worked, worried, was promiscuous and penitent, gambled and groaned, and obsessively searched his mind and soul for some chink of light and logic that would illuminate and reconcile his inconsistencies. A promotion in May 1775 had disconcerted him: Henry Dundas, at the age of thirty-three, had been made Lord Advocate. Boswell himself was thirty-five, and could not 'help being angry and somewhat fretful.' That the preferment should have gone to a slightly younger man, one whom Boswell had mocked when he was younger and bouncier, one whom Boswell indeed still considered 'a coarse, unlettered, fanciful dog,' was shocking. The news is incomprehensible. Why is Harry Dundas so lucky? He is a Whig, a favourite of Lord Mansfield, which may partly account for the matter. Is it wrong, Boswell wails to Temple, to be resentful of the success Dundas enjoys? He does not go so far as to say that the appointment may have been made at the expense of some better man, but that is the clear inference. Meanwhile, Boswell still must mumble his dinners at the Inner Temple with other aspirants below the salt.

Boswell liked to be liked: to be a good fellow among good fellows. He could argue, interrogate, plead, and enjoy a triumph or bear with fortitude a defeat. But, in court as in social life, he was conscious of his dignity. It was sometimes impaired by drink – but a lapse of that nature among equally hard drinkers was no serious disgrace. Pranks in the press could do no serious harm: if they were sometimes incautious, they at least attracted attention and gave public fame to the name of Mr Boswell. Domestically, it was a different matter: there, on his feet or his knees, he could

Boswell, his wife Peggie and their children,
a family portrait by Henry Singleton

indulge a violence of temper and be sure of wifely forgiveness. In
public, there was a face to be maintained: in private, the mask of
precarious decorum could be dropped.

On 9 December, Peggie did not yield readily over some trifling
matter and Boswell's 'passion rose to a pitch that I could not quite
command. I started up and threw an egg in the fire and some beer
after it. My inclination was to break and destroy everything. But I
checked it.' He made up the quarrel with Peggie, but 'begged of

her to be more attentive again.' Peggie was getting used to sitting up anxiously all night waiting for Boswell to choose to come home after drinking and losing money at cards. He was usually in a sorry state when he did, and not only fell ill himself but caused his wife to take to her bed. She justly complained, and Boswell 'pacified her by sincere promises of future attention,' though he doubted how long such resolution might last. 'My good practice is never of sufficiently long continuance to have a stable consistency. It is shaken loose by occasional repetitions of licentiousness. The wounds of vice break out afresh.' The figure of speech is revealing: Boswell felt as though, like some venereal disease, he had contracted some moral infection that could hardly be cured but might merely lie dormant until it broke out to disorient him.

Between reneging on his oaths to Temple and Peggie, and falling into paroxysms of passion when he was liable, on one occasion at least, to throw the dining room chairs around the room, to beat about the house with a walking stick until it broke, or to throw a guinea note into the fire (though with presence of mind enough to retrieve it and later get its value from the Royal Bank), he was obliged to apply to Lord Auchinleck for aid in meeting debts amounting to £1300 – equivalent to £300 over and above a year's income from the estate of Auchinleck. Auchinleck's reaction was to threaten to reduce Boswell's allowance from the £300 per annum he had allowed him on marriage to £100, and to threaten to have the debt paid by a trustee whom Auchinleck would then immediately instruct to recover it from Boswell who, since he could have no hope of paying it, would therefore be thrown into prison. With considerable understatement, Boswell noted in his Journal, 'He was in a shocking humour today.' The depth of Lord Auchinleck's rage was fathomless. He was very serious in his intentions, and Boswell knew it. Mere anger might have led Auchinleck, on the spur of the moment, to threaten to proceed against Boswell personally for repayment of the debt, should he choose to take it over himself. But, conscious that such unpaternal behaviour might cause a scandal, he had taken time and thought to consider how best to humiliate Boswell and simultaneously protect himself from blame.

Boswell claims to have remained calm, and to have explained that he had tried to follow the course of life recommended by his father: it was disagreeable, but Boswell was, in his own opinion, succeeding better than might have been expected. Hanging between them had been the question of the entail of the estate on the heirs male. Something Boswell said suddenly made Lord Auchinleck fall into a fierce passion, 'I see you have been consulting lawyers,' he screamed, 'I will guard against you.' There was more. Diabolically, Lord Auchinleck threatened to sell off the estate entirely 'and do with the money what I please.' The interview concluded with imprecations being thrown at the heads of Johnson and Mountstuart, and Auchinleck spoke con-temptuously of Boswell's consorting with London *geniuses* who despised him merely.

'I was a good deal agitated inwardly,' confessed Boswell who nevertheless had attempted to keep cool. 'He appeared truly odious as an unjust and tyrannical man . . . It was an abominable altercation.' Boswell did not doubt that his father had the power and the will to do precisely as he had threatened. Auchinleck might seem to soften from time to time, but however easily Boswell might put the past behind him, convinced that the morrow would confirm his conversion to duty and virtue, Lord Auchinleck had forgotten and forgiven nothing and put no faith in promises when the example of the past spoke so firmly against the possibility of their being fulfilled. In the event, the quarrel rumbled on like stage thunder from the wings for some time without either father or son rushing to act impulsively. Lord Auchinleck would not: Boswell could not.

Boswell endured a period of gloom before setting out for London on 11 March. Life was not only depressing, it was getting to be quite dangerous. Having worked himself up to a pitch about a remark made by Henry Dundas which he had taken as an insult on his father's professional and judicial integrity, Boswell had written a letter which more or less amounted to a challenge, and the prospect of a duel between himself and the Lord Advocate was alarming. It did not come to that extreme, but Boswell had taken piteous leave of Peggie (who had doubtless fallen into a faint again), exclaiming, 'God grant we may meet in a better world.' Whether or not Peggie hoped for a world in which chairs stayed safely put under the dining table, and guinea notes were not liable to conflagration, we may not inquire. From London, Boswell accompanied Dr Johnson on a trip to Oxford and then to his birthplace at Lichfield. The conversation and the companions they met with are, as ever, comprehensively chronicled in the *Life*.

It is scarcely necessary to follow Boswell through the labyrinth of his habitual diversions in London – Paoli, Johnson, the Club, drink, drabs, dinners, and Dilly. To do so would be to act as an ant in pursuit of a blob of honey through the whorls and coils of a Nautilus shell. Once may be novel and entertaining, but after a while the weary ant should be able to find its own way through the labyrinth. The trip of spring 1776 was notable, however, for its *envoi*: Johnson, for some reason wishing to recommend himself to Peggie, enjoyed the satisfaction of relinquishing Boswell to her care by writing a letter thanking her for the loan, as it were, of her husband. 'You will now have Mr Boswell home; it is well that you have him; he has led a wild life . . . Pray take care of him and tame him; the only thing in which I have the honour to agree with you is in loving him.' It is just possible that Peggie's lips tightened perceptibly to repress the words 'dawmed impidence'. Boswell returned in the third week of May, having been away for near enough ten weeks.

In that time, he had contrived to introduce Johnson to Wilkes and to interview the glamorous adventuress Mrs Margaret Caroline Rudd. In the *Life* the scene of 15 May in which Wilkes solicitously fills Johnson's plate with veal and condiments is a masterpiece of dialogue and dramatic timing of which the interview with Princess Blair has given us a mere inkling of Boswell's genius for the miniature. On a broader canvas, it is of the greatest interest to follow the Doctor's seasons through dinner, from the dank spirit of winter through the faint warmth of spring giving way to the glow of summer and the ample, mellow fruitfulness of autumn into which, by the end of dinner, Johnson had contentedly sunk, basking in the glow of Wilkes's gay geniality. That devil Wilkes had adopted his near-Mephistophelean charm and ease of manner, coaxing along his great adversary with perfect skill, scholarly wit, gentlemanly relish, and exquisite nicety. Johnson unfolded, blossomed, and was enchanted. He and Wilkes cannot be said to have become friends, but they were ever after amiable towards one another. But Johnson knew when he was being set up. He had permitted Boswell to orchestrate with the most consummate diplomacy the evening with Wilkes: he would not go so far as to be persuaded into a meeting with Mrs Macaulay, the historian, no matter how ardently Boswell might desire to see the sparks fly. His function in life was not solely to gratify Boswell's unquenchable enthusiasm for novelty.

The day after the satisfactory dinner at Dilly's, Boswell met with Mrs Rudd who was not merely notable for having been the mistress of one, or both, of the brothers Perreau who were hanged for forgery, but for having conducted her own defence after having informed on her lovers. The jury had acquitted her after she had assured them that she felt safe in their hands, since they were honest men. And so she was, perfectly safe, being pathetic, beautiful, affecting and able. Boswell had composed a song in her honour, which of course he sang to her, and then enjoyed a lengthy and intimate conversation which was terminated when Boswell closed her pretty mouth by pressing several passionate kisses upon it. Boswell wrote a full account of his interview for Peggie, mentioning only one chaste kiss, but forbore to send it.

The return to humdrum routine affected Boswell much as he must have come to expect. The Court of Session began to sit on 12 June, and Boswell was obliged to be back at work. He wrote thrice to Johnson during the summer, and once to Mrs Thrale to solicit any Johnsonian scraps she might care to share. The year was marked by the death of David Hume which unsettled Boswell who had 'a strong curiosity to be satisfied if he [Hume] persisted in disbelieving a future state even when he had death before his eyes.' To Bennet Langton, Boswell wrote, 'I am sorry to say that I believe he persisted to the last in his wretched notions, and died in great tranquillity.' Hume's persistence in disbelief disturbed Boswell's own optimism about immortality. Meanwhile, he was romping with whores picked up in the streets and even, to

Peggie's mortification, with her young orphaned niece, Annie
Cunningham, who happened to be staying with the Boswells. But
the Old Testament patriarchs marched in licentious procession
across his mind, with their strumpets in tow, and his guilt was
faintly diminished.

A second son, David, was born on 15 November 1776, but
lived only until the end of March the next year. It was a blow, and
Boswell's gloom was punctuated by a number of funerals which
he attended more or less dramatically, on one occasion arriving
drunk and kissing a girl in full view of a congregation of Methodists. Boswell loved a pious and lachrymose funeral as much as a
good hanging – both affected him deeply and gave rise to
opportunity for morbid philosophy. But there were bursts of
euphoria, when the weather was fine, things fell into place, and
Boswell experienced the ideal state to which he aspired – 'that
philosophical calm, that *aisance du monde*' – but for which he
scarcely hoped. Relations with Auchinleck had somewhat improved, and the Boswells had moved to a new house on the south
side of The Meadows in Edinburgh. The Meadows is a stretch of
urban grass, a rather flat and uninteresting park. In Boswell's time
it was more pastoral, *rus in urbe*, and less densely surrounded by
dwellings. The house had a garden, but it did Peggie little good:
she was displaying the first symptoms of consumption. She saw no
good reason why her husband should wish to go jaunting and
leave his family, but on 10 September Boswell set off, having
invited himself to meet Dr Johnson at Ashbourne, fondling
women on the way and guiltily reflecting, 'How inconsistent is it
for me to be making a pilgrimage to meet Dr Johnson, and
licentiously loving wenches by the way.' Though Boswell berates
himself for having failed to pay his usual devoted attention to
noting Johnsoniana, he amply made up for the omission the next
year when, in March 1778, he returned to London to record what
have been called the 'Great Dialogues' that form the centrepiece
of the *Life*.

At Ashbourne, Boswell was on the wagon, more or less. He
continually had solicited Johnson's opinion of wine and women,
carefully posing his questions and eliciting the answers in a

generalised manner without specific references to his own pre-occupation and experience with both. In October 1777 he began to write a series of essays, published over the next six years in the *London Magazine*, under the appellation of 'The Hypochondriack'. To Boswell and his contemporaries, a hypochondriac was less a man beset by ailments, imaginary or actual, than a man afflicted with melancholy. 'The Hypochondriack' was an essayist who, though pursued and plagued, and laid low by morbidity of mind, was able now and again to extract some moral reflections from his interesting condition. The condition itself was a fruitful soil for the growth of philosophy and a heightened sensitivity. To describe oneself as 'hypochondriack' was at once to allow that one might fall from grace, but also to mitigate the consequences by claiming a more than usual delicacy of perception – at least, if the victim suffered, he could enjoy the satisfaction of analysing the causes and effects if not achieving the cure for his melancholy. Boswell's subjects are much as might be expected – *On Hypochon-dria, On Conscience, On Love, On Death, On Marriage, On Living in the Country, On Religion, On Dedications, On Disputation*, and a good deal *On Drinking*. The four essays *On Drinking* were published from March to June 1780, and may be assumed to reflect Boswell's attitude towards the subject fairly frankly, since he immediately admits his qualification to write upon the theme.

'I do fairly acknowledge that I love Drinking . . . and that if it were not for the restraints of reason and religion I am afraid I should be as constant a votary of Bacchus as any man . . . An Hypochondriack is under peculiar temptations to participate freely of wine. For the impatience of his temper under his sufferings which are sometimes almost intolerable, urges him to fly to what will give him immediate relief . . . or at least insensi-bility . . . Writing upon Drinking is in one respect, I think, like Drinking itself: one goes on imperceptibly without knowing where to stop;' and Boswell rambles on among the thickets of classical quotation and curious sociological and anthropological example, to make his apparently general but in fact particularly personal *apologia* for drink.

By the beginning of January 1778, Boswell was seriously

worried about Peggie's health: she was spitting blood and thought she was done for. He fussed over her, repented the injuries he had done her, prayed earnestly, and was 'in state of wildness'. The doctor, Sandy Wood, was grave about her tubercular condition, but towards the end of the month Peggie had rallied and Boswell wrote to Johnson on 26 February to thank him for the offer of his London apartments: he doubted if Peggie could be persuaded to visit London, since she disliked travelling, and Boswell thought she would prefer to go to the country in Scotland with the children. The newspapers of 27 and 28 February had published ominous reports that Johnson was critically ill and on the point of death. Boswell was seriously alarmed, but relieved that the intimations of imminent mortality had been much exaggerated: Johnson had had a cold. Nevertheless, Boswell paid an anxious visit to London in mid-March. Despite the affecting farewells his family had given him, and his anxiety about Peggie, he stayed until 19 May.

Boswell, before his trip, was drinking only water. It was difficult to stick to this new regime, but Johnson had been teetotal for years, and his example no doubt buoyed up Boswell's resolution. The trip to London this year was sober and generally respectable, and Boswell's clear head may have been responsible for the more than usually assiduous note-taking that recorded Johnson's conversational oratory, and that of the supporting chorus that surrounded him. He was staying with Paoli, and dining with Dilly: on 19 March he was shown 'a good portion of the *Life of Cowley* by Dr Johnson' which caused Boswell almost to faint with pleasure, as if he held in his hands a venerable relic. The felicity of Johnson in all his aspects was strongly borne in upon Boswell who discovered, 'I really *worshipped* him, not *idolatrously*, but with profound reverence, in the ancient Jewish sense of the word.' The next day, in Johnson's company, Boswell felt an inevitable deflation of his awe. 'I had a sort of regret that we were so easy. I missed that awful reverence with which I used to contemplate *Mr Samuel Johnson* in the complex magnitude of his literary, moral, and religious character. I have a wonderful superstitious love of *mystery*.'

The letter Boswell received from Johnson in July, after he had been two months in Edinburgh, may have rekindled a little of the holy dread with which he liked to season the great man. Boswell had been pestering Johnson for a flow of letters which he did not care to provide, on the ground that when he had something to say he would say it, and not before. Johnson did not prattle to fill the idle hour, and Boswell should not require constant reassurance that he enjoyed Johnson's affection and esteem. Softening a little, Johnson wrote, 'I have heard you mentioned as *a man whom everybody likes*. I think life has little more to give.' Boswell had been complaining that Edinburgh was narrow, but Johnson was impatient with Boswell's epicureanism. 'I wish you would a little correct or restrain your imagination, and imagine that happiness, such as life admits, may be had at other places as well as London . . . I do not blame your preference of London to other places, for it is really to be preferred, if the choice is free; but few have the choice of their place, or their manner of life; and mere pleasure ought not to be the prime motive of action.' Besides, Johnson has his own woes which, in a very short paragraph, he no more than relates. As a tart reminder to Boswell that others may occasionally be afflicted, it is worth more than an ampler account.

Peggie was again pregnant, and on 15 September 1778 she gave birth to a third son, James. Her pregnancy seemed to have coincided with a significant improvement in her health – though pregnancy is apt to distort the symptoms of tuberculosis – and Boswell was less worried on that score. By January 1779, he was taking a little wine and decided to fortify his spirits further by travelling to London in the spring. Relations with Auchinleck were mending, and altogether things seemed a little brighter. Even the death of Garrick, in early 1779, did not depress Boswell unduly. But during his visit to London, Boswell fell into thoroughly low spirits, exacerbated by an inflammation of his foot caused by an ingrowing toenail. Gratifyingly, however, he was visited by Johnson and Sir Joshua Reynolds to relieve his agony of flesh and spirit: they were better than an opiate. He returned, hobbling, to Edinburgh in early May and on 17 July, after bearing with hypochondria as best he could for two months, wrote piteously to Johnson.

He described his existence as 'a supine indolence of mind,' and complained of Johnson's neglect which Boswell admitted that he had tested by neglecting to write to Johnson. Johnson had been concerned at Boswell's unaccustomed silence, and had made enquiry of Mr Dilly before writing to Boswell to ask whether he was merely piqued or the victim of some awful disaster. Johnson was furious at having been duped by Boswell's test of his friendship, and condemned the experiment in his roundest and most economical tones. Boswell never dared try this trick again. Boswell was back in London in early October, having come down in the exciting military train of Colonel James Stuart who was on a recruiting tour, and returning to Edinburgh by way of Chester and Lichfield.

The autumn visit had cheered Boswell, and he promised Dr Johnson that he would attempt to bear Edinburgh and Ulubrae as best he could. Peggie was glad to have her wandering husband at home, and Boswell was looking forward to a winter of profitable legal activity. To Temple, in January 1780, he wrote, 'My mind is at present in a state of tranquillity, or rather good insensibility. I have neither elevation nor gayety; but I am easy.' Lord Auchinleck's health had given rise to concern – he had been 'seised with a fever,' his pulse had been dangerously high at 95, and fears had been entertained of his demise. Evidently his wife had been attentive, for he pulled through and was as much 'sadly influenced' by her as ever, to Boswell's impotent rage and dismay.

Boswell's finances were in dire straits. Peggie's nephews had drained his pockets to the tune of some £700 to £800, which Boswell had had to borrow at 5%, the debt being due for repayment in early February. There was no question of appealing successfully to Auchinleck's munificence: best to keep it quiet. It was simply impossible to consider a visit to London: there was no money to spare. Johnson bore with the news manfully, and counselled Boswell to be discreet about his depressions, since he regarded constant harping on the theme as an indication that Boswell really was fond of his melancholy. 'When you talk of them [mental diseases], it is plain that you want either praise or pity; for praise there is no room, and pity will do you no good; therefore, from this hour speak no more, think no more, about them.' There is a nub of truth in this. It can be alleged against Boswell that, though there may have been no help for his melancholy, he did make use of it. There is little doubt that he sensually wallowed in it, with no nobility of quiet endurance.

At some level of his consciousness, Boswell was perhaps convinced that his fits of gloom, his sensitivity and susceptibility to melancholy, made him interesting. The constant reassurance he needed from Johnson that he was valuable, and that people liked him, betrayed a profound insecurity against which depression was a shield. Nobody, after all, would care to kick a man when he was down. The early ailments that blackmailed his mother into tenderly caring for him disappeared in adolescence, but it can be no coincidence that they were replaced by depressive periods for the rest of his life. Amateur psychoanalysis is a blunt tool to explain Boswell's feelings of personal inadequacy, but it is important to point out, however perfunctorily, that Boswell's vanity, self-importance, near-alcoholism, melancholy, promiscuity, aspirations to political and legal eminence, and shaky self-esteem, are all part and parcel of a basic, deep-rooted insecurity that nothing could bolster for very long. It is in large part attributable to early parental influences, but a full consideration of Boswell's psyche must be left to the inquiries of the Freudians and a spirit of scientific inquiry which, unlike the moral judgements of Boswell's critics, will not lay blame upon him for his excesses. For the most part, we may simply take it that his sufferings were no less real for having been self-inflicted. He could no more resist them than the moth can resist the candle.

A third daughter was born to the Boswells in 1780, Elizabeth, who was generally known as Betsy. Boswell was in receipt of a parental allowance of £300 a year, and there were now five children and an appearance of gentility to be maintained. Boswell regretted his incautious opposition to Lord Auchinleck's second marriage, and had behaved with meritorious politeness lately to his stepmother – but Auchinleck still maintained an unrelenting coldness towards Peggie and as much chilliness towards his grandchildren as he had shown to their father. Boswell was setting his ambition in a political direction, as it seemed unlikely that he could expect preferment in the law. To Temple, he mumbled that advice to be content with promotion in Scotland was very wise, and that to expect to embark in a new sphere at the age of forty was not wholly advisable. 'Yet, my dear Temple, ambition to be in Parliament or in the metropolis is very allowable.' Pro and con, Edinburgh or London, Boswell dithered, presenting arguments equally convincing for either course, on the one hand . . . on the other hand . . .

We need not put ourselves to so much trouble as Boswell did to pursue the course of his attempt to be elected as candidate for a Parliamentary seat as the representative for Ayrshire. His hopes were based on the family fame of the Boswells as well-known, well-entrenched and well-respected in the county. However, the chosen candidate was a Major Hugh Montgomerie on whose behalf Boswell assiduously canvassed with an eye to establishing himself as the coming man in future elections. In the event, though Montgomerie was apparently elected as Tory Member of Parliament, his election was overturned on appeal to the Court of Session in favour of Adam Fergusson of Kilkerran whom Boswell had so much resented on an earlier occasion.

1780 marks, more or less, Boswell's attempts to gain some salaried public office – a stipendiary badge of respectability. He was about to discover who his real friends were and the fickleness of the promised interest of the great. His legal practice was falling off distressingly, which only added to the desirability of a regular income from the government. But his character, like that of the scorned blackguard and pimping dog Derrick's, caught up with him – he was well known as a flighty, indiscreet, gossiping, excessive man and, though a competent advocate, a man not steadily devoted to the delights of the law. He turned again and again to Mountstuart who promised much and then, vaguely, disappointingly, failed to deliver either the Clerkship to the Register of Sasines or one of the Commissaries of Edinburgh. Henry Dundas was also a broken reed. However much Boswell had resented and despised Dundas, there was no denying he was a power in the land and set fair to increase that influence. He assured Boswell that nobody wished him better than he did, but a hearty handshake was all Boswell got for his hopes. Good wishes were something to build an airy castle upon, but they were less substantial than required.

Boswell cast his net wide and high: Paoli was pressed to inform the King that Boswell would be pleased to serve near him; Lord Bute was solicited for the considerable pleasure of his agreeable company and the gratification of his great person – not, heaven forfend!, for any base desire to press the Boswell claim to political advancement. Even Edmund Burke, with whom Boswell had never been intimate and really only knew as a fellow-Club member, was importuned and he murmured, 'We must do something for you for our own sakes,' but did little but write Boswell a glowing letter of reference to General Conway who had places in his gift. But, nothing. To Charles James Fox, on 19 April 1782, Boswell wrote asking his interest to be deployed in Boswell's favour for the office of Judge Advocate of Scotland. Dempster's Parliamentary influence was invoked; Burke responded by referring to Conway, and to Boswell's dismay a Mr Mark Pringle was preferred to the plump, forty-ish advocate who so ardently reminded Burke of his detestation of the Ministry that the Rockingham administration had replaced. That Boswell had reservations about Rockingham's own policies was a matter best suppressed for the time being.

In the spring of 1781, Boswell managed to visit London to see Johnson and divert himself with his usual merry round. The visit had been prefaced by a letter from Boswell 'complaining of having been troubled by a recurrence of the perplexing question of Liberty and Necessity; and mentioning that I hoped soon to meet him [Johnson] again in London.' Johnson did not wait for Boswell's arrival to ask, 'What have you to do with Liberty and Necessity? Or what more than to hold your tongue about it? Do not doubt but I shall be most heartily glad to see you here again, for I love every part about you but your affectation of distress.' Boswell met him in Fleet Street, walking along in his distinctive fashion, 'with the constant roll of his head, and the concomitant motion of his body, he appeared to make his way by that motion, independent of his feet.' His gait was perhaps less confident now, since his health was failing and he was, after all, a man of seventy-two years. He now, occasionally, enjoyed a glass of wine with greedy relish. Boswell says of him, 'He could practise abstinence, but not temperance.'

Boswell by this time was again no abstainer from liquor, and had to be restrained, tactfully, by Johnson from making more of an ass of himself at dinner than he had begun to prove himself to be by refusing to be drawn on the subject of an improbable attachment between Boswell and the Duchess of Devonshire. Boswell had become loud and boisterous and had bounced expansively in the presence of the noble, stately, decorous Miss Monckton and her guests of exalted rank. Johnson could have been forgiven if he had imagined himself to be in charge of a romping puppy likely at any moment to disgrace himself and his master beyond any redemption or charming apology – which, in the form of an amusing poem, Boswell delivered the next day. Boswell, as ever, was generously and readily forgiven. On 5 June he set off for Edinburgh, well pleased by his visit.

The beginning of 1782 was difficult: during the first half of the year, Peggie showed unmistakable signs of being seriously consumptive, Lord Auchinleck was failing in health, Johnson wrote to mention (but not to complain about) his tottering health, and Boswell himself, in late June and early July, was laid low with influenza. The Boswells and Johnson recovered somewhat, but Lord Auchinleck succumbed on 30 August.

Boswell was now the Laird of Auchinleck, and Johnson, when he wrote to condole with Boswell was sensible enough not to express extravagant grief. 'Your father's death,' he wrote, 'had every circumstance that could enable you to bear it.'

The Laird of Ulubrae

The Master of Ulubrae, as he termed himself in a letter to Wilkes, was two months short of his forty-second birthday. He regretted the lack of affection between himself and his father who had died unreconciled to Boswell's imprudence and intemperance. He wept, but there was no occasion for inappropriately excessive grief. Johnson put it frankly when he wrote to describe Auchinleck as a kind, though not a fond father. Age had not softened the old autocrat's mind, morality or tyrannous temper. In a rather gossipy way, Johnson was avid to know how Lord Auchinleck had disposed of his fortune. In the event, a sense of feudal duty had triumphed over moral disgust and Boswell assumed the dignity of a Scotch landlord together with its responsibilities. Boswell's 'new station,' as Dr Johnson remarked, was attended with 'new cares and new employments'. Careful to curb Boswell's vanity, Johnson cautioned the new Laird to 'Begin your new course of life with the least show, and the least expence possible; you may at pleasure encrease both, but you cannot easily diminish them.'

He may have had in mind the grandiose views that had been published by The Hypochondriack in 1780. 'He who is master of land sees all around him obedient to his will, not only can he totally change the face of inanimate nature, but can command the animals of each species, and even the human race itself, to multiply or diminish, to continue or to migrate, according to his pleasure.' Had Boswell's prospective tenants read these baronial reflections on the Divine Right of Lairdship, they might reasonably have had cause for alarm. In practice, this self-appointed

agent of the Creator behaved admirably. As a landlord, Boswell
was kind, discreet, humanitarian and economical. He took his
lairdly duties too seriously to imperil the estate or the comfort of
the tenantry. He took time to acquaint himself thoroughly with
the management of the land: he learned as best he could about
forestry, the mysteries of his colliery, the advantages of liming the
soil, and took pains to become familiar with the particular
problems and personalities of his dependants. Towards those
genuinely in distress, he displayed a sincere and spontaneous
generosity. But the Laird was not to be taken advantage of – with a
nice discrimination, Boswell held firmly to his legal rights and
gave no quarter to mere malcontents. Aside from a faintly
pompous adherence to the custom of family prayers and the
demand to be addressed respectfully as 'Sir,' rather than the more
familiar 'Good Sir,' he was, in effect, the perfect patriarch.

The annual income of about £1600 per annum from the
estate was not sufficient to permit extravagance. The rents of
Auchinleck and the rewards of his profession were enough to
allow Boswell to live modestly with his family in town and country,
attending to his business as advocate and landlord, consolidating
a reputation as a liberal but prudent laird and a diligent man of the
law. It was an opportunity to settle to an ordered life, and the
chorus of advice was for Boswell to stay put and content himself
with his good fortune. Johnson, Peggie, and his brother David all
urged him to be responsible and discreet. Peggie went to an
extreme length to keep her husband at home: she herself wrote to
Johnson to invite him to Auchinleck.

Johnson was greatly moved by Peggie's readiness to accommodate him: he had not forgotten her dislike of him, and he wrote
back with gratitude, gracefully declining the invitation on the
ground of ill-health. Boswell therefore set off for London on 24
September, but was hurriedly recalled from the road to attend to
Peggie who had suffered 'a violent fit of spitting of blood'. A letter
from Johnson on 27 September urged Boswell to remain in
Scotland and it was not, therefore, until March 1783 that Boswell
was again in London. Johnson's 'wisdom was highly requisite'
and a consultation could not be longer postponed. Johnson was

with Mrs Thrale, in his own room in her house in Argyll Street. He was pale, had difficulty breathing, and confessed to being 'very ill'. But Boswell cheered him, and he was immediately full of good advice about enjoying the superiority of a country gentleman over his tenants. Boswell, not to be denied the pleasures of jaunts to town, countered with the observation that great proprietors of land preferred living in London, and Johnson was obliged to admit that something might be said for the intellectual superiority of London and diverted smartly into another topic of conversation.

Johnson was still capable of knocking Boswell down with a well-aimed blow – on the occasion of this visit, for his bumptious vanity: but Boswell records, almost in the same breath as he relates the knock, Johnson's spontaneously affectionate compliment, 'Boswell, I think I am easier with you than with almost everybody.' He might not have been so generous, had he been aware of Boswell's excursion into verse on the occasion, in the spring of 1781, of the death of Mrs Thrale's husband. He had composed an *Ode by Dr Johnson to Mrs Thrale, upon their Supposed Approaching Nuptials*, a parody of Johnson's own style. It was a disgraceful piece of verse, a defamatory and jealous squib, so ingenious that D. B. Wyndham Lewis suspects the involvement of Wilkes in its composition, and that Wilkes himself egged Boswell on in 1788 actually to publish the appalling piece of impertinence. However it was done, it was a satisfactory pie in the face for Mrs Thrale-Piozzi four years after Johnson had been safely dead.

Boswell left Johnson to return to Scotland on 30 May 1783, worried about the Doctor's precarious state of health. Soon afterwards, Johnson suffered a 'dreadful stroke of the palsy' which deprived him of speech and might soon, Johnson feared, 'deprive me soon of my senses'. He recovered somewhat, sufficiently to visit Bennet Langton at Rochester and a friend, William Bowles, at Salisbury. Boswell, back in Edinburgh, began to adjust his sights: he had hoped, in London, for support from Mountstuart in his ambition to gain a seat in Parliament. Mountstuart took the time to listen and advise, but took no trouble to give any practical assistance. Johnson, applied to for his seal of approval on the venture, doubted whether Boswell could afford financially to enter Parliament without attaching himself to the administration in power.

The Doctor's lack of enthusiasm did not dampen Boswell's desire to cut a significant political figure, and when Henry Dundas was dismissed as Lord Advocate, Boswell besought the support of Burke in an attempt to catch this plum job for himself or, at least, the post of Solicitor-General. By this time, too, Boswell was bored with being a landlord. 'Upon the whole,' he wrote in his Journal for 21 September, 'I led a life of wretched insignificance in my own estimation, though indeed it was perhaps no worse than that of many gentlemen of fortune. My valuable wife and agreeable children were constant objects of satisfaction. But my mental eye was often too dim or confused to relish them sufficiently. I began to despair of acquiring any knowledge in country affairs, and apprehended that my affairs would go into confusion.' Johnson's ill-health was a constant worry. 'I thought of his death with dreadful gloom. It appeared to me that if he were gone, I should find life quite vapid and myself quite at a loss what to do, or how to think.' On 12 November, to Boswell's great vexation, the Hon. Henry Erskine and a Mr Wight were respectively received as Lord Advocate and Solicitor-General.

On December 24, Johnson wrote to Boswell to say, 'Like all other men who have great friends, you begin to feel the pangs of neglected merit; and all the comfort I can give you is, by telling you that you have probably more pangs to feel, and more neglect to suffer.' He went on to advise Boswell, again, to 'wrap yourself up in your hereditary possessions, which, though less than you may wish, are more than you can want . . . content yourself with your station, without neglecting your profession. Your estate and the Courts will find you full employment; and your mind, well occupied, will be quiet.'

But the busy mind of Mr Boswell was already preparing its next diversion: the writing, printing and publication, on 31 December 1783, of *A Letter to the People of Scotland on the Present State of the*

Nation. It was a competent piece of work, aimed less at the people of Scotland than their rulers in London. It argued against the East India Bill of Fox, which had been defeated in the Commons and was well received by Pitt who, through Dundas, had preferment in his gift for up and coming zealous and loyal Scotch lawyers. Johnson thought Boswell's pamphlet a creditable performance, neat in its knowledge of history and the Constitution. 'It will certainly raise your character, though perhaps it may not make you a Minister of State.' Boswell was puffed up with Pitt's praise and took a more sanguine view of fulfilling his ambitions than Johnson did: Boswell's euphoric confidence was not dented, his political agitations continued to rally support and effusions of loyalty for the King and monarchical privileges. In an address to the freeholders of Ayrshire, he described himself roundly as a Royalist and, a little more *sotto voce*, as 'animated with genuine feelings of liberty.' He curried favour with the powerful Henry Dundas, in effect Pitt's major-domo in Scotland, and eulogised him in verse.

On 5 May 1784, Boswell was in London. He found Johnson 'greatly recovered'. He brought news from doctors whom Johnson had urged him to consult in Scotland about his case, and 'so far as they were encouraging, communicated to Johnson.' He accompanied Johnson to Oxford, where he attempted to get Johnson's blessing on 'the subject of my trying my fortune at the English bar,' but Johnson had a good deal to say in general and 'nothing particular to say to you on the subject.' Johnson, on more than one occasion, had been morbid. He felt the approach of death, and the thought occurred to him that a sojourn in Italy might help to postpone the inevitable, however briefly. On 24 June, Boswell wrote to Lord Thurlow to enlist his aid in suggesting to the King that 'the royal bounty would be extended in a suitable manner' if it were applied to defraying the expenses of a winter in Italy where Johnson might enjoy 'the benignant influence of a southern climate'. Johnson was so tenderly touched by this attention to his interests that he was moved to tears, so much so that he was obliged to leave the room. With delight, later, he discussed the prospective journey to Italy: but the royal purse remained closed, and pride would not allow Johnson to accept even an advance against his pension from friends eager to relieve his disappointment.

On 30 June 1784, he and Boswell took leave of one another. 'I accompanied him in Sir Joshua Reynolds's coach,' writes Boswell in the *Life*, 'to the entry of Bolt-court. He asked me whether I would not go in with him to his house; I declined it, from an apprehension that my spirits would sink. We bade adieu to each other affectionately in the carriage. When he had got down upon the foot-pavement, he called out, "Fare you well;" and without looking back, sprung away with a kind of pathetick briskness, if I may use that expression, which seemed to indicate a struggle to conceal uneasiness, and impressed me with a foreboding of our long, long separation.' That last little leap, that brave little show of pulling himself together, was the last Boswell saw of Johnson. Six months later, in December 1784, the Doctor was dead.

In the six months remaining to his friendship with Johnson, Boswell contrived at last, in September, to get Johnson's sanction for the plan to leave Scotland and make a career at the English bar. 'The condition on which you have my consent to settle in London is,' wrote Johnson, 'that your expence never exceeds your annual income. Fixing this basis of security, you cannot be hurt, and you may be very much advanced. The loss of your Scottish business, which is all that you can lose, is not to be reckoned as any equivalent to the hopes and possibilities that open here upon you. If you succeed, the question of prudence is at an end.' In the *Life*, Boswell pleads, as the cause of his failure to write regularly to Johnson, indisposition and a desire not to express 'such complaints as offended him'. Johnson, in his last letter to Boswell, complained on 3 November of neglect. 'Are you sick, or are you sullen?'

Boswell was at least preoccupied: in July, in a letter to Temple, Boswell wrote of his resolution to 'try my fortune at the English bar' and detailed his anxieties. 'The difficulties are to keep the family seat in good repair, to be once a year there for some months with my family, the travelling expenses amounting to £120 annually, to get my debts kept quiet and gradually cleared off. To restrain my eagerness for variety of scenes, to conduct myself with prudence. But strict economy will, I trust, do a great deal, and a determined attendance on Westminster Hall, and a course of study and practice of the English law will give me a desirable steadiness.' Boswell, somewhat mysteriously, follows up this flight of fancy with the phrase, 'My retreat to the bench in Scotland will, I trust, be secured.' On 4 June, Boswell had had an audience with the King and 'talked over my scheme fairly . . . His Majesty was graciously pleased to listen to me, and talked of it afterwards to the Lord in Waiting. I think my pretensions to employment as a lawyer of fifteen years' good practice in Scotland in all questions of the law of that country should be strong.'

This can only mean, on a *prima facie* interpretation, that in early June Boswell had not given up hope – indeed was actively canvassing – for judicial office in Scotland. It is certain that he could not be appointed, as a member of the English bar, to the bench of the Court of Session. Boswell may have been hedging his bets.

By 20 July, Boswell was in low spirits. Despite the encouragement of Johnson and his own optimism, 'I have been harassed by the arguments of relations and friends against my animated scheme of going to the English bar. I have lost all heart for it. My happiness when last in London seems a delirium . . . I have at that time thought of English law as of an *end* without perceiving the *means*; for upon endeavouring to acquire it I perceive myself incapable of the task, at least I imagine so. Then upon making out a State of My Affairs I find my debts amount to so large a sum that the interest of them and a moderate annual appropriation of rents for a sinking-fund will leave me no more than what will maintain my family in Scotland, but would by no means support it in London unless I could submit to live in penurious privacy, which my wife with her admirable good sense observes would deprive me of all the felicity which London now yields me.'

There is more. 'When I go thither at present as a gentleman of fortune I am on a footing with the first people, easy, independent, gay. But were I settled as a man of business, labouring uphill and anxious for practice, my situation would be quite different. Add to all this, the weakness of her [Peggie's] lungs renders her very unfit to live in the smoke of London. Last night she had a return of spitting of blood. In short, my friend, I tell you *in confidence* I am *satisfied* that my airy scheme will not do. And moreover, that if I cannot obtain an office from His Majesty, I must drag on a life of difficulties.' The letter concludes with a moan, 'But alas! what is to become of my ambition? What of my love of England, where I am *absolutely certain* that I enjoy life, whereas *here* it is *insipid*, nay, *disgusting*. . . . May I not get into Parliament for a few sessions?' A postscript, dated 22 July, is typical of Boswell's sharp ups and downs: 'I am rather better and my scheme revives. Oh, would but *rex meus* patronize me!'

On 9 December, Lord Rockville, a judge of the Court of Session, advised Boswell's wife 'that my jocularity was against me in my claim for a judge's place, as also my openly declaring my antipathies to many people. He was very desirous I should have a more sedate behaviour.' Peggie had written to Henry Dundas on the subject of her husband's intention to settle in London, and on 12 December Dundas invited Boswell to breakfast with him. He spoke approvingly of Boswell's notion of settling in London, but 'he took it for granted I had £1000 or £1200 a year to spend . . . But as I had now informed him I had not above £500 a year to spend, his opinion was different.' Dundas promised to talk with Pitt, with the Attorney-General, and with the Chancellor, Lord Thurlow, 'and see whether I could get an office of some hundreds a year, or could be assured of immediate practice; either of which was indispensably necessary to make my settling in London rational.'

Peggie was sceptical: she 'thought all this might be artful, to keep me off from interfering with his numerous claimants of a seat on the bench.' But Boswell did not doubt that Dundas was sincere in his offer of aid. Peggie was right not to place her faith in princes: Dundas did nothing. In this frame of mind, now buoyed up, now cast down, Boswell was devastated on 17 December to hear of the death of Johnson. For the moment, he was paralysed and went through the motions of daily life 'stunned, and in a kind of amaze . . . I did not shed tears. I was not tenderly affected. My feeling was just one large expanse of stupor. I know that I should afterwards have sorer sensations.' Despite an immediate resolution to respect Johnson's memory by 'doing as much as I could to fulfil his noble precepts of religion and morality,' Boswell was instead rendered insensible of 'spiritual feeling' and indifferent 'to the awful subject of religion.'

On 18 December, Dilly wrote to mention Johnson's death; 'in the true spirit of the trade' urging Boswell to supply an octavo volume of 400 pages of Johnson's conversations by February. Boswell wrote back to refuse the commission, saying that he had 'a large collection of materials for his life, but would write it deliberately.' The fact of Johnson's death had registered in Boswell's mind, but even by the time Johnson's will was published on 23–25 and 26 December in the London newspapers, he was not emotionally convinced that the event had occurred. He noticed that his name did not appear as a beneficiary in the will, but he comforted himself with the thought that he had had books from Johnson in his lifetime, and later noticed that other intimate friends had not been mentioned. On the night of 5 and 6 February, Boswell dreamed of Johnson and was powerfully and happily affected that the dream seemed to imply that he had not, at the last, been forgotten by his old friend.

On 20 March, at Auchinleck, Boswell sat down to write to the Right Reverend Thomas Percy, with whom he had long been in correspondence, to reflect upon the death of Johnson. 'I certainly need not enlarge on the shock it gave my mind. I do not expect to recover from it. I mean, I do not expect that I can ever in this world have so mighty a loss supplied. I gaze after him with an eager eye; and I hope again to be with him.' The work of making a memorial to his memory has begun. 'It is a great consolation to me now, that I was so assiduous in collecting the wisdom and wit of that wonderful man. It is long since I resolved to write his life – I may say, his life and conversation. He was well informed of my intention, and communicated to me a thousand particulars from his earliest years upwards to that dignified intellectual state in which we have beheld him with awe and admiration.' Percy is begged to provide some Johnsoniana.

But, first, Boswell intends to publish, at last, his *Journal of a Tour to the Hebrides*. In order to prepare the book for publication, Boswell arrived in London on 30 March 1785. Here, in addition to finishing writing the *Tour*, he was busy scribbling another pamphlet to follow up his first *Letter to the People of Scotland* of 1784. This *Letter* inveighed against the proposed reduction of the number of judges of the Court of Session from fifteen to ten, and the consequent increase in salary for the remaining lordships. In this *Letter*, Boswell laid into Dundas, dwelt upon the personal grievance Boswell held against that grandee, extolled Boswell's own grandeur of lineage, and frankly admitted his own vaunting ambition. It was a ludicrous, crackpot performance that effectively wrecked any remaining prospect of public office.

On 13 May, Boswell was 'shocked and pleased' to witness the ascent heavenwards of the celebrated aerialist Monsieur Vincent Lunardi, whose balloon took off from the grounds of Bethlehem Hospital. Later, Boswell took an opportunity to sing with the inmates of Bedlam, and at night he got drunk. He found himself in St Paul's Churchyard where he sang ballads with two women in red cloaks, had his pocket picked, fell down, and was assisted home by a couple of worthy fellows. The Lunardi experiment, though not the rest, formed a convenient topic of regal conversation on 20 May when Mr Boswell presented himself at Court, dressed in a scarlet suit and looking baronial. The King, having exhausted aerial topics, was graciously pleased to inquire how Mr Boswell's account of his friend Johnson was going on. Eagerly, Boswell replied, '"Sir, I am going first to give my *log-book*, my journal kept *de die in diem* of the curious journey which Dr Johnson and I made through a remote part of *Your Majesty's dominions*, our Highlands and Islands," (thus connecting them with the King – throwing them into his bosom).'

'It will be more a journal of Dr Johnson than of what I saw,' added Boswell, promising a copy of the book to the King who, fortified by this burst of generosity, nodded and asked, 'But when are we to have your other work?' [meaning the *Life*]. Boswell had his answer ready. 'Sir, Your Majesty a little ago remarked that people were sometimes in too great a hurry before they had collected facts. I mean to avoid that fault, and shall take time, as I intend to give a very full account of Dr Johnson.' 'There will be many before you,' remarked the King. 'There will be many foolish lives first. Do you make the best.' Boswell promised to do as well as he could.

Immensely gratified by this expression of the royal regard and confidence, Boswell addressed a letter to George III enquiring, with the utmost delicacy, what might be His Majesty's pleasure in the matter of the references in the *Tour* to 'that person who in 1745–46 attempted to recover the throne upon which his ancestors sat.' Declaring his allegiance to the present occupant and denying the validity of any Stuart claim to replace the Hanoverian bottom with that of Charles Edward Stuart, Boswell requested guidance as to whether 'Prince Charles' or the more insulting 'Pretender' might be the preferred appellation. There was, in all conscience, no need for this letter, except that it kept Mr Boswell as a loyal subject prominently before the popping blue eyes of the King.

On 15 June, Boswell gained his reward: at a royal levee, the King 'contrived to get himself and me so much aside that nobody could hear us,' and the King declared frankly that he had never before been questioned on the designation of Charles Edward Stuart and, what did Mr Boswell think? 'How do you feel yourself?' Mr Boswell, reading all manner of subtle implications into the question, was fairly taken aback. He bowed, and enigmatically replied, 'That, Sir, I have already stated in writing to Your Majesty.' Possibly unable to recall for the moment exactly what Mr Boswell had written, His Majesty parried by leaning a little forward and, giving 'a benignant smile equal to that of any of Correggio's angels,' said, 'I think and I feel as you do.' 'Then, Sir, I may do as I have proposed?' asked Boswell who had just marginally favoured one suggestion over another but had, in fact, plumped for neither one nor the other. The King, not to be bested, now asked, 'But what designation do you mean to give?' 'Why, Sir, "Prince Charles" I think is the common expression.' A slight hesitation or faint expression of disapproval on the royal countenance moved Boswell to think fast. 'Or shall it be "the

grandson of King James the Second"?' 'Yes,' declared His
Majesty, adding 'I do not think it a matter of consequence to my
family how they are called.' This grand dismissal of the entire
question of the right of the Stuarts to the throne moved Boswell to
confess what he had probably been longing to impart from the
beginning. 'Sir, allow me to inform you that I am his cousin in the
seventh degree.' The intelligence of such a remote Jacobite
connection caused no terror in the royal bosom and the pleasant
little *tête à tête* was terminated with the utmost goodwill on both
sides.

With the editorial assistance of Edmond Malone, Boswell
continued throughout the summer to write and revise the manuscript of the *Tour*, and finished it on 8 September. He made some
additions thereafter, but finally the book was published on 1
October to considerable acclaim. The first edition of 1500 copies
sold out in just over a fortnight, it was serialised in magazines and
newspapers, lengthily reviewed, and by the end of the year two
more editions were printed. Reviewers found some fault with the
book – notably, Boswell's egregious self-advertisement, his continuous popping up between the reader and Johnson, and his
insistent detailing of the most minor matters. The book was
treated, too, as an appetite-whetter for the larger, comprehensive
Life of Johnson which was expected from Boswell, and which was
impatiently awaited.

Meanwhile, Boswell had been planning his removal to
London. On 7 June, he had written to Sir Joshua Reynolds who,
now that Johnson was dead, became almost a substitute for the
Doctor. Boswell frankly acknowledged his debts which, 'contracted in my father's lifetime will not be cleared off by me for
some years,' and despite a reluctance 'to indulge in any expensive
article of elegant luxury,' bespoke a portrait of himself to be paid
for out of 'the first fees which I receive as a barrister in Westminster Hall,' or, failing that, within five years. It was a matter of
sure certainty in Boswell's mind that he would be called to the
English bar in February 1786, although the general feeling
among family and friends was firmly against any such move.

But on 27 January 1786 Boswell departed for London, and on

13 February he was called to the English bar where immediately he felt ambition swell in the familiar manner: he 'did not despair of yet being a Judge' of the King's Bench. His 'mind was firm and serene, and my imagination bright.' Little or nothing need be said about Boswell's career as a barrister. His practice in Scotland, as an advocate, had been dwindling: his practice in England was non-existent save for a single brief and, on Malone's advice, an optimistic but ultimately fruitless tour of the Northern circuit to York and Lancaster in the spring of 1786. It is tempting to give more detailed consideration to Boswell's political activities and aspirations, for the light they shed upon his character: but they are largely irrelevant in terms of achievement.

On 12 July, Boswell's hopes of success at the English bar were wavering. To Thomas Percy, he wrote, 'How long I shall continue will depend upon circumstances.' Peggie and the children were in Scotland, and he missed them sorely. With the distracted mind of a man who has made a fatal misstep, Boswell on one occasion at least wandered the streets of London with tears of frustration and loneliness streaming down his face. Paoli attempted to cheer him by counselling him to abandon ambition and to settle to middle age and to enjoy the advantages that remained to him. But Boswell could not admit defeat: he had an indefatigable optimism that the next day would be better, or that he himself would be better able to seize its opportunities. He took a house in Great Queen Street to prepare for the advent of his wife and children. It was not ideal, but for the moment it would do.

At this point, James Lowther, Earl of Lonsdale, invited Boswell to dinner. Immediately a vision of what the future might hold under the flattering interest of Lonsdale ignited Boswell's imagination and spirits. He fairly bounced, 'The great Lowther has taken me up! I may be raised to eminence in the State!' Boswell, according to social etiquette, could not accept the summons to dinner since he and Lonsdale had not met, but the implication was clear: Mr Boswell's pamphleteering had attracted the eagle eye of an agent wielding considerable political power. Boswell had paid passing tribute to the Lowther family in the *Tour*, and that may also have helped. The memory of the Earl of Lonsdale is not notably adorned with even modest tributes to generosity of pocket, heart or spirit. Even his contemporaries took care, when they could, to steer clear of the man Alexander Carlyle characterised as 'a shameless political sharper, a domestic bashaw, and an intolerable tyrant over his tenants and dependants.'

This man of ambition, wholly without scruple, lordly owner of great estates and princely wielder of influence in the north-west of England, had cast his glamour over the bedazzled Boswell who, if he had been less desperate, might have been a little more cautious. Still, Lonsdale had more or less launched Pitt – what could he not do for a Boswell? In a flush of excitement, Boswell bustled Peggie and the children from Auchinleck on 20 September and bundled them into two postchaises which arrived in London five days later. In late November, the formal summons to meet Lonsdale at Grosvenor Square arrived. In a flurry, Boswell took himself off, panting for preferment. Lonsdale had in his pocket a minor appointment, the Recordership of Carlisle. Perhaps to test Boswell, Lonsdale declined to meet him personally on this occasion, instructing him through his agent, Mr Garforth, to employ himself as Mayor's Counsel during the Carlisle elections which Lonsdale was directing more or less as a matter of mere form. Boswell sped to Carlisle, performed his duties adequately, and after the week's activities, returned for his reward.

The experience had been a premonitory foretaste of what Boswell might expect as Lonsdale's lackey: Boswell found himself defending the right of the borough Corporation to make honorary freemen, as many as they liked, to create an electorate ostensibly with the right to vote freely – but, in reality, to get Lonsdale's man into Parliament. Boswell had repeatedly attacked this practice in Ayrshire, and though he had some qualms about turning devil's advocate on this occasion, did so 'with animation and force'. In December 1787, Boswell was given the Recordership of Carlisle, a post he had earned, and a first step on the road to becoming a Member of Parliament. It was also, as Boswell fully realised, a step down a corrupt path. Boswell had already tempted fate so many times, convinced of his capacity to remain personally unsullied by sordid means to a virtuous end, that he accepted the post. But he was not wholly innocent of the danger to which he exposed himself as a lamb lying down with the Lowther lion. Lonsdale's power was immense: it is almost impossible to comprehend it today. He was a northern Nabob of awesome proportions and Boswell took his lowly place at a court in which, for a while, he displayed all the reflected glory of his master.

Increasingly, however, Boswell was becoming uneasy. The Member of Parliament for Ayrshire, Colonel Hugh Montgomerie, gained an appointment as Inspector for Roads in North Britain in June 1789, and Boswell hoped that by supporting the new candidate in the by-election he would drum up support for his own candidacy in the following election. His candidate failed to be elected, and Boswell was obliged to subside back into the thrall of Lonsdale. The Recordership involved legal duties as the principal legal officer of Carlisle and judicial duties as the sole judge of civil and criminal cases at the Carlisle quarterly sessions. The salary was £20 per annum, and the Recorder was able to live in London when duty did not require his presence in Carlisle. Boswell, for the moment, contented himself with his lot: in February 1788, a month after he had been appointed, Boswell wrote to Thomas Percy to say that 'Lord Lonsdale's recommending me to that office [the Recordership] was an honourable proof of his Lordship's regard for me, and I may hope that this may lead to future promotion. I have indeed no claim upon his Lordship; but I shall endeavour to deserve his countenance.' The Sun King, Louis XIV, could have asked no more of a minion. The Bishop of Kilaloe, with whom Boswell was on cordial terms, wrote on 28 February 1788 to congratulate Boswell on his appointment, mentioning that he had 'always heard that His Lordship is very generous *where he Likes*: And though perhaps he may not be the very first Man one would chuse for a Patron, he is no bad one as Times go.'

Peggie had not taken kindly to London. She was suffering the final stages of tuberculosis, and Boswell clung to the hope offered by her occasional rallies. To Temple, in February 1788, he wrote, 'My wife is, I thank God, much better; but is it not cruel to keep her in this pernicious air, when she might be so much better at Auchinleck?' Peggie was a woman imbued with the Scotch scorn for idleness and vacillation: she knew where her own, and her husband's duty lay; and it was not in London scribbling at a book or toadying to the likes of Lonsdale: there would be no good got out of him, we may be sure was her opinion, as there had been no good to be had from Dundas or Mountstuart or Pitt or Bute or any other coat-tail to which Boswell had attached himself. It did her no good, either, to see her husband relieving his distress in drink, or dining with his fancy friends. They had it out with one another in February, and whatever may have been said, Peggie returned to Auchinleck with her three daughters on 15 May 1788.

Despite considerable efforts and patience, Boswell was making no impact and no inroads on Westminster Hall. He was almost discouraged, but ever at the back of his brain, bobbing up and down, were visions of future glory: it was all very well to be 'Baron of Auchinleck, with a good income for a gentleman in Scotland,' but the fever of ambition still raged in his veins. 'In the country I should sink into wretched gloom, or at best into listless dullness and sordid abstraction.' Peggie, unaccountably, was wholly at ease in the country, 'The country air, asses' milk, the little amusements of ordering about her family, gentle exercise, and the comfort of being at home amongst old and valuable friends, had,' Boswell reported to Edmond Malone in July 1788, 'a very benignant effect upon her.' Boswell was still anxious about her health, but though 'I sometimes upbraid myself for leaving her . . . tenderness should yield to the active engagements of ambitious exercise.'

However it was done, Peggie had been induced, by January 1789, to attempt to live again in London. The best house Boswell could find was a small lodging in Queen Anne Street, at a rent of £50 a year, that would 'serve as a sort of camp lodging till better could be had.' The financial and domestic situation was parlous: the house could not accommodate all the family, and what little Boswell had managed to pick up of 'the *forms*, the *quirks and the quiddities*' of English law would not stand the test of a Westminster Hall trial. But still Boswell is floating along, 'driven along the tide of life, with a good deal of caution not to be much hurt, and still flattering myself that an unexpectedly lucky chance may at last place me so that the prediction by a *fortunate* cap appearing on my head at my birth will be fulfilled.' Boswell was constantly convinced that, one way or another, he was marked for greatness.

In February 1789, Peggie had suffered a recurrence of 'her asthmatick fever', so never came to London. By 5 March, when he wrote to Temple, Boswell was frantic with worry about his wife's health. He had resolved to set out for Auchinleck, but had been eased in his mind slightly by a letter from Peggie and another from his daughter, Veronica. A visit to Auchinleck would be a distraction from work on the *Life of Johnson*, though by 10 March further reports were alarming: Peggie's legs had swelled, she sweated copiously, and coughed severely. These were not new symptoms, but each relapse made her condition more parlous. Boswell resolved to go to Auchinleck, should Peggie be in immediate danger but, as he remarked to Temple, 'as London is the best place when one is happy, it is equally so when one is the reverse.'

Peggie herself bade Boswell not to hasten to leave London, though 'I should have a heart as hard as stone were I to remain here; and should the fatal event happen in my absence, I should have a just upbraiding gloom upon my mind for the rest of my life.' He decided to set out for Auchinleck on 1 April. Peggie, when he got to her bedside, was 'miserably emaciated and weak'. The doctors gave no hope of her recovery, though they could not with confidence say how long she might live. Short carriage rides afforded her some relief by distracting her attention from her illness, but Boswell himself was prey to remorseful memories of a 'thousand instances of *inconsistent* conduct' which had plagued Peggy and distressed her during her married life. 'I can justify my removing to the great sphere of England, upon a principle of laudable ambition. But the frequent scenes of what I must call *dissolute* conduct are inexcuseable. Often and often when she was very ill in London have I been indulging in festivity with Sir Joshua Reynolds, Courtenay, Malone, &c. &c. &c., and have come home late, and disturbed her repose. Nay, when I was last in

Auchinleck on purpose to soothe and console her, I repeatedly
went from home and both on those occasions, and when neighbours visited me, drank a great deal too much wine.'

In mid-May, when all these anxieties and recriminations were
crowding his brain, Boswell was summoned from Auchinleck by
Lonsdale to accompany him to London. Boswell was in a considerable dilemma: whether to offend Peggie by leaving her, or to
offend Lonsdale by refusing to go. Peggie generously gave
Boswell leave to tag along with Lonsdale, and though Lonsdale
made Boswell await his lordly pleasure by delaying the journey for
a few days, Boswell finally scrambled into the carriage and was
immediately powerfully reanimated by the glamour of Lonsdale's
'great Parliamentary influence' which was such that, 'be the
minister who will, he may, when he pleases, get almost anything
for a friend. I have no right to expect that he will give me a seat in
Parliament, but I shall not be surprised if he does.' Boswell feared
that he had not only lost the support of Dundas, who had been
notably avoiding him, but that Pitt had actively been prejudiced
against him. Lonsdale was the only card left in the pack, and even
his value was not wholly certain.

Boswell's state was pitiful, 'full of ambition and projects to
attain wealth and eminence, yet embarrassed in my circumstances
and depressed with family distress.' On 4 June, Peggie died.
Boswell and his two sons had made a dash in a postchaise from
London, travelling day and night 'in 64 hours. But alas! our haste
was all in vain. The fatal stroke had taken place before we set out.'
They were met at Auchinleck House by Euphemia, who ran out in
tears to tell them that her mother was dead. Boswell was beside
himself with conflicting passions and emotions that swayed him
now this way, now that: the unavailing but earnest wish to have
Peggie back for a day to assure her of Boswell's love, the regret at
not having been with her at the last, the distress she had suffered
from illness and her husband's irregularities, the love, the remorse, the sincerity of regret, the impossibility of making amends.
The funeral, which Boswell attended though it was not the
custom for a husband to be present at his wife's funeral, brought
the occupants of nineteen carriages, the tenants of 'all my lands,' a

large body of horsemen, and the family together to pay their last respects. Boswell, who took much of the proceedings into his own hands, was very much comforted by the ceremony.

Boswell's brother David was all for educating the children in Scotland, but Boswell had grander ideas. 'Should I or could I be satisfied with narrow provinciality, which was formerly so irksome, and must now be much more so?' The disposals he intends to make, he tells Temple, are that Euphemia will finish her education in Edinburgh, since that is her wish (though Boswell has reservations about '*Edinburgh-mannered girls*' in whose company he takes no satisfaction); Betsy will be boarded at a quiet school in Ayr; Veronica's desire to be boarded during the winter with a lady in London will be gratified; and Alexander will go to Eton. James will remain at the Soho Academy.

Lonsdale had sent his condolences, but the death of a wife was no impediment to the demands he made on his satellite: Boswell was to report to Lowther at his own convenience, and in August he joined a house party there where his wig was abducted and could by no means be found. Poor Boswell was the butt of the company which grinned behind its gloves at his distress, beseeching search to be made and being obliged to go out bareheaded until he could post twenty-five miles to Carlisle to get a new wig fitted to cover his confused embarrassment. It was a childish trick to play on an afflicted man, and Boswell felt it keenly. Peggie would have been disgusted, but Boswell could not afford to show his pique.

A letter to Temple, on 23 August 1790, unleashed not only an account of this silly practical joke, but also a torrent of morbid grief. 'I have an *avidity* for death. I *eagerly* wish to be laid by my dear, dear wife. Years of life seem insupportable ... Every prospect that I turn my mind's eye upon is dreary. *Why* should I struggle? I am *constitutionally* unfit for any employment . . .' and Boswell, very thoroughly, fairly drowns in a welter of despair and grief. His aching distress was not relieved by more immediate claims upon his anxiety: indeed, money worries only compounded the misery. Boswell, totting up the charges on his income, reckoned the expense of his children at £100 each, £500 in total, after which he had about £350 left for himself. 'How unpleasant it is to be straitened in our *circumstances*,' he wrote to Temple who knew all too well what it was to be constantly in financial distress. 'Yet this I have been for twenty years, and, I dread, must be so I know not how long.'

On 22 March 1790, Boswell gave a farewell dinner for Paoli who was about to return to Corsica. Paoli had been constantly supportive throughout Boswell's many desolations of spirit, irregularities of conduct, and vagaries of direction. On Paoli's departure, a considerable force for good was removed from Boswell's life: they would never meet again. As if Nemesis had been saving up her artillery for one final, shattering fusillade, Lonsdale insisted that Boswell accompany him to Carlisle to give support in electioneering. Boswell asked to be excused: he had reasons for wishing to remain in London, notably that he did not want to be interrupted in his research and writing of the *Life of Johnson*, Temple was staying with him in London, he was still distressed by the death of Peggie, and not least he had been informed by an acquaintance at Lonsdale's court that Lonsdale had expressed the opinion that if ever he put Boswell into Parliament, Boswell would only get drunk and talk foolishly.

Even to Boswell, prepared to overlook snubs that would have had other men rushing for their pistols, this was a considerable affront. Presenting himself to Lonsdale in London, Boswell had the mortification to hear the insult more or less repeated to his face. 'I suppose you thought I was to bring you into Parliament. I never had any such intention.' Indeed, Boswell had hoped for just that, but Lonsdale's remark, expressed 'in the most degrading manner, in presence of a low man from Carlisle and one of his menial servants,' finally made Boswell 'almost sink under such unexpected, insulting behaviour.'

Boswell there and then attempted to resign the Recordership, but Lonsdale insisted that Boswell had solicited the office and could not peremptorily give it up. To his disgust, Boswell was caught. 'Thus was I dragged away, as wretched as a convict,' and Lonsdale returned to the offensive. Boswell's spirit had somewhat returned, and 'in my fretfulness I used such expressions as irritated him almost to fury, so that he used such expressions towards me' that, until tempers had cooled, almost resulted in a duel. Lonsdale, in response to some Boswellian babblings of 'liberal and independent views and of their inconsistency' with Lonsdale's corrupt practices, accused Boswell of having 'kept low company all your life! What are *you*, Sir?' To this potentate, Boswell replied, 'A gentleman, my Lord, and a man of honour; and I hope to show myself such.' Lonsdale, in a fit of rage, shouted, 'You will be settled when you have a bullet in your belly.'

Boswell had no pistol, but he demanded one of Lonsdale's which was refused him. At Barnet, there was no pistol to be had in the neighbourhood, so the duel was postponed, and over dinner at the inn the quarrel cooled, though Lonsdale insisted on the satisfaction of Boswell owning himself to have begun the quarrel. Boswell refused, but offered to apologise for the quickness of his temper. It would have to do: Lonsdale was no more eager than Boswell for a bullet in his belly, and they cautiously shook hands. But the association was at an end: Lonsdale took off to attend to his electioneering, Boswell repaired to Carlisle where he was 'in wretched spirits, and ashamed and sunk on account of the disappointment of hopes which led me to endure such grievances. I deserve all that I suffer.'

On 28 June, to the Mayor, Aldermen, Bailiffs, and Capital Citizens of Carlisle, Boswell tendered his formal resignation as Recorder of Carlisle. Lonsdale had not quite finished with the worm that had turned: he peevishly pursued Boswell until mid-July with imprecations of neglect of duty, almost got his satellite stoned by a mob of disgruntled Carlisle men incensed by Lonsdale's tyranny, and reviled him for pretending to the favours in Lonsdale's gift. On 15 July, Boswell was gratefully out of Carlisle, safely in a post-chaise bound for London where, under the benign solace of Malone's ingenious philosophic balm, he recovered a good deal of his poise and responded to the solicitous attentions of Reynolds and the sympathy of Temple. To Temple, he promised, though he had 'parted from the Northern Tyrant in a strange equivocal state; for he was half irritated, half reconciled,' that 'I shall keep myself quite independent of him.' And so he did.

Boswell's relief at having escaped from the toils of Lonsdale did not inhibit any further excursions into the vexed business of politics. In an article for the *European Magazine* he confirmed what he took for granted to be general astonishment. 'It was generally supposed that Mr Boswell would have had a seat in Parliament; and indeed his not being amongst the Representatives of the Commons is one of those strange things which occasionally happen in the complex operations of our mixed Government. That he had not been *brought into Parliament* by some great man is not to be wondered at when we persue his publick declarations.' This was one in the eye for Lonsdale, Dundas, Pitt, Burke, Mountstuart, and all the rest who, having been made uneasy by Mr Boswell's independence of mind and spirit, had judged him too much of a danger to attempt to woo to their causes.

The article also reminded them that Mr Boswell was now free to consider any courtship that might be made in his direction. In July, never despairing of being the Member for Ayrshire, he offered his valuable services as one of the county's grandees, being patriarch of 'one of the oldest families' and possessing 'extensive property and a very fine place.' Mortifyingly, 'the power of the Minister for Scotland was exerted for another person, and some of those whose support he might have expected could not withstand its influence.' The malignant influence of Dundas had again foiled Boswell's hopes. A rumour reached his ears that the candidate might step down, and Boswell immediately appealed to Dundas for the place, invoking promises made in the past, but Dundas turned a deaf ear.

The last, desperate course was to catch the direct attention of Pitt. The opportunity presented itself at the Lord Mayor's Banquet in 1790 where Pitt was guest of honour. When the guests were about to tuck into their pudding, Boswell was easily persuaded to get to his feet and burst forth into song 'in praise of Mr Pitt's conduct in the dispute with Spain.' The ballad selected by Boswell as most appropriate to this great Guildhall occasion was his own composition, entitled *The Grocer of London*. He prefaced it with a eulogistic speech, and launched into his song which, astonishingly, was encored six times. By one account, Pitt remained unmoved except, towards the end of the sixth performance, for a wintry smile. By another account, he had left the table before the Boswellian tribute was started. However, Boswell regarded the event as a wonderful triumph.

Pitt had ignored several prayerful letters from Boswell, and, though the public performance of the singing barrister was more difficult to disregard, Pitt contrived to do so. What Boswell hoped to gain by this effort is open to speculation: evidently Pitt had no ready response, or at least had the discretion to give none. Boswell was disappointed. In a letter to Dundas, he complained bitterly of Pitt's arrogant and ungrateful treatment. Boswell was genuinely at a loss to know the reason for being so disgracefully overlooked. It was hard, perhaps, to recognise that a great political career was not about to begin on the back of a happy little song.

Parliament was not likely to be rejoiced by his presence: Westminster Hall had learned to live with the loss of Mr Boswell's lingering, gossiping, hopeful, but briefless presence: Mr Boswell's 'attention to the business of Westminster Hall has been chiefly interrupted,' he informed the curious readership of the *European Magazine*, 'by his great literary work in which he was engaged for many years, *The Life of Dr Johnson*, which has at last been published, in two volumes quarto, and which has been received by the world with extraordinary approbation.' The eagerly awaited work had been published on 16 May 1791.

[10]

⟶⟨⟩⟵

Boswell and *The Life*

⟶⟨⟩⟵

Boswell's desire to write a *Life of Johnson* was of long standing. He had mentioned it as early as 1782, and on 9 July of that year he wrote to Mrs Thrale, guilelessly or otherwise, 'May I presume more upon your kindness, and beg that you may write to me at more length? I do not mean to put you to a great deal of trouble; but you write so easily that you might by a small expence of time give me much pleasure. Anecdotes of our literary or gay freinds, but particularly of our illustrious Imlac, would delight me.' On 20 July, he followed up with a more direct appeal, '. . . may I again intreat to hear from you how Dr Johnson does, from time to time? I express myself inelegantly. But I trust you think me worthy of that attention; and I know I am grateful for your goodness.'

Mrs Thrale was Johnson's friend and, as such, she scarcely could avoid coming into annual contact with Boswell if she wished to see the Doctor. Like Boswell, she was a collector of Johnsoniana and a fairly natural jealous rivalry, well concealed behind a façade of politeness, existed between them. In 1786, Mrs Thrale published *Anecdotes of the late Samuel Johnson* which attracted public attention and gave Boswell a bad moment or two. For one thing, Mrs Thrale took her opportunity to swipe at Boswell's alleged 'trick . . . of sitting down at the other end of the room, to write at the moment what should be said in company, either by Dr Johnson or to him.' Mrs Thrale was careful to say that she never did such an ill-bred thing herself, and considered that treacherous conduct of this kind 'were it commonly adopted,' would exile all confidence from society.

Hester Thrale is also alleged to have deliberately suppressed

Hester Lynch Piozzi (Mrs Thrale),
portrait by an unknown Italian, 1785

Boswell's name from a conversation with Johnson in which names
of his possible biographers were canvassed and variously disparaged, the consensus being that either Mrs Thrale or Johnson
himself was best suited to the business of memorialising his life
for posterity. Boswell reacted to her anecdotical emphases, which
to his mind featured Mr and Mrs Thrale too philanthropically
and flatteringly, by a notable cooling of enthusiasm for the

authoress who had succeeded in selling out her first edition in one day. A few years after, in the *Life*, he amply took his revenge.

1787 was ornamented by the appearance of *The Life of Samuel Johnson, LL D* by Sir John Hawkins, commissioned by the London book trade. This was intended as the 'official' biography, and Boswell had again been pipped at the post. Fortunately, the Hawkins opus, although it had some success in two editions, was dull and discursive and struck Boswell as giving Dr Johnson a 'dark uncharitable cast'. It was occasionally gratuitously offensive, so that Boswell could appeal to Johnson's manservant, Francis Barber, for the truth about Johnson. 'Sir John Hawkins having done gross injustice to the character of the great and good Dr Johnson, and having written so injuriously of you and Mrs Barber, as to deserve severe animadversion, and perhaps to be brought before the spiritual court, I cannot doubt of your inclination to afford me all the helps you can to state the truth fairly, in the work which I am now preparing for the press.'

Hawkins had accused Frank Barber of being a 'loose fellow' in the opinion of Johnson, and of being grasping. Frank was a negro, and Mrs Barber had been characterised by Hawkins as 'one of those creatures with whom, in the disposal of themselves, no contrariety of colour is an obstacle.' He continued thereafter to libel Mrs Barber's honour. To get back at Hawkins would not merely be a duty, it would be a pleasure and Boswell felt he could rely on Barber's co-operation.

The co-operation of many of Johnson's friends was necessary. Immediately on Johnson's death, Boswell began his campaign to collect every possible scrap of paper, every faintest memory, every anecdote, and every particular pertaining to the life of Johnson. From the end of 1784, from the moment he heard of Johnson's death, to mid-April 1791, he was busy collecting first-hand material for the book. The flood of correspondence in response to his petitions fills a book: his own, requesting, begging, pleading, and reminding, would fill another. Throughout the period of debt, drinking, Peggie's illness, abandoning his practice as an advocate and coming to the English bar, throughout the elections in Ayrshire, and the Lonsdale boot-licking, Boswell persevered

James Boswell, portrait by Joshua Reynolds, 1785

with his *Life of Johnson*. The *Life* itself, in the first edition, refers to the time and trouble taken. 'Were I to detail the number of books I have consulted, and the inquiries which I have found it necessary to make by various channels, I should probably be thought ridiculously ostentatious. Let me only observe, as a specimen of my trouble, that I have sometimes been obliged to run half over London, in order to fix a date correctly.'

Not only London – to Windsor also, after seeing Alexander at

Eton. Here Fanny Burney, maid of honour to Queen Charlotte and daughter to the distinguished musician Dr Charles Burney, an intimate of Johnson, was to be found. Fanny Burney was alternately exasperated and amused by Boswell, whom she labelled 'the anecdotical memorandummer,' and she had been fond of Dr Johnson. It is good to have an accurate, if astringent, first-hand account of Boswell's conversational manner, and Fanny Burney gives it without stint. Boswell panted up to her at the choir gate of St George's Chapel, and immediately, impatiently, burst into flood. 'I am happy to find you, Madam. I was told you were lost! – closed in the unscaleable walls of a royal convent! But let me tell you, Madam, it won't do. You must come forth, Madam! You mut abscond from your princely monastery and come forth. You were not born to be immured, like a tabby cat, in yon august cell! We want you for the world! . . .'

But why had Boswell come? Why was he suddenly pulling a bundle of proof-sheets from his pockets, showering them, and pointing, and exclaiming, 'yes, Ma'am! The finest book in the world! Do but listen to this conversation – this letter! Is not this elegant? Is not this astonishing? In his own manner – positively his own manner, I assure you!' Was Miss Burney to listen to the collected oratory and anecdotes and aphorisms there and then? An audience was collecting, giggling at the gabbling Mr Boswell – worse! pointing and remarking on the confusion of Miss Burney. Boswell was in Windsor to get permission to publish Johnson's interview with George III, but Miss Burney was a fortuitous sugar plum, a rich store of anecdote, to gild the greatness of Johnson. 'Yes, Madam: you must give me some of your choice little notes of the Doctor's; we have seen him long enough upon stilts; I want to show him in a new light! Grave Sam, and great Sam, and solemn Sam, and learned Sam – all these he has appeared over and over. Now I want to entwine a wreath of graces across his brow; I want to show him as gay Sam, agreeable Sam, pleasant Sam!' There was no telling how long this parade of multi-faceted Sams might have continued to be conjured had not the figure of Mrs Schwallenberg, matron and sergeant-major of the maids of honour appeared, stout and stern as the Queen of Spades, at her

window and there – oh! confusion! – came the King and Queen
and a train of attendants and family from the terrace. Miss Burney
bolted, and Mr Boswell billowed off in pursuit of his proof sheets
and anecdotical memoranda.

Boswell was unstoppable: he would hardly take no for an
answer, and an answer was demanded even if it had nothing to
relate. He had suffered one mild snub from Horace Walpole in
Paris when he wanted information about Corsica, and he put
himself in the way of another when Walpole's teeth and doors
were, on a second occasion, an insufficient barricade against
Boswell's breezy persistence. He was liable to stop people in the
street and, in the case of Mr Mauritius Lowe, hurry after them to
get sight of a note in Johnson's hand, no matter how trivial the
content. And, no matter how inconvenient the conditions, he
would work: at the house in Queen Anne Street that he was
preparing to receive his wife and family, he would sit dining on tea
and toast.

On 10 January 1789, Boswell reported to Temple that 'I am
now very near the conclusion of my rough draught of *Johnson's
Life*. On Saturday I finished the Introduction and Dedication to
Sir Joshua, both of which had appeared very difficult to be
accomplished. I am confident they are well done. Whenever I
have completed the rough draught, by which I mean the work
without nice correction, Malone and I are to prepare one half
perfectly, and then it goes to press, where I hope to have it early in
February, so as to be out by the end of May. I do not believe that
Malone's Shakespeare will be much before me.' Edmond
Malone, who was selflessly helping Boswell to arrange the materials for the *Life* was also occupied with his own editorial work on
Shakespeare at this time. By the time Boswell was again writing to
Temple on 16 February 1789, the report was that the 'book is now
very near the conclusion of the rough draft,' and in a PS Boswell
asks, 'Pray (by return of post) help me with a word. In censuring
Sir J. Hawkins's book I say "there is throughout the whole of it a
dark uncharitable cast which puts the most unfavourable con-
struction on almost every circumstance of my illustrious friend's
conduct." Malone maintains *cast* will not do. He will have

malignancy. Is that not too strong? How would *disposition* do? . . .
Hawky is no doubt very malevolent. Observe how he talks of me as
if quite unknown.'

In Hawkins's *Life of Johnson*, Boswell had been referred to only
once, and then only glancingly in connection with the trip to the
Hebrides, as 'Mr Boswell, a native of Scotland'. The slighted
Boswell protested to Hawkins, 'Surely, surely, Mr *James*
Boswell;' marginally better than bare Mr Boswell. Sir John was
sympathetic, 'I know what you mean, Mr Boswell; you would have
had me say that Johnson undertook this tour with *The* Boswell?'
Boswell, since he does not report any crushing retort, we may take
as being fairly stumped. He brooded upon the clip he had been
given, and in Boswell's *Life of Johnson*, there is a bland reference
to Mr John Hawkins, thus stripped of his knighthood, whom
Boswell claims never to have seen more than twice in
Johnson's company.

On 14 October 1789, Boswell informed Temple that the day
before he and Malone 'revised and made ready for the press the
first thirty pages of *Johnson's Life*.' Boswell was now grieving for
the loss of Peggie, and had been counting up the cost of educating
his children, so that despite the labour and achievement of his
work on the *Life* Boswell felt 'a sad indifference' and Malone had
remarked with some justification, since Boswell had been drinking, that he had not the use of his faculties. On 28 November,
Boswell was at a low ebb: Temple learned that his friend had
'been endeavouring to seek relief in dissipation and in wine,'
though self-disgust had set him lately on a more moderate course
of conduct. With Malone's assistance, invaluable since he was 'so
acute and knowing a critick' and '*Johnsonianissimus*,' a third of the
work had been settled ready for the press.

But it had been a prodigious labour. 'You cannot imagine what
labour, what perplexity, what vexation, I have endured in arrang-
ing a prodigious multiplicity of materials, in supplying omissions,
in searching for papers, buried in different masses – and all this
besides the exertion of composing and polishing. Many a time
have I thought of giving it up. However, though I shall be uneasily
sensible of its many deficiencies, it will certainly be to the world a

Edmond Malone, portrait by Joshua Reynolds, 1778

very valuable and peculiar volume of biography, full of literary and characteristical anecdotes . . . told with authenticity and in a lively manner. Would that it were in the booksellers' shops. Methinks, if I had this *Magnum Opus* launched, the publick has no further claim upon me; for I have promised no more, and I may die in peace or retire into dull obscurity, *reddarque tenebris*.'

To be sure, Boswell had promised the world, in the first edition of the *Tour to the Hebrides* in 1785, *The Life of Samuel Johnson LL D*, advertised as a literary monument to a great author and an excellent man, based not only on materials which Boswell solicited in the advertisement but on materials he himself had been collecting for twenty years, during which time 'he was honoured with the friendship of Dr Johnson.' The blasting of his political hopes in 1790, after the discreditable Lonsdale episode and the performance of his ballad at the Guildhall banquet, and the disillusionment of his ambition to set Westminster Hall by its judicial ears as a barrister, forced Boswell back on his literary work. He pressed on with the *Life* which generally delighted him: Temple was informed in February 1790 that it would be 800 pages long (in fact, with additions, it amounted to more than 1000), and 'I think it will be, without exception, the most entertaining book you ever read.' At this time, he was alternately drinking with Lonsdale and revising with Malone, entertaining high hopes of political preferment and 'high expectations both as to fame and profit' from the *Life*. 'I surely have the art of writing agreably. The Lord Chancellor [Lord Thurlow] told me, "he had read *every word* of my Hebridean journal; he could not help it."'

To Bennet Langton, in early April 1790, Boswell crowed, 'Only think what an offer I have for it [the *Life*] – *a cool thousand*. But I am advised to retain the property myself.' Towards the end of this year, Boswell pledged that his daily ration of wine should not exceed four good glasses at dinner. His spirits were not good, Malone was in Ireland and his contribution to the *Life* was missed, and above all Boswell was sunk in debt. To Malone, in January 1791, he explained the urgency of the matter: £500 had been borrowed in order to lend it to an unfortunate cousin; repayment was now due. After allowing for his children's expenses, all that Boswell could reckon on out of his estate was £900 a year net. Besides, he had been improvident enough to buy the small estate of Knockaroon in Ayrshire and owed £1000 on that. Mr Dilly was owed £300, Temple was owed £200, and Wilkes £100. The total came well in excess of £2000. Twice, to Malone, Boswell wrote to ask whether it might not be wise to sell the copyright of the *Life* for

1000 guineas. The quandary as to what should be done to ensure the best income was compounded by the disquieting notion that interest in Johnson, so long after his death, and after two biographies and some pamphlets had appeared to gratify public interest, might have diminished. Curiosity about Johnson was not, after all, limitless and might well by now be confined to a small circle of friends and devotees.

In February Boswell went out and bought himself, desperately, a lottery ticket, paying £16/8/- for it. A handbill advertising the lottery had been circulated claiming that a ticket bought from Nicholson's, to which Boswell immediately repaired to buy his, had been drawn to win a prize of £5000. To Malone, Boswell wrote, 'calculating that mine must certainly be one of 100, or at most 200, sold by Nicholson the day before, made me look at the two last figures of it, which, alas, were 48, whereas those of the fortunate one were 33 ... O, could I but get a few thousands, what a difference it would make upon my state of mind, which is harrassed by thinking of my debts.'

By 25 February 1791 Boswell thought 'I should accept even of £500' for the *Life*. The date in March, by which Boswell hoped to have published his book, passed without its appearance. People, in a sort of straw poll, had tended to shake their heads at the prospect of two quartos at a price of two guineas, and there had been no luck in the lottery. There was still the matter of the precise wording of the title page to be settled with Malone, and at the beginning of April Boswell was likely to wake up in the small hours of the morning, or in the dead watches of the night, to brood upon his complaints. One resolution he is able to make is that, when the book is published on 25 April, as is hoped, he will force himself to sit several hours a day in his shabby little rooms in the Temple, at Inner Temple Lane, and frequent Westminster Hall in hopes of getting fees if only to cover the cost of £40 rent, furniture, and a lad to attend him occasionally as a clerk.

There is another prospect: a Miss Bagnal, sister-in-law to Sir William Scott, the King's Advocate who is seven and twenty, lively and gay, '*a Ranelagh girl*,' and possessed of six or seven hundred a year in addition to excellent principles that move her on Sunday evenings to read prayers to the servants in her father's family. Boswell's immediate reaction is predictable. 'Let me see such a woman' who has, so far, refused young and fine gentlemen. The Boswell brain and bravado moves into top gear. 'Here now, my Temple, I am, my fluttering self – A scheme – an adventure seises my fancy. Perhaps I may not like her; and what should I do with such a companion, unless she should really take a particular liking to me, which is surely not probable; and as I am conscious of my distempered mind, could I *honestly* persuade her to unite her fate with mine?' Evidently he could not, or would not.

On 19 April 1791, Boswell wrote to his old friend George Dempster to announce the imminent event. 'My *Magnum Opus*, the *Life of Dr Johnson*, is to be published on Monday 16th May,' as it duly was. 1200 copies, of the 1700 printed of the first edition, were sold by 22 August and Boswell was hopeful of having sold the balance by Christmas. Joseph Farington, RA, a later friend of Boswell, records that the first edition of two quartos at two guineas made £1550 for the author, and that this was increased to £2000 on account of the later octavo edition. Fortunately, Boswell had not sold his copyright and the book was a fair success. It had not the immediate fame or novel sensation of the *Account of Corsica* or the *Tour to the Hebrides*, but it was a much larger and a much greater work and did not strike with so much immediacy the tinder of the public imagination: in any case, Johnson was now a familiar figure through previous accounts of his life, and a dimmer figure since his demise. Nevertheless, the success was gratifying and better than Boswell had, in his worst moments, expected.

The reviews were mixed: at one end of the spectrum of contemporary critical opinion, the *Quarterly Review* and the *Edinburgh Review* praised it as one of the best imaginable books: at the other, Boswell was nitpickingly derogated for most of the literary sins in the catalogue of reviewers' imprecations. He was personally reviled for impropriety and indiscretion – and, to be sure, the *Life* was not short of imprudent references to the quick and the dead. Johnson himself, as might have been expected, came under the reviewers' fire when the *Monthly Review* reviled

him for dogmatism and bigotry. They might have made out a case
according to their lights, but spoiled it by the immoderacy of their
blanket condemnation.

Notoriety never harmed the sales of a book, and the *Life* was no
exception: it sold steadily, and it has continued to do so for near
enough two hundred years. Posterity has not yet exhausted the
last editions of Sir John Hawkins or Mrs Thrale. Boswell's
sternest critics may attack his morals and his character, but they
are on a hiding to nothing when they attempt to attack the *Life of
Johnson*: it may be assaulted in particulars, but it remains generally impregnable as the monument it was intended to be, and
has in truth become. That it depicts the Doctor merely emerging,
like a Michelangelo statue, from the stone, may be true: it is a
product of one man and one editor and, as such, is a selective
portrait in much the same manner as a portrait by Reynolds may
be said to be partial in its depiction of its subject.

Whether Boswell himself was conscious of his artistry as the
author of the *Life* is a question overshadowed by the fact of his
achievement and the judgement of posterity: it is for academics,
and not a biographer, to answer. All that can be said here is that
Boswell, with the aid of Malone, took the greatest pains over the
collection and ordering of materials: but that alone will not make a
good book. The spark of Boswell ignites the book and animates,
illuminates, and throws its subject into relief against a vivid and
vast background cast of minor characters (including the author)
painted in with the utmost geniality, frankness, and precision.
Boswell himself, though now and again delighted with his work
on the book, was never wholly immodest about it: contrary to his
self-delight in other departments of his life. If he was satisfied
with any aspect of the *Life* and congratulated himself on it, it was
the amount of effort he put into the research and writing over a
long period. Boswell, who fluttered like a moth from one career,
one hope, one ambition and one prospect, to another, could take
proper pride in his assiduity and his devotion to the self-imposed
task of giving Johnson to the world.

It cannot be said without doubt that Boswell was serving his
own interest: for one, Johnson would never have put up for long

with a fawner pure and simple. Boswell had a respect bordering on idolatry for Johnson, and he pursued him perhaps as he had first pursued Paoli, Rousseau, or Voltaire: it is always interesting and sometimes instructive to meet a philosopher. But, as with Paoli, the impulse to associate with a great man became subsumed into something deeper and more lasting: reverential awe became warm friendship, valuable to both parties. Though Paoli and Johnson were both put in a book apiece, Boswell was thoroughly annoyed by any imputation that, as Mrs Thrale had suggested in her book, he took advantage of the confidences of society. He did overstep the mark in the *Life of Johnson*, unblushingly publishing a good number of remarks that Johnson made unguardedly and 'off the record,' but his objective care to show the dangerous side of Sam as much as his learned or gay aspects perhaps overrode temporary discretion. In the long run, had Boswell considered the matter, he might have realised that we, as much as he, seize upon every spark that even marginally illuminates a corner of the life of Johnson or, indeed, of his contemporaries. Discretion is not the better part of biography: in the short term, it may avoid a good deal of trouble, but in the long term it is an irreparable mothhole in an otherwise complete canvas.

To Sir William Scott, on 9 August 1791, Boswell irritably replied to explain why he refused an invitation to dine. Sir William, though desirous of Boswell's company, had taken care to caution him not to embarrass fellow-guests by recording their conversation. Boswell did not care to have the reputation of a fellow who went about in society merely as a scribbling gossip, and reminded Sir William that anything he had published of his conversation in the *Life* had been revised in advance by Sir William himself. Boswell took the opportunity to assert his principle of conduct which Sir William could probably be relied upon to broadcast to others.

'If others, as well as myself, sometimes appear as shades to the Great Intellectual Light [i.e. as minor characters and foils to Johnson in the *Life*], I beg to be fairly understood, and that you and my other friends will inculcate upon persons of timidity and reserve, that my recording the conversation of so extraordinary a man as Johnson, with its concomitant circumstances, was a *peculiar* undertaking, attended with much anxiety and labour, and that the conversations of people in general are by no means of that nature as to bear being registered, and that the task of doing it would be exceedingly irksome to me.' The members of London society should not, in short, suppose that Mr Boswell, having taken considerable trouble to record the oracular sayings of Tiresias, would now bother to chronicle the twitterings of bloodless shades, tattling round the dinner tables of London.

In May 1791, having seen the *Life* through the press and to the booksellers and now receiving letters of congratulation and criticism which contained information that would have to be considered for future editions, Boswell set out on the Home Circuit, round Hertfordshire, Essex, Kent and Surrey, as a barrister – 'though I did not get a single brief,' he informed Temple on 22 August. Bravely, and to cover his disappointment, Boswell claimed not to grudge the expense since the exercise showed him to be 'desireous of business, and imbibing legal knowledge'. It was at least important for Boswell to show his face in legal circuits. Temple had asked Boswell to solicit the interest of Dundas on behalf of his son, Francis Temple, who wished to gain promotion from midshipman to lieutenant. Boswell visited Portsmouth 'and viewed the grand fleet; and there I was assured that the most difficult step in the navy is from midshipman to lieutenant.' Boswell had no reason to believe that Dundas would do anything for him, much less for a son of a friend, but Dundas made a memorandum to see if the promotion could be achieved.

By this time, Miss Bagnal had faded in favour of a number of alternative matrimonial schemes, including 'Miss Milles, daughter of the late Dean of Exeter, a most agreeable woman *d'une certaine âge*, and with a fortune of £10,000.' She was not seven and twenty, like Miss Bagnal, but neither was Mr Boswell at fifty years of age. Miss Milles, like the rest, stuck to her fortune and, perhaps, bestowed it and herself elsewhere: it was not applied to bind up the fortunes or the spirits of James Boswell who, in the autumn of 1791, returned to Auchinleck, to a house 'deserted and

melancholy,' redolent with memories of Peggie and reminding
Boswell of his loss. To relieve his 'langour and gloom' and restore
his energies, he rode about the county visiting neighbours and
friends – but his spirits refused to be roused.

London, on his return, was not much better. 'I keep chambers
open in the Temple. I attend in Westminster Hall. But there is
not the least prospect of my having business.' He was depressed,
too, by the 'visible wearing away of Sir Joshua Reynolds' who died
three months later, in February 1792, almost blind. Later that
year Boswell totted up the losses. 'No General Paoli – no Sir
Joshua Reynolds – no Sir John Pringle – no General Oglethorpe.'
All these men were a good deal older than Boswell and might
naturally be expected to predecease him – but the fall of the
mighty was a series of concussive blows to Boswell's imagination,
though Paoli was still alive, but living in Corsica. Not that he
lacked friends; for each loss there were two or three new or old
acquaintances to be brought up to fill the front ranks. He had, too,
his children: the Boswells had installed themselves comfortably at
47 Great Portland Street. Boswell was devoted to his children,
entertaining great hopes of his eldest son, Sandie, and lavishing
indulgent affection on Veronica, Euphemia and Betsy. They were
lively children, advanced for their years according to Boswell's
own testimony, and his authority over them was precarious. 'My
only hold is their *affection*,' he complained. That it should be so
perhaps gratified him more than it shocked him: he would not
have cared to treat them as his own father had treated Boswell and
his brothers.

By 21 June 1793 Boswell was hoping to see a second edition of
the *Life* published at the end of the month, and he was planning a
trip to Holland and Flanders. The tour was perhaps postponed,
and subsequently abandoned, after Boswell was mugged in early
June, knocked down, robbed of a few shillings, and left lying,
stunned, in Great Tichfield Street. A newspaper report on 12
June detailed the injuries, 'a severe cut on the back part of his
head, and a contusion on both his arms; he has ever since been
almost constantly confined to his bed, with a considerable degree
of pain and fever.' To Temple, Boswell wrote, 'This, however,

shall be a *crisis* in my life. I trust I shall henceforth be a sober, regular man. Indeed, my indulgence in wine has, of late years especially, been excessive.' Evidently Boswell had been drunk at the time of the attack, and had been seriously frightened by the violence of the assault. Temple was worried that Boswell might, if the occasion were to be repeated, be carried off, the legs caught from under him by the scythe of the Grim Reaper, while intoxicated: an awful prospect, as Boswell readily agreed, and not unlikely since the streets of London after nightfall were patrolled by thugs not averse to cutting a throat or fracturing a skull for a small reward. The resolve to give up drink was, like the promises of repentance and reformation of the past, a well-intentioned but temporary expedient more to quiet alarm than to rule future behaviour.

Boswell continued to circumambulate the legal circuit, but he was bored. To divert himself in July, he visited Warley Camp where Pitt's Militia, a band of volunteer recruits as brave and enthusiastic as they were haphazard and inadequate, had assembled for annual training. Boswell was received with civility and even enthusiasm by the officers, who included Bennet Langton, but the old military fire had been quenched in Boswell: he caught cold, and rushed back to town after two days, later exclaiming in a letter to Langton on 24 July, 'O London! London! there let me be; there let me see my friends; there a fair chance is given for pleasing and being pleased.'

Boswell was perfectly capable of pleasing and being pleased: a glance at his journal for this period shows no diminution of his alacrity in accepting invitations and in thoroughly enjoying himself. His social manner was practised, but never perfunctory: he was rarely bored by society and rarely boring, and so his company was eagerly sought throughout town. His eye for a pretty woman had not dimmed, nor his taste for a Mass, nor his appetite for rambling philosophical discussion. He regularly gave himself little treats, such as visits to the theatre, or following a young lady home, at a respectful and discreet distance behind her pretty back, for the sheer pleasure of middle-aged Don Juanism. But there were black spots: in October, Boswell learned of the suicide

of Andrew Erskine, with whom he had rioted and corresponded
so entertainingly as a young man. The news depressed him, as did
all intimations of mortality, but equally some of the gaiety of life
had been removed: there was less to look forward to than to look
back upon. The candles were being extinguished, one by one,
behind his back.

He was not idle, however: the *Life*, in its second edition, was
selling briskly and as a result of publication he had involved
himself, with enormous pleasure, in a quarrel with Anna Seward,
the poetess, known to her supporters as the 'Swan of Lichfield'.
She claimed to know the circumstances surrounding Johnson's
verses, composed in youth, addressed to 'a Lady, on receiving
from her a Sprig of Myrtle.' Miss Seward alleged that the verses
were for one Lucy Porter, with whom Johnson had been infatu-
ated before his marriage. The twenty-year-old Johnson was said
to have presented his verse tribute to Lucy Porter in the presence
of Miss Seward's mother, and Boswell in all good faith printed the
anecdote as accurate. Mrs Thrale had, on the contrary, asserted
that Johnson had written the verses for a friend, Edmund Hector,
to give to a girl Hector was keen to impress. On application to
Hector, Mrs Thrale's version of the incident was confirmed:
Hector had in turn given them to another friend to give to *his* girl.
The Swan was furious, and continued to brood and fulminate
against Boswell for having dared to prefer her pretty fable to the
less romantic facts of the matter. This quarrel occupied a good
deal of Boswell's time very pleasantly, beguiling his leisure
moments and affording his malice employment and acute satisfaction. The Third edition of the *Life* incorporated a good deal of
new or revised matter, and Boswell was busy preparing it for the
press in the latter half of 1793, after the appearance of the Second
edition. He exerted himself, too, on behalf of others: his industry,
fired by a tender heart, on behalf of alleged criminals whom he
believed to be wrongly arrested, held in detention, or convicted
improperly, is recorded in his journals. 'Much satisfied by my
benevolent exertions,' he may write – but Boswell was all his life
given to gratuitous and spontaneous benefactions and a phrase
such as this is self-congratulatory, to be sure; but though Boswell

James Boswell, engraving by William Daniell
after a drawing by George Dance, 1793

may take satisfaction in a benevolent exercise of his powers, the
original impulse rarely stems from any thought of gathering
subsequent laurels.

Though his practice as a barrister was non-existent, Boswell
could take pride in some considerable achievements: his sac-

rifices for his children were laudable, he had achieved fame as an author, and he had contrived to contain his debts. Though he had abandoned any attempt at direct management of the estates of Auchinleck in 1786, they were competently managed by his overseer, Andrew Gibb, who reported regularly to Boswell and received detailed instructions by word of mouth when the Laird happened to be at Auchinleck, or by letter when he was in London. By good management and judicious enterprise, the income accruing from the estate had nearly doubled by 1795. If Boswell still cherished hopes, they were of advancement in other fields of endeavour that would crown his head with laurel and win wealth and fame, and bring credit to the name of Boswell.

An opportunity appeared to present itself in March 1794. Corsica had been occupied by the British after Paoli, as President, had appealed for help from Britain in his struggle with the Buonapartes who supported France in the civil war that had broken out in the island. President Paoli, and the island's governing body, the Cortes, had offered Corsica to the British Crown and, accordingly, a British administration was to be introduced. On 17 March Boswell wrote excitedly to Henry Dundas, Secretary of State, reminding Dundas not only of their friendship and the remarkable restraint of Boswell's claim upon that connection, but also pressing his qualification to be appointed Minister or Commissioner for Corsica. His long acquaintance with Corsica and Paoli was mustered to support his application, and reference was made to the delight with which the Corsicans and Paoli would receive news of the appointment of Mr Corsica Boswell. There could hardly be any competition in the matter.

Dundas, with as little trouble as he had put aside previous claims by Boswell to his attention and favour, put aside this latest application. Sir Gilbert Elliot of Minto was appointed as Viceroy of Corsica. The official reply informing Boswell of the appointment was the full stop to his hopes of political or public office. Boswell had some claim to the Corsican appointment, but more on the ground of 'auld lang syne' than for any evidence of an ability to administer a parish or a province. It was a final flutter towards the glittering prospect that had always excited his imagination, towards the thing that would prove his worth to the world, give him a stage on which to play the principal part that would bring the house down with the applause of the audience he wished so ardently to acquaint with his marvellous abilities. The chance would be a fine thing.

The disappointment may have contributed to another bout of indulgence in wine, because on 31 May 1794 Boswell was writing to Temple to pledge himself anew, once again, to be temperate, 'upon my guard'. But there are things to be done, people to see, dinners to eat, and children to be raised, not to say debts to be paid. Boswell busily attends to the day-to-day affairs of his life, and he has not yet wholly given up the pursuit of women or matrimony: to Lady Orkney, on 22 March 1795, Boswell wrote to remember himself to her and to solicit an invitation to dine.

By mid-April 1795, however, Boswell had fallen ill. After a visit to the Literary Club, he had been too ill to walk home and, having been assisted to Great Portland Street, he contracted 'a fever of cold attended with a severe shivering and violent headache, disorder in his stomach and throwing up.' Boswell was put to bed, and there he stayed doubtful as to when he should recover. That he would recover, he did not for a moment doubt: a warm letter of congratulations to Warren Hastings on the occasion of his acquittal promised that Mr Boswell, 'the moment that he is able to go abroad, he will fly to Mr Hastings, and expand his soul in the purest satisfaction.' But three weeks later, on 16 May, Boswell's son James wrote to Temple to say that Boswell had been unable to read Temple's last letter unaided – though there were hopes of Boswell's recovery. Boswell's constitution, despite lifelong assaults on its health and strength, had withstood astonishing punishment. For all that Boswell had been afflicted with venereal diseases, hangovers, the energy-draining attacks of hypochondria, he had never been seriously ill, hardly ever confined for more than a few days to his bed with influenza or misery. On 18 May, James wrote again to Temple with the news that Boswell had weakened and was unable to keep food in his stomach. He had complained of being confined to bed, and had asked to be lifted out: but the effort had been too great. Boswell had fainted away, and his condition had deteriorated quickly.

On 19 May, Boswell's brother David wrote to Temple, 'I have now the painful task of informing you that my dear brother expired this morning at two o'clock; we have both lost a kind, affectionate friend, and I shall never have such another. He has suffered a great deal during his illness which has lasted five weeks, but not much in his last moments; may God Almighty have mercy upon his soul, and receive him into his heavenly kingdom. He is to be buried at Auchinleck, for which place his sons will set out in two or three days; they and his two eldest daughters have behaved in the most affectionate, exemplary manner during his confinement; they all desire to be kindly remembered to you and Miss Temple; and beg your sympathy on this melancholy occasion.'

According to William Ober, who has considered Boswell's medical history at some length, with particular references to his recurring bouts of clap, his death was due to uraemia provoked by an acute recrudescence of chronic urinary tract infections. Ober identifies 'nineteen episodes of urethral disease, of which at least twelve must be reckoned as new primary cases of gonorrhea, one a nonspecific urethritis, one the development of a urethral stricture about thirty years after his first attack, and the others as recrudescences of subsiding recent infections'. Boswell's persistent vomiting seems to indicate 'that uraemia had developed as the kidneys were being destroyed by pressure and infection . . . It is not inaccurate to say that Boswell died of the complications of his many episodes of gonorrhea.'

On Malone's testimony, Boswell died without pain or effort. His had been a life of considerable struggle and effort, and if we are to take Malone's word for the comparative peacefulness of Boswell's relatively quick death, perhaps dying was the only thing he had easily accomplished in his strenuous life.

Envoi

It is pious to wish that Boswell could have had the full value of his reward as a biographer and a journalist: but it is doubtful whether even the applause of posterity would be enough to satisfy his uneasy shade. However he might swoon with pleasure at the compliments the sourest critics are obliged to heap on his *Life of Johnson*, he would be mortified at the scorn they have regularly poured on his own life. If Boswell can be said to have been consciously artful in the writing of the *Life of Johnson* he was artless to the point of naïveté in the conduct of his own.

Boswell could never seriously believe that a will to repentance and a resolution to reform would not wipe out the errors and indiscretions of the past: having a good heart and a forgiving, fallible nature himself, he could not readily imagine that others might be less generous. That Boswell never learned from his mistakes cannot be denied – but the reason for his apparent perseverance in perversity is not difficult to discover: he acted always, however absurdly, in utter sincerity; sometimes in the rational belief that what he was doing was proper, sometimes quite on instinct and impulsively.

He could, without any apparent trouble, believe any number of improbable things before breakfast: even when the facts were staring him in the face, he was immediately able to assemble them into an alternative pattern, another reality, to justify his acting apparently in flat contradiction of plain common sense. Johnson had the measure of it when, on his ramble round the Western Isles, he had occasion to boom 'Sir, are you so grossly ignorant of human nature as not to know that a man may be perfectly sincere in good principles, without having good practice?' It is a difficult concept to grasp, and few enough manage to do so. But one thing is evident: Boswell may have acted thoughtlessly on many occasions, to the detriment of himself and others, causing grief and pain – but to suppose that it was his conscious intention to injure is seriously to distort and malign his character. Repentance does not, of course, make a wrong action right, nor does it give licence to repeat the action. To continue in wrong-headedness does not inspire confidence in others, and Boswell lived at a slight angle to life. For all his sophistication, Boswell never quite learned how the world wagged, nor how to manipulate it to his advantage.

He took it for granted, and rightly, that his social position granted automatic privilege, and time and again he saw many a morally inferior and more unscrupulous man promoted over his head, building rapidly and with ease on a natural social distinction. This properly galled Boswell, though undoubtedly he often overestimated his own capacity to fulfil the demands and responsibilities of the post he had unavailingly sought to gain. He knew, in a practical sense, that the influence of friends and the opposition of enemies in society and public life could make or break a man, but Boswell took little or no heed of his own character as a determining factor in the shaping of his career.

He constantly got things subtly wrong: other men were no less foolish in youth, others drank and were dissipated, others fawned and flattered, and appeared to reap a good harvest. Why should Mr Boswell of Auchinleck be the exception? Perhaps a partial answer is that Boswell had no guile: he took no care to cover his tracks or conceal his character. On the other hand, Boswell associated with some of the best people, the most learned, the most aristocratic, the most powerful in the land. That, at least, was some evidence that Boswell was worthwhile. Johnson, an honest friend, tried on at least one occasion to point out to Boswell that contact with men of merit did not automatically confer merit, and that Boswell could expect disappointment in his ambitions. But Boswell could not, right to the end, be contented with 'literary fame, and social enjoyments. I must still hope for some credible employment; and perhaps I may yet attain to it.'

That was written in November 1794, only six months before his death.

Boswell, to the last, believed that his credibility as a candidate for legal, political or parliamentary position could be retrieved. All that was needed was an opportunity to display his gifts to best advantage, though by no means could anyone be induced to provide the chance so urgently sought and so long desired. It was his ambition as an adult, as it had been in childhood, to be 'good for something'. He wanted to 'be someone' – he wanted to be Johnson, or Paoli, or Lord Auchinleck, or Sir David Dalrymple, or Rousseau, or any one of a hundred models of achievement. Boswell wanted to be solid.

The life of Boswell, on one reading, ends on a pathetic note: the ill-conceived and fruitless attempt to be appointed as Minister or Commissioner for Corsica. The snub to his self-esteem, delivered without compunction, by Dundas, was but one of a long list of keenly-felt rejections for which Boswell more or less set himself up. In a sense, he colluded with his detractors and with life itself to experience its reversals. If, at heart, Boswell was convinced that he was fit for nothing, then he set out to satisfy that unconscious conviction. It was a form of masochism that could never be wholly sated – Boswell, time and again, came back off the ropes for a further dose of punishment.

Yet the will to succeed was strong: an alternative reading of his life is possible – that, with the publication of the *Life of Johnson* towards the end of his life, he had succeeded in achieving at least one, and perhaps the most significant, of his ambitions. It is certain that Boswell was satisfied, more or less, that he had written a good book: it brought him much of the applause he so ardently desired, and through periods of despair and distress he had salvaged some self-esteem and diverted his mind in the hard and dedicated work it had taken to complete the book he antici-pated would be his '*Magnum Opus*'. Its success was gratifying, but nevertheless it was, in his mind, no greater than the achievement of a Parliamentary seat or a place on the bench, whether in Scotland or England.

To posterity, Boswell's success is as an author of a biography that, it can be argued, has no rival. But, in the context of Boswell's own life, it will not do to make too much of this. In worldly terms, Boswell died with the reputation of a foolish failure: that is to put it at its worst, and his critics did no less. To some, he died as a man whom many had loved but few had respected. To none did he appear to have been a man who had fulfilled his own expectations.

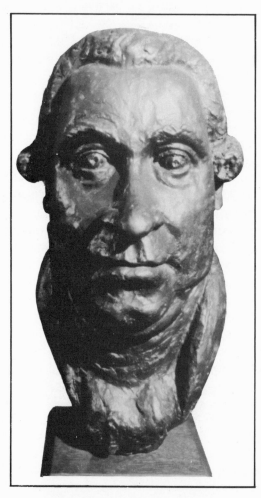

Sculpture of James Boswell at Auchinleck

To be mentally unstable, to the point almost of lunacy is, as D. B. Wyndham Lewis remarks, not necessarily a hindrance – but to be merely eccentric, like Boswell, 'all his life . . . teetering on the verge of complete sanity,' is to lack the solidity of apparent sanity or evident madness. Either end of the spectrum is more or less reassuring to a public eager to classify its members as either trustworthy and reliable or plainly certifiable. Boswell was caught all his life between the examples of madness in his own family and the reassuring, comforting sanity of Paoli, Johnson, Lord Auchinleck, and other exemplars. He personally inclined to believe that he might easily lapse into madness, though in his writings, of all kinds, he notably avoids discussion of the topic. But Boswell's feeling that there was no substance to support his brilliance may be accounted for, at least in part, by the fact that he took no trouble to hide his feelings.

When Boswell groaned, the world heard it; when he was gay, he exhibited that gaiety publicly. There are few who would be prepared to write, even to a close friend, so openly as Boswell wrote to Temple. Every new friend was a lapel to be buttonholed and, to give Boswell credit, he rarely bored: Johnson had no time or patience for Boswell's moanings and introspections, but by and large a man is flattered to be regarded as a confidant – in which case, Boswell's flattery was spread thick and wide. But the danger is that to reveal oneself reveals not only sincerity of motive but the inconsistencies of action. Boswell's self-revelatory impulses more often than not spoke against his worldly interests. He was never capable of telling less than the terrible truth.

D. B. Wyndham Lewis says, with some truth, that Boswell has been roughly handled by moralising critics of his private life, as though such a dog had no business to be a genius or even tolerated by those he counted as his friends. But it is precisely because Boswell has no academic gown, and no robe of scarlet or ermine to pull around him to cloak his imprudence or conceal his excesses that he is easily reviled as a wretch. Boswell has no order paper to wave in the face of insult, no clerk of the court hurriedly to declare his proceedings *in camera*, no regiments to send into the field to cover up indiscretions with the noise of cannon and the smoke of battle. Platitudinous parliamentarians, jurisprudential judges, meretricious military officers, pious public officials, and dissipated divines all may point grandly to the edifice of their public careers to reduce criticism to a murmur or a mumble. The cruel humour of Lord Kames is a case in point: his appalling behaviour on the bench is explained by his biographer, Lord Woodhouselee, as 'due to a certain humorous manner,' and 'the pleasing relaxations of a great mind'.

Boswell had no seat on the bench and no great legal mind to set against his alleged misbehaviour. Like any artist – writer, painter, actor, or other inconsiderable dog, he is fair game and may be kicked with impunity by any passer-by. It cannot, in truth, be maintained that Boswell led a quiet or a blameless life. It is not much to the point to wish that he might have been better than he was, or to imagine that he was capable of 'pulling himself together' by a water diet or a course of cold baths. It is, however, to the point to refer critics to his ability to attach himself to men of the sternest moral character and to hold not only their attention but actively to inspire and retain their affection and concern, not as a licensed jester but as a sincere and a good man with the impulse, if not the ability, to be a better man. '*Spero meliora*,' wrote Boswell towards the end of his life, 'I hope for better things.' The intention behind the phrase may more likely have been a material than a spiritual improvement in circumstances – but it can be taken to include all Boswell's longings to do and to be better. That he did his best, and that his best in one area of his life at least was superlative, he never had the satisfaction of knowing. In that sense, and in that sense only, he had failed: he never loved himself as much as he loved and was loved by others.

Bibliography

BOSWELL, JAMES, *Boswell's Column*, ed. M. Bailey, William Kimber, London, 1951
— *Boswelliana*, ed. Charles Rogers, Grampian Club, London, 1874
— *Life of Johnson*, ed. R. W. Chapman, Oxford University Press, London & N.Y. 1970.
— *The Journal of a Tour to Corsica; and Memoirs of Pascal Paoli*, ed. M. Bishop, Williams & Norgate, London 1951
— *Journal of a Tour to the Hebrides with Samuel Johnson, LL.D*, ed. R. W. Chapman, Oxford University Press, Oxford, 1924
BRADY, F., & POTTLE, F. A. (eds), *Boswell in Search of a Wife, 1766–1769*, Heinemann, London, 1957; McGraw Hill, N.Y., 1956 (Yale Ed.)
— *Boswell on the Grand Tour: Italy, Corsica and France 1765–1766*, Heinemann, London, 1955; McGraw Hill, N.Y., 1955 (Yale Ed.)
DAICHES, DAVID, *James Boswell and his world*, Thames & Hudson, London, 1976; Scribners, N.Y., 1976
FIFER, C. N. (ed.), *The Correspondence of James Boswell with Certain Members of the Club*, Heinemann, London, 1976; McGraw Hill, N.Y., 1974 (Yale Ed.)
GRAHAM, H. G., *The Social Life of Scotland in the 18th Century*, A. & C. Black, London, 1901
HYDE, MARY, *The Impossible Friendship: Boswell and Mrs Thrale*, Chatto & Windus, London, 1973; Harvard Univ. Press, Camb. Mass, 1972
JOHNSON, SAMUEL, *Journal to the Western Islands of Scotland*, ed. R. W. Chapman, Oxford University Press, Oxford, 1924
LEWIS, D. B. WYNDHAM, *The Hooded Hawk*, Eyre & Spottiswoode, London, 1946
LUSTIG, I. S., & POTTLE, F. A. (eds), *Boswell: The Applause of the Jury, 1782–1785*, Heinemann, London, 1982; McGraw Hill, N.Y., 1982 (Yale Ed.)

POTTLE, F. A. (ed.), *Boswell in Holland, 1763–1764*, Heinemann, London, 1952; McGraw Hill, N.Y., 1963 (Yale Ed.)
— *Boswell on the Grand Tour: Germany and Switzerland, 1764*, Heinemann, London, 1953; McGraw Hill, N.Y., 1953
— *Boswell's London Journal, 1762–1763*, Heinemann, London, 1950; McGraw Hill, N.Y., 1950
— *James Boswell: The Earlier Years, 1740–1769*, Heinemann, London, 1966; McGraw Hill, N.Y., 1966
QUENNELL, PETER, *Four Portraits*, Collins, London, 1945; Viking Press, N.Y., 1945
— *Samuel Johnson*, Thames & Hudson, London, 1972; American Heritage Press, N.Y., 1973
REED, JOSEPH W. & POTTLE, FREDERICK A., *Boswell, Laird of Auchinleck, 1778–1782*, McGraw Hill, London and N.Y., 1977 (Yale Ed.)
RYSKAMP, C., & POTTLE, F. A. (eds), *Boswell: The Ominous Years, 1774–1776*, Heinemann, London, 1963; McGraw Hill, N.Y., 1963 (Yale Ed.)
SCOTT, G., & POTTLE, F. A. (eds), *Private Papers of James Boswell from Malahide Castle*, Privately printed, New York, 1928–34
TINKER, C. B. (ed.), *Letters of James Boswell*, (2 vols), The Clarendon Press, Oxford, 1924
TINKER, C. B., *Young Boswell*, Putnam, Boston, 1922
VULLIAMY, C. E., *James Boswell*, Geoffrey Bles, London, 1932; Books for Libraries Press, Freeport N.Y., 1971
WAINGROW, M. (ed.), *The Correspondence and Other Papers of James Boswell Relating to the Making of the* Life *of Johnson*, Heinemann, London, 1969; McGraw Hill, N.Y., 1969
WALKER, R. S. (ed.), *The Correspondence of James Boswell and John Johnston of Grange*, Heinemann, London, 1966 (Yale Ed.)
WEIS, C. MCC., & POTTLE, F. A. (eds), *Boswell in Extremes, 1776–1778*, Heinemann, London, 1971; McGraw Hill, N.Y., 1971 (Yale Ed.)
WIMSATT, W. K., & POTTLE, F. A. (eds), *Boswell for the Defence, 1769–1774*, Heinemann, London, 1960; McGraw Hill, N.Y., 1959 (Yale Ed.)

Index

Numbers in italic refer to illustrations

Addison, Joseph, 55, 92
Alford, Lord (Sir John Graham), 126
Antonetti, Signor Antonio, 109–10, 111
Argyll, Duke and Duchess of, 25, 184–5
Arthur's Seat, Edinburgh, 35–6
Auchinleck, Alexander Boswell, Lord
  (father), 1–3, 4, 6–7, 9, 18, 24, 25–6,
  27, 54, 102, 116, 132, 135, 139, 144;
  Ramsay's portrait of, *3*, 7; appointed
  Sheriff of Wigtownshire, 6; appointed
  judge of Court of Sessions, 16–17;
  Boswell's relations with, 20, 21–2,
  32–4, 35, 44–5, 56, 67–8, 75–6, 96,
  123–4, 129–30, 136, 164, 165, 168,
  198, 202–3, 206, 211, 215; death of
  wife, 126, 129; and Boswell returns
  home to Scotland, 129; Douglas Cause,
  150–51; second marriage to Elizabeth
  Boswell, 153–5, 165; Boswell stays in
  Auchinleck with, 167–8; Paoli's visit to
  Auchinleck, 168–9; and Johnson's visit
  to Auchinleck, 185–90; Boswell's
  opposition on choice of parliamentary
  candidate, 191–2; and quarrel over
  Boswell's debts, 202–3; illness of, 210,
  214; and death of, 214–15; Auchinleck,
  Lady Elizabeth (*née* Boswell), 210, 211;
  marriage to Lord Auchinleck, 153–5,
  165
Auchinleck estate, Ayrshire, 4, 6, 16, 26,
  27, 129, 132, 167–8, 251–2, 256; size
  and income from, 4, 256; Paoli's visit
  to, 168–9; Johnson's visit to, 185–90;
  Boswell becomes Laird of, 214–16;
  Peggie's illness and death at, 230–33;
  Boswell buried at, 258; sculpture of
  Boswell at, *262*

Baden-Durlach, Prince of, 74
Bagnal, Miss, 247–8, 251
Barber, Francis (and Mrs), Johnson's
  manservant, 240
Barry, James, portrait of Dr Johnson, *158*
Bastelica, Corsica, 113

Bastia, Corsica, 122–3
Batoni, Pompeo, 98
Bavarian Chapel, London, 23
Beauclerk, Lady Diana, 175
Beauclerk, Hon. Topham, 173, 174, 175
Beafsteak Club, Covent Garden, 39
'Belle de Zuylen' *see* Serooskerken
Bellegarde, Marquis de, 65, 105, 130,
  132, 149
Berlin, Boswell's visit to, 69, 73–4
Billon, Monsieur, 90–91
Black, Lion, Fleet Street, 41
Blair, Miss Catherine (Princess),
  Boswell's courting of, 138–9, 140–43,
  149, 153, 204
Blair, Hugh, 44, 52
Boily, Monsieur, 77
Bolingbroke, Viscount, 175
Bosville, Miss Elizabeth, 133, 138, 148
Boswell, Alexander (father) *see*
  Auchinleck, Lord
Boswell, Alexander (son), 198, *201*, 233,
  241–2
Boswell, Claud, of Balmuto, 132, 153
Boswell, David (uncle), 10
Boswell, David (son), 206
Boswell, Elizabeth/Betsy (daughter), 211,
  233
Boswell, Euphemia (*née* Erskine: mother),
  1, 2–3, 7–8, 9, 17; Mosman's portrait
  of, *2*, 7; death of, 126, 129, 130
Boswell, Euphemia (daughter), 192, *201*,
  232, 233
Boswell, James: birth (1740), 1; and
  family, 1–4, 6–8, 9–10, 16–17, 28;
  character and appearance (including
  description of self), 5, 14, 15, 34–5, 55,
  59, 60, 62, 130–31, 149, 200–201,
  210–11, 253, 259–64; education, 6, 9,
  10–11, 20; trips to Moffat Wells, 9,
  14–15, 132, 133, 136; Willison's
  portrait of, 15, *80*, 98; theatrical
  acquaintances, 15–16, 18; trip on the
  North Circuit, 18; falls in love with Mrs

Boswell, James: – cont.
  Cowper, 19; becomes Freemason, 20;
  relations with his father, 20, 21–2,
  32–4, 44–5, 56, 67–8, 75–6, 123–4,
  129–30, 136, 164–5, 168, 198, 202–3,
  206, 211, 215; enrolled as student at
  Glasgow University, 20; his conversion
  to Catholicism, 21, 22–3, 81, 97–8;
  goes to London, 22, 23; and stays with
  Eglinton, 24–5; catches VD, 26, 28;
  amorous adventures of, 30–32, 38,
  40–42, 61–7, 68–9, 89–91, 92–3,
  94–5, 101–4, 126–7, 132–3, 137, 145,
  148–9, 205–6; death of son Charles,
  32, 61–2; passes Civil Law
  examination, 34; moves to London,
  35–8; love affair with Mrs Lewis,
  40–42; first meeting with Dr Johnson,
  48–9, 50–51; and Johnson's friendship
  with, 52–4, 56, 62, 156–9, 160, 161–2,
  164–5, 169–71, 173–4, 175–90, 197,
  204–5, 208–11, 213–14, 216–20; trip
  to Holland, 54, 55–6; and studies civil
  law in Utrecht, 59–73; relationship
  with 'Belle de Zuylen', 62–7, 70–73,
  81–2, 96–7, 130–32, 148–9;
  European tour, 73–127; visits
  Rousseau at Môtiers, 77–83; and visits
  Voltaire at Ferney, 83–7; caricature of
  Rousseau by, 86; Italian tour, 89–104,
  123–4; and meetings with Wilkes, 92,
  93–5; Mountstuart's friendship with,
  93, 99–102, 103; commissions painting
  from Hamilton, 98; love affair with
  'Momina', 103–4, 123; Corsican trip,
  104, 105–23, 125, 127–8; and meeting
  with General Paoli, 114–22; Miller's
  engraving of, *119*; Paris visit, 125–6;
  mother's death, 126, 129, 130; affair
  with Thérèse Le Vasseur, 126–7;
  returns to England, 126–8; and to
  Scotland, 128–9; affair with Mrs
  Dodds, 133, 134, 136, 137, 138–40;
  passes Scots Law exam and admitted to
  Bar, 133–4; represents John Reid in
  two criminal trials, 134–6, 194;
  courtship of Catherine Blair, 138–9,
  140–43; *Account of Corsica* published
  (1768), 143–4, 146; Stratford
  Shakespeare Jubilee celebrations,
  146–8; Douglas Cause, 149–51; trip to
  Ireland, 151–3; courtship of and
  marriage to Margaret Montgomerie,
  151–5, 165; and father's second
  marriage, 153–5, 165; visits Johnson in
  Oxford, 156–9; Paoli's friendship in
  London, 161, 165, 169–70;
  antagonism between Mrs Thrale and,
  163–4, 199–200, 217, 238–40;
  undergoes operation, 164; married life

  in Edinburgh, 165–7; admitted to Bar
  of General Assembly, 166, 167; death
  of son at birth, 166; visits father at
  Auchinleck, 167–8; buys interest in
  London Magazine, 168; General Paoli's
  visit to Scotland, 168–9; appears for
  client before House of Lords, 169;
  attends Lord Mayor's ball, 171–2; birth
  of daughter Veronica, 173; at Sir
  Joshua Reynolds' literary party, *174*;
  elected member of Literary Club,
  174–5; Johnson's tour of Scotland
  with, 175–90, 191; Rowlandson's
  drawing of Johnson and, *177*; opposes
  father's choice of parliamentary
  candidate, 191–2; birth of daughter
  Euphemia, 192; his drinking (and
  gambling) excesses, 193–5, 200, 202,
  207, 214, 253, 257; anonymous paper
  in *London Chronicle* by, 195; Peggie's
  relationship with, 195–6, 201–2,
  203–4, 229–33; visits brother John in
  Newcastle, 196; visits Temple at
  Mamhead, 197; birth of son Alexander,
  198; Singleton's family portrait, *201*;
  financial difficulties, 202, 210, 246–7;
  quarrels with father over debts, 202–3;
  introduces Johnson to Wilkes, 204–5;
  birth and death of son David, 206;
  meets Johnson at Ashbourne, 206; his
  anxiety over Peggie's ill-health, 208;
  birth of son James, 209; inflammation
  of his foot, 209; birth of daughter Betsy,
  211; his vain attempts to gain public
  office, 212–13, 217–19, 221, 222,
  236–7, 256–7; death of father, 214;
  and becomes Laird of Auchinleck,
  214–16, 218; death of Dr Johnson,
  220, 222–3; talks with George III,
  224–6; called to English Bar, 226–7;
  Great Queen Street house of, 227; Earl
  of Lonsdale's patronage of, 227–9,
  234–6; wife and family join him in
  London, 228, 229–30; acts as Mayor's
  Counsel in Carlisle election, 228; and
  appointed Recorder of Carlisle, 228–9,
  234; illness and death of his wife,
  229–33, 234; Queen Anne St house of,
  230, 243; gives farewell dinner to Paoli,
  234; quarrels with Lonsdale, 234–5;
  and resigns Recordership of Carlisle,
  235; his tribute to Pitt, 236–7; *Life of
  Johnson* published (1791), 237–8,
  240–51; Reynolds' portrait of, *241*;
  buys Knockaroon estate, 246; returns
  to Auchinleck, 251–2; Great Portland
  Street home of, 252, 257; and his
  devotion to his children, 252; mugged
  and robbed, 252–3; Daniell's engraving
  of, *255*; Anna Seward's quarrel with,

254; application for job of minister for Corsica turned down, 256–7, 261; illness and death (1795), 257–8; sculpture at Auchinleck of, 262

Boswell, James: *Written works: Account of Corsica (Journal of a Tour to Corsica)*, 139, 143–4, 146, 156, 157, 160, 248; *The Cub at Newmarket*, 29–30, 38; *De supellectile legata* (legal thesis), 133–4; *Dorando* (pamphlet), 139, 150; 'Erskine Correspondence', 30, 34–5, 43–5; 'The Hypochondriack' essays, 207, 215; 'Inviolable Plan', 59, 68; *Journal of a Tour to the Hebrides*, 5, 179, 199, 224, 225, 226, 227, 246, 248; *Letter to the People of Scotland on the Present State of the Nation*, (1784), 218–19, 224; *Letter* (1785), 224; *Life of Johnson*, 52, 53, 162, 170, 173–4, 198–9, 204, 220, 224–5, 226, 231, 234, 237, 238–51, 252, 254, 259, 261; *London Magazine* articles, 168, 207, 215; *Memorabilia*, 149; *Ode by Dr Johnson to Mrs Thrale . . .*, 217; *Ode to Tragedy*, 29, 34; *On the Profession of a Player*, 168; pamphlets, 28–9, 139, 150, 218–19, 224; poetry, 19, 28, 29; *Remarks*, 198–9; *Scots Magazine*, letter in, 29

Boswell, James (son), 209, 233, 257
Boswell, John (uncle), 10
Boswell, John, 1, 10, 28; derangement of, 196

Boswell, Mrs Margaret (Peggie: *née* Montgomerie), 216, 227; courtship and marriage to Boswell, 151–5, 168; life in Edinburgh, 165–7; death of son at birth (1770), 166; suffers miscarriage, 169, 172; birth of daughter Veronica, 172–3; Johnson's visit to Scotland, 176–9, 190, 191, 193; birth of daughter Euphemia, 192; Boswell's relationship with, 195–6, 201–2, 203–4, 229–33; birth of son Alexander, 198; Singleton's family portrait, 201; birth and death of son David, 206; illness (tuberculosis), 208, 209, 214, 216, 222, 229–32; birth of son James, 209; birth of daughter Elizabeth, 211; joins Boswell in London, 228, 229–30; and returns to Auchinleck, 230; and death of, 232–3, 234

Boswell, Thomas, 189
Boswell, Thomas David (brother), 1, 28, 216, 233, 258
Boswell, Veronica (daughter), 173, 201, 233
Bothwell Castle, 154, 155
Bowles, William, 217
Bowyer, publisher, 29
Boyd, Mary Ann, Boswell's infatuation for, 148–9, 151, 152, 153

Braxfield, Lord, 7
Brooke, Mrs, actress, 31
Brown, Rev. Robert, 59–60
Bruce, Euphemia, 132–3
Brunswick, Duke of, 73
Burgaretta, Countess, 90–91
Burke, Edmund, 174, 175, 213, 218, 236
Burney, Dr Charles, 242
Burney, Fanny, 115–16, 242–3
Burns, Robert, 12
Bute, Lord, 23, 43, 58, 93, 213, 230
Buttafoco, Matteo, 109

Carlisle, 234; Boswell employed as Mayor's Counsel, 228; and appointed Recorder of, 228–9, 234; and resigns Recordership, 235
Carlyle, Alexander, 228
Charlemont, Lord, 153, 174
Charles Edward Stuart, Prince, 98, 225–6
Charles Emmanuel I, King of Sardinia, 92
Charlotte, Queen, 242, 243
Châtelet, Mme du, 66
Chessel's Buildings, Canongate, Boswell's home at, 165, 166
Churchill, Charles, 39, 52, 53
Cockburn, Lord, 147
Colonna, Signor, 116, 122
Constant, Benjamin, 149
Conway, General, 213
Corsica, 133, 134, 138; Boswell's visit to, 89, 104, 105–23, 125, 127–8; and Boswell's *Account* of, 143–4, 146, 156, 157, 160, 248; Genoese interest sold to French, 146; British occupation of, 256
Cosway, Richard, portrait of General Paoli, 108
Cowper, Mrs, actress, 19–20, 21, 23
Clement XIII, Pope, 97
Corte, Corsica, 111–12, 122
Crawford, Countess of, 143
Cunningham, Annie, 206

Dalrymple, Sir David (later Lord Hailes), 17–18, 34, 45, 55, 72, 134, 136, 143
Dance, James (alias Mr Love), 18
Dance, George, portrait-engraving of Boswell after, 255
Dance, Nathaniel, 93
Daniell, William, portrait-engraving of Boswell, 255
Davies, Tom and Mrs, bookseller, 46–7, 48–9, 160
Delyre, Alexandre, 92, 99, 102
Dempster, George, 38, 56, 81, 170, 248
Dempster, Miss, 38
Denis, Mme (Voltaire's niece and

Denis, Mme – *cont.*
    housekeeper), 83, 85
Derrick, Samuel, 24, 39, 44, 46
Digges, West, actor-manager, 18, 55
Dilly, Edward, bookseller, 139, 143, 145,
    160, 161, 170, 171, 175, 197, 204, 208,
    210, 223
Dodds, Mrs, Boswell's affair with, 133,
    134, 136, 137, 138–40
Dodds, Sally (Boswell's daughter), 140, 149
Dodsley, publisher, 38, 47
Doig, Charles (Boswell's son), death of,
    32, 61–2
Doig, Peggy, 32
Douglas, Archibald, Duke of, 150, 154
Douglas, Duchess of, 32–3
Douglas, Lady Jane, 150
Douglas Cause, 149–51
Doyle, James E., *174*
Drury Lane Theatre, 36
Dun, John, 6, 9
Dundas, Henry, 134, 194, 200, 203,
    212–13, 218, 219, 222, 224, 230, 232,
    236, 237, 251, 256, 261

Edinburgh, 22, 136, 169; social activities
    in, 11–12, 16; and theatre, 15–16,
    18–20; Boswell in, 10–20, 25–6,
    28–36, 128, 129, 136, 150–51, 153–5,
    165–7, 175–9, 190–96, 197–203,
    205–6, 208–9, 210–13, 214–16,
    217–19; Douglas Cause riot in,
    150–51; Johnson's visit to, 175–9, 190
Edinburgh Advertiser, 135
Edinburgh Review, 248
Edinburgh University, Boswell's studies
    at, 10–11
Edmonstone, Colonel James, 100–102
Eglinton, Earl of, 24–5, 29, 30, 33, 38–9,
    43, 44, 192
Elliot of Minto, Sir Gilbert, 256
Erskine, Andrew, 34, 38, 40; Boswell's
    friendship with, 30, 153; *Letters*
    (Boswell/Erskine), 30, 33–4, 43–4, 53;
    suicide of, 254
Erskine, Lady Anne, 38
Erskine, Hon. Henry, 218
Erskine, *Institutes of the Law of Scotland*,
    68–9
The Essence of the Douglas Cause, 150
European Magazine, 236, 237

Farington, Joseph, RA, 248
Fergusson, Sir Adam, 166, 191–2, 212
Fergusson, Joseph, 6, 9, 13
Ferney (Switzerland), Boswell's visits to
    Voltaire at, 83–7
Florence, 125; Boswell's visit to, 102–3
Foote, Samuel, 147, 170
Forbes, Duncan, surgeon, 164

Forrester, Sally, whore, 24, 38
Fox, Charles James, 213, 219
France, Boswell's travels through, 125–7
Frederick the Great of Prussia, 69–70,
    73–4, 76
Fullerton, William, 140–41

Gaffori, Gian Pietro, 108–9
Garrick, David, 36, 46, 49, 144, 146, 148,
    161, 164, 168, 170, 173, 174, *174*, 175,
    191, 209
Geelvinck, Madame, 61, 64, 66
General Election (1769), 145
Genoa, 125; Boswell's stay in, 123–4
Gentleman, Francis, 20, 24
George III, King, 93, 172, 219, 221, 222,
    224–6, 242, 243
Gibb, Andrew, 256
Gibson, Mr, attorney, hanging of, 145
Glasgow University, 20, 35
Goldsmith, Oliver, 47, 170, 174, *174*,
    175, 191; *She Stoops to Conquer*, 173
Gordon, Sir Alexander, 181
Graham, H. G., *Social Life of Scotland in
    the Eighteenth Century*, 12
Grant of Ballindalloch, Mrs, 198
Gray, Thomas, 133, 143, 144

Hahn, Johannes David, 69
Hailes, Lord *see* Dalrymple, Sir David
Hamilton, Duke of, 150
Hamilton, Gavin, 98
Hänni, Jacob, Boswell's manservant, 73,
    75, 122, 123, 124–5
Harrison, Commander, 105
Hastings, Warren, 257
Hawkins, Sir John, 47; *The Life of Samuel
    Johnson*, 240, 243–4, 249
Hector, Edmund, 254
Hequet, Mme, 126
d'Hermenches, Constant, 65, 71, 72, 75,
    84, 149
Heron, Mrs Jean, 31
Hoare, William, portrait of Lord
    Mountstuart, *94*
Hogarth, William, satirical portrait of
    Wilkes, *57*
Holland, Boswell's stay in, 55–6, 59–73
Holyroodhouse, 18, 35
Home, John, 44; *Douglas*, 16
Houston, Lady, *The Coquettes, or The
    Gallant in the Closet*, 19, 21
Hume, David, 17, 44, 46, 85, *86*, 126,
    138, 167, 171, 205
Hunter, Robert, 10–11

Idler, Johnson's essays in, 47
Ireland, Boswell's trip to, 151–3
Italy, Boswell's tour of, 76, 89–105,
    123–4

Jachone, Boswell's dog, 122, 124
James III and VIII, Old Pretender, 99
Johnson, Dr Samuel, 4–5, 23, 27, 39,
    47–54, 55, 115, 116, 127, 133, 144,
    145, 147, 160, 169, 172, 174, 193,
    259–60; *Rambler* and *Idler* essays, 47,
    56; *Rasselas*, 47–8; Dictionary, 48; first
    meeting with Boswell, 48–9, 50–51;
    and Boswell's friendship with, 52–4,
    56, 62, 75, 156–9, 160, 161–2, 164–5,
    169–71, 173–4, 175–90, 197–8,
    204–5, 208–11, 213–14, 216–20;
    Wilkes's criticism of, 95; Boswell's legal
    thesis criticized by, 133–4; and
    Boswell's *Account of Corsica*, 144, 156,
    157, 160; Boswell's meeting in Oxford
    with, 156–9; Barry's portrait of, *158*;
    Thrale family's friendship with, 162–3,
    177, 199–200, 217; tour of Scotland
    with Boswell, 175–90, 191;
    Rowlandson's caricatures of, *177–8*;
    appearance, 176; *Journey to the Western
    Islands of Scotland*, 179, 181, 191, 199;
    in a Highland hut, *180*; visit to
    Auchinleck, 185–90; Paris excursion
    with Mrs Thrale, 199–200; Wilkes
    dines with, 204–5; *Life of Cowley*, 208;
    ill-health of, 214, 217, 218, 219–20;
    and death of (1784), 217, 220, 222–3,
    244; Mrs Thrale's *Anecdotes* of, 238,
    240; Sir John Hawkins's *Life* of, 240,
    243–4; Boswell's *Life* of, 237–51
Johnston, John, 20, 32, 34, 36, 43, 139;
    Boswell's friendship with, 11, 12–13,
    23, 166; Boswell sends his journal to,
    37; Boswell's correspondence with, 45,
    62, 164, 167
Jones, Sir William, 175
Juel, Jens, portrait of 'La Belle Zuylen', *63*

Kames, Lord, 7, 31, 44, 264
Kauffmann, Angelica, 93
Keith, Lord Marischal, 67, 69–70, 73, 75,
    76, 77, 82
Kennedy, David, 192
Kennedy, Dr, 155, 159, 160
Kilaloe, Bishop of, 229
Kincardine, second Earl of, 3
Kincardine, third Earl of, 9
Kinloch, Marguerite, 64, 70
Knockaroon estate, Ayrshire, 246
Knox, John, 180

Lainshaw House, 155
Langton, Bennet, 170, 191, 199–200,
    205, 217, 246, 253
Lawrence, Sir Thomas, pencil drawing of
    Boswell, *frontispiece*
Le Vasseur, Thérèse (Rousseau's
    mistress), 76–7, 79, 81, 83, 126;

Boswell's affair with, 126–7
Leghorn, 104, 105, 107
Leinster, Duke of, 153
Lewis, D. B., Wyndham, *The Hooded
    Mask*, xiii, 22–3, 24, 110, 144, 147,
    171, 179, 217, 263
Lewis, Mrs, actress, 40–42
Lisbon Diet Drink, 155, 159, 160
Literary Club, 191, 204, 257; Boswell
    becomes member of, 174–5, 197
Lloyd, Robert, 52, 53
London Chronicle, 44–5, 136, 144;
    Boswell's (anonymous) paper in, 195
London Magazine, 147; Boswell buys
    interest in, 168; and 'The
    Hypochondriack' essays (Boswell) in,
    207
Lonsdale, James Lowther, Earl of, 227–9,
    230, 232, 233, 234–6, 246
Loudon, Earl of, 192
Love, Mr and Mrs, 31, 38
Lowe, Mauritius, 243
Lumisden, Andrew, 98–9
Lunardi, M. Vincent, balloonist, 224
Lyttelton, Lord, 144

Macaulay, Mrs, historian, 144, 205
Macdonald, Flora, 183
Macfarlane, Lady Betty, 38, 44
Macfarlane, Laire of, 44
Macleod, Malcolm, 182–3
Macpherson, James 'Ossian', 46, 181
Mallet, David, 100–102
Malone, Edmond, 226, 227, 230, 235,
    243–4, 246–7, 249, 258; Reynolds'
    portrait of, *245*
Mansfield, Lord, 169, 170, 200
Mar, Earl of, 3
Marboeuf, Comte de, 106, 123
Marseilles, Boswell's visit to, 125
Martin, Guillaume, 92–3
Mary Queen of Scots, 98
Mazerac, François, Boswell's servant,
    72–3
The Meadows, Edinburgh, Boswell's
    home near, 206
Meighan, Thomas, 23
Melancthon, tomb of, Wittenberg, 75
Michieli, Madame, 101
Milan, Boswell's visits to, 92, 102
Miller, J., engraving of Boswell dressed as
    Corsican, *119*
Milles, Miss, 251
Mitchell, Andrew, 67, 75
Mitre Tavern, London, 53–4, 161
Moffat wells (spa), Boswell's visits to, 9,
    14–15, 132, 133, 136
Monboddo, Lord, 180–81
Montgomerie, Colonel Hugh, 212, 229
Montgomerie, Margaret *see* Boswell, Mrs

Monthly Review, 248–9
Morison, Colin, 97
Mosman, William, portrait of Boswell's mother, *2*
Môtiers, Switzerland, Boswell visits Rousseau at, 77–83
Mountstuart, Lord, 170, 203, 230, 236; Hoare's portrait of, *94*; Boswell's friendship with, 93, 99–102, 103, 153, 211, 217–18; Boswell's legal thesis dedicated to, 133
Mundell's School, Edinburgh, 6, 9
Murphy, Arthur, *Essay on the Life and Genius of Samuel Johnson*, 52
Murray, Peter, 193

Naples, Boswell's visit to, 94–5
Nash, Beau, 24
Nassau, Countess of, 64
Neill, Adam, printer, 143
Newgate prison, 46
North Briton, 39, 46, 53, 58, 95
Northumberland, Duchess of, 43
Nugent, Dr, 175

Ogden on Prayer, 179
Oglethorpe, General, 170, 252
Orkney, Lady, 257
Oroonoko (Southerne), adaptation dedicated to Boswell, 20–21

Paoli, Clemente, 108–9
Paoli, Giacinto, 108
Paoli, General Pasquale, 4, 105, 106, 107–9, 111, 112, 124, 128, 138, 146, *174*, 213, 227, 250, 252; Cosway's portrait of, *108*; Boswell's meeting in Sollacarò with, 113–22; and Boswell's *Memoirs* of, 139, 143; settles as refugee in London, 146, 161; and Boswell's friendship with, 161, 165, 169–70, 197, 204, 208; meets Johnson, 164; visit to Scotland, 168–9; returns to Corsica, 234
Paris: John Wilkes exiled in, 58; Boswell's visit to, 125–6; Johnson's excursion with Mrs Thrale to, 199
Parma, Boswell's visits to, 92, 102
Percy, Right Reverend Thomas, Boswell's correspondence with, 223, 227, 229
Piccolomini, Girolama ('Momina'), 103–4, 123, 140
'The Picturesque Beauties of Boswell', *186–8*
Piozzi, Gabriel, 163
Piozzi, Hester *see* Thrale, Mrs
Pitt, William, Earl of Chatham, 128, 134, 139, 219, 222, 228, 230, 236–7
Porter, Lucy, 254
Pottle, Professor Frederick A., *James Boswell, The Earlier Years*, xiii, 18, 24, 31, 32, 74, 113, 140
Presbyterian Church of Scotland, 13, 185
Preston, Sir George, 193
Pringle, Sir John, 159, 185, 190, 197, 252
Pringle, Mark, 213
Public Advertiser, 53, 172

Quarterly Review, 248
Queensberry, Duke of, 33–4, 42–3

Rambler, Johnson's essays in, 47, 56, 59
Ramsay, Allan: portrait of Lord Auchinleck, *3*, 7; portrait of Rousseau, *78*
Ramsay of Ochtertyre, 151
Ranelagh gardens, 36
Reid, John, 195; first trial of (1766), 134–5; second trial of (1774), 135–6, 194
Reynolds, Sir Joshua, 174, 209, 220, 226, 231, 235, 243; literary party at (engraving), *174*; portrait of Boswell, *241*; portrait of Edmond Malone, *245*; death of, 252
Ritter, Joseph, Boswell's servant, 179, 184
Rivarola, Count Antonio, 105, 109, 114
Robert the Bruce, 1
Rockville, Lord, 222
Roman Catholicism, Boswell's conversion to, 21, 22–3, 81, 97–8, 110
Rome, Boswell's visits to, 92–3, 97–100
Rose, James, 59–60
Rostini, Abbé, 116
Rotterdam, Boswell's visit to, 55, 56, 68
Rousseau, Jean-Jacques, 8, 9, 21, 31, 68, 75, 76–83, 89, 92, 94, 97, 99, 100, 101, 102, 104, 105, 126, 127, 138, 162, 250; *Emile*, 76, 81; *The New Héloïse*, 76; *Discourse on the Arts and Sciences*, 76; *Letters Written from the Mountain*, 77; Ramsay's portrait of, *78*; Boswell's visit to Môtiers, 77–83; Boswell's caricature of, *86*; *Le Contrat Social*, 107; and Corsica, 107, 109, 114; and Thérèse Le Vasseur, 126–7
Rowlandson, Thomas, caricatures of Boswell and Johnson, *177–8*
Rudd, Mrs Margaret Caroline, 204, 205

St Gilles, Comtesse de, 89–91
St James's Chronicle, 126
St James's Court, Lawnmarket, Edinburgh, Boswell's home in, 167
Saint-Pierre, Abbé de, 81
Salusbury, Hester *see* Thrale, Mrs
Salusbury, Mrs, 162
Sandwich, Lord, 39, 58
Sansedoni, Porzia, 103
Scots Magazine, 19, 29

Scott, Sir Walter, 168
Scott, Sir William, 247, 250
Serooskerken, Isabella Agneta Elisabeth;
    van Tuyll van (Belle de Zuylen/Zélide:
    later Mme de Charrière): Jens Juel's
    portrait of, 63; Boswell's relationship
    with, 62–3, 64–7, 70–73, 81–2, 96–7,
    104; self-portrait of, 65–6; Boswell's
    marriage proposal, 130–32, 148–9
Seven Years' War, 25, 107
Seward, Anna, 'Swan of Lichfield',
    Boswell's quarrel with, 254
Sheridan, Mrs, The Discovery, 39
Sheridan, Thomas, 44, 160; Boswell's
    friendship with, 30, 39–40, 46
Siena, Boswell's visit to, 103–4, 105
Simpson, Miss, 145
Singleton, Henry, portrait of Boswell and
    family, 201
Skarnavis, Countess, 91
Skye, Boswell and Johnson's visit to,
    182–4
Smith, Adam, 20, 35, 44
Smith, Gregory, 149
Soaping Club, 34
Sollarcarò, Corsica, 111, 112, 113–22
Somerville, Lord, 16, 18
Sommelsdyck family, van, 3, 60, 61
Steele, Sir Richard, 55
Sterne, Laurence, 25, 29; Tristram
    Shandy, 25
Stevenson, John, 10
Stratford Shakespeare Jubilee
    celebrations, 146–8
Stuart, Colonel James, 210
Stuart, Lady Mary, 3
Switzerland, Boswell's trip to, 75–87

Temple, Francis, 251
Temple, William Johnson, 18, 19–20, 72,
    179; Boswell's friendship with, 13, 140,
    141, 212; and Boswell's
    correspondence with, 17, 25, 56, 64–5,
    67–8, 69, 70, 73, 85, 95, 132, 136,
    137–8, 140, 141–2, 146–7, 148, 152,
    155, 166, 192, 198, 210, 220, 229–30,
    231, 233–4, 243, 246, 252–3, 257,
    263; Mamhead living (Exeter)
    presented to, 136; Boswell's visits to
    Mamhead, 155, 197; visits Boswells in
    Edinburgh, 166–7; stays with Boswell
    in London, 234, 235
Terrie family, Boswell rooms in Downing
    Street home of, 37
Thornton, Bonnell, 52, 53
Thrale, Henry, 160, 162–3; Boswell visits
    Streatham Park villa of, 162; death of,

163, 217
Thrale, Mrs Hester (later Mrs Piozzi),
    160, 205; Johnson's friendship with,
    162–3, 177, 199–200, 217; Miscellany,
    163; Thraliana, 163, 199; death of
    husband and marriage to Gabriel
    Piozzi, 163; Boswell's relations with,
    163–4, 199–200, 217, 238–40;
    Anecdotes of the late Samuel Johnson, 238,
    240, 249, 250, 254; portrait of, 239
Thurlow, Lord, 219, 222, 246
Tomasi family of Corsica, 111
Trotz, Professor, of Utrecht, 59, 73
Turin, 125; Boswell's visit to, 89–92
Tyburn, 46

Utrecht, Boswell's stay in, 45–6, 56,
    59–73

Venice, Boswell's visit to, 101–2
Voltaire, 66, 68, 75, 77, 83, 86, 101, 127,
    250; Candide, 48; Boswell's visit to
    Ferney, 83–7; portrait of, 84

Wale, S., portrait of Boswell, 119
Walker, W., 174
Walpole, Horace, 56, 126, 133, 143, 144,
    146, 243
Warley Camp, Pitt's Militia trained at,
    253
Weir, Major, warlock, 9
Whyte, Martha, 17, 18, 19
Wight, Mr, Solicitor-General, 218
Wilkes, John, 5, 39, 46, 47, 52, 53, 56, 58,
    90, 92, 93, 101, 102, 127–8, 129, 145,
    162, 217; North Briton, 39, 46, 95;
    Hogarth's satirical portrait of, 57; An
    Essay on Women, 58; exiled in Paris, 58;
    Boswell's meetings in Italy with, 90, 92,
    93–5; criticism of Johnson by, 95, 171;
    Boswell's meeting in Paris with, 126;
    and in London, 172, 197, 204; elected
    Lord Mayor of London, 172, 197;
    dinner with Johnson arranged by
    Boswell, 204–5
Williamson, John, 14–15
Willison, George, portrait of Boswell, 15,
    80, 98
Wittenberg, Boswell's visit to, 75
Wodrow, Robert, 16
Wood, Dr Sandy, 208
Woodcock, Mr, perfumer, 159

York, Duke of, 25, 30

Zélide/Zuylen, Belle de see Serooskerken
Zuylen, Monsieur de, 96, 97, 130